RETIRED

French Writers
and the Politics of Complicity

French Writers
and the Politics of Complicity

Crises of Democracy in the 1940s and 1990s

RICHARD J. GOLSAN

The Johns Hopkins University Press
Baltimore

© 2006 The Johns Hopkins University Press
All rights reserved. Published 2006
Printed in the United States of America on acid-free paper

2 4 6 8 9 7 5 3 1

The Johns Hopkins University Press
2715 North Charles Street
Baltimore, Maryland 21218-4363
www.press.jhu.edu

Library of Congress Cataloging-in-Publication Data
Golsan, Richard Joseph, 1952–
French writers and the politics of complicity : crises of democracy in the 1940s
and 1990s / Richard J. Golsan.
p.   cm.
Includes bibliographical references and index.
ISBN 0-8018-8258-3 (hardcover : alk. paper)
1. Authors, French—20th century—Political and social views. I. Title.
PQ146.G56 2006
840.9'0091—dc22   2005014178

A catalog record for this book is available from the British Library.

For Nancy

"Paris at Night"

Trois allumettes une à une allumées dans la nuit
La première pour voir ton visage tout entier
La seconde pour voir tes yeux
La dernière pour voir ta bouche
Et l'obscurité tout entière pour me rappeler tout cela
En te serrant dans me bras.

—*Jacques Prévert*

Contents

Acknowledgments

It is a great pleasure on completing a project such as this to have the opportunity to thank colleagues, friends, and family for their encouragement, support, and many helpful suggestions. The writing of this book afforded me numerous opportunities to test ideas and pick the brains of people more knowledgeable than myself on both sides of the Atlantic.

In France, I have enjoyed discussing the ideas and historical circumstances examined here in many conversations with Tzvetan Todorov, Henry Rousso, Annette Lévy-Willard, and Marc and Sylvie Dambre. My understanding of French attitudes and especially French political views has benefited over the years from discussions with Guy Hareau, Michel Wieviorka, Rémy Desquesnes, Pascal Bruckner, and especially old friends Pat and Hervé Picton and Jean-Jacques Fleury. I would also like to express my thanks to Nicholas Werth for spending a morning with me discussing the background and stakes of the *Black Book of Communism* controversy.

Outside France, I have benefited greatly from the knowledge and expertise of many people working in the field of French studies. These include colleagues and friends such as Chris and Joan Flood, Van and Mary Kelly, Leah Hewitt, and Rosemarie Scullion. At Texas A&M, they include Nathan Bracher, Ruth Larson, Melanie Hawthorne, and especially Ralph Schoolcraft, who offered careful and thoughtful readings of several of the chapters included here (as well as sharing my passion for the music of Delbert McClinton). I also wish to thank Susan Suleiman at Harvard, Ora Avni at Yale, Anke Finger and Roger Celestin at the University of Connecticut, and Luis Costa at Fresno State for inviting me to talk about the "politics of complicity" on their campuses and for offering their own ideas on the subject. I am especially indebted to Lynn Higgins and Mary Jean Green at Dartmouth. Hosting me at Dartmouth to lecture on complicity is just one of the many kindnesses both have shown me over the years. Lynn was also a careful, thoughtful, and rigorous reader of the manuscript of this book, and for her comments as well as many other things I owe her my thanks.

In Bryan–College Station, tennis buddies David Ogden, Joe Ward, and Doug Goodgame have tolerated bad tennis and irrational outbursts from me on the court and have even let me win a little along the way. My administrative assistant Ede Hilton-Lowe has put the wheels back on and bailed me out so many times I've lost count. Three friends in particular—Wayne Ahr, Terry Anderson, and Larry Reynolds—have generously shared their wit, intelligence, and wisdom with me over many years. Wayne has tried—and failed—to teach me many valuable practical skills as well as the true history of the Great State of Texas. Terry and Larry have been exemplary tennis partners, excellent colleagues, astute critics of my writing, and much more. *Merci, chers amis.*

Finally, I want to thank my family. My mother Lucy, my sisters Katie and Maryanne, and my niece Sonia, francophiles all, have shared my love of France for as long as I can remember. Most of all, I wish to thank my sons James and Jody and my wife Nancy for their support, love, and patience. They are the reasons why.

Earlier versions of several chapters have been published previously. I wish to thank the editors of *Nottingham French Studies* (chapter 2), *SubStance* (chapter 3), and *Contemporary French Civilization* (chapter 4) for permission to incorporate those essays in this book.

French Writers
and the Politics of Complicity

Introduction

Complicity is a disturbing word. According to most dictionary definitions, it signifies participation or involvement in a crime or other form of wrongdoing. In its French usage, it can also mean a deep, conspiratorial bond between individuals. The *Robert* dictionary gives "connivance" as a synonym. But these definitions do not do justice to the full range of intentions and behaviors associated with complicity. This is especially the case in attempts to characterize and assess the moral, legal, or political implications of complicity in difficult and even life-threatening historical circumstances. For example, in experiencing military defeat and occupation by a foreign power, most citizens of the defeated and occupied country are constrained to "go along with" or, to use Philippe Burrin's expression, to "accommodate themselves" to the abuses and even the criminal actions of the occupying power.[1] There are of course degrees of willingness involved, but accommodation in any form still implies a level of complicity—in refusing to oppose or resist a particular politics, the individual allows for and even participates in its perpetuation.[2]

In *France under the Germans*, Burrin demonstrates that accommodation of this sort was the lot of the French during World War II. He emphasizes that no profession, class, or walk of life managed to avoid accommodation and that no other country in Hitler's Europe succeeded in avoiding France's fate. As Burrin claims, "despite their great diversity, there was not a single country in Nazi Europe that did not, to some degree, witness the emergence of accommodating behavior."[3]

The historical record backs Burrin's claim, and many extraordinary literary and cinematic works appearing in the long postwar period also testify to the often terrible and dehumanizing consequences of accommodation or complicity with Nazi tyranny. The continuing impact of many of these works confirms that the problem of complicity in a wide variety of forms with Hitlerian evil remains a source of moral unrest and soul-searching more than a half century after the experience of occupation and accommodation.

If political complicity is acute during periods of occupation by a foreign power, it becomes nothing less than a permanent and integral feature of life in totalitarian societies. The effects of constant ideological indoctrination and the omnipresence of terror are such that no one and nothing remains outside "the political." As a result, all individuals are implicated to some extent in the perpetuation as well as the projects and actions of the regime. But as Tzvetan Todorov points out in a remarkable essay on the totalitarian experience, the average citizen remains oblivious to this fact because, in totalitarian societies, power never reveals its true source.[4] (Indeed, Claude Lefort insists that it is the very essence of totalitarianism that power is always "unlocatable.")[5] The average citizen participates in the totalitarian exercise while remaining oblivious to one degree or another to his or her complicity. *Homo sovieticus*, as Todorov labels such a citizen (or at least the former Soviet variety), automatically identifies with political authority as well as its affirmations and undertakings yet never feels responsible, since it is always "others who decide."[6]

But what of systems or historical circumstances that are much less coercive or constraining, such as modern capitalist democracies? What forms of complicity are prevalent and perhaps characteristic? In his controversial book *The Gulf War Did Not Take Place*, Jean Baudrillard argues that during the conflict in Kuwait (the first "Gulf War") the war was essentially *invisible* to the public because all media coverage and images produced were tightly controlled. Nonetheless, all in the West were made complicitous in the conflict through an endless media barrage that showed *nothing* of the death and destruction taking place. In a colorful if disturbing metaphor, Baudrillard compares the television-viewing public in the European and U.S. democracies to "seabird[s] glued in an oil spill, blinded and helpless," in front of their screens. One was an "accomplice" to this "anorexic war," he continued, in the same way that one was an abettor in a ubiquitous publicity campaign.[7]

Baudrillard may well be stretching the notion of complicity to the breaking point in declaring virtually everyone complicitous in the Gulf War simply because they were inundated with sanitized news of a conflict they did not necessarily understand or condone. But the complexity of a mediatized world in which, as Alain Finkielkraut has stressed, we are all beamed into the immediacy of faraway and often incomprehensible conflicts certainly complicates our status as mere spectators, or "bystanders." Our "presence," so to speak, can force us into the role of participants. If we do not react to stop ethnic cleansing in the former Yugoslavia, for example (this was Finkielkraut's context), we are arguably a party to it.

As if the dilemma of complicity through media saturation in contemporary democracies were not enough, there are other, equally troubling forms of complicity that are not necessarily "media induced." These forms of complicity go more directly to the heart of individual responsibility. In his illuminating study titled *Complicity*, the legal philosopher Christopher Kutz offers a number of examples of such complicitous behavior on an individual scale. These include "buying a table of tropical wood that comes from a defoliated rain forest, or owning stock in a company that does business with a country that jails political dissenters; being a citizen of a nation that bombs another country's factories in a reckless attack on terrorists, or inhabiting a region seized long ago from its aboriginal occupants; helping to design an automobile the manufacturer knowingly sells with a dangerously defective fuel system, or administering a national health care bureaucracy that carelessly allows the distribution of HIV-contaminated blood."[8]

What is fascinating in Kutz's examples of complicity is not only the range of individual actions described but, among other things, the degree of moral ambiguity associated with all of them. Kutz notes that in each of the cases alluded to, the individual may "stand outside the shadow of evil," but that does not mean that he or she stands "in the full light of good." Moreover, Kutz continues, in democratic societies generally speaking, there is an absence of an integrated legal framework to deal justly with such "mediated relations to harms."[9]

Kutz's examples also underscore the potential degree of ignorance on the part of the individual implicated in these actions. For example, the person buying the table made of tropical wood may not know about the defoliated rain forest, just as the individual designing one component for the automobile may not know about the defective fuel system and its dangers. Similarly, a person buying stock in a company that deals with a politically oppressive regime may be either unaware of the corporation's dealings with that regime or uninformed as to the political abuses in which the regime indulges, and thus that person will not be aware of his or her own political complicity. Ignorance is of course no excuse, at least under the law, but in assessing an individual's complicity in wrongdoing, ignorance of that wrongdoing would certainly appear to be an extenuating circumstance. It would also appear to make a clear-cut determination of responsibility or culpability more difficult.

If ignorance of one's complicity muddies the moral as well as the intellectual waters (not to mention the legal waters), so, too, does the problem of motive. One can become complicitous in the most terrible of crimes—indeed, one may even precipitate them—through justifiable acts of self-defense or through the urge to protect what one loves. A person can also become complicitous in crime through baser motives or even through sheer accident, in which case there is no real motive at all. Finally, one can become complicitous in a crime through a combination of these and other motives. This can certainly occur in any political circumstances, but the stakes are often much higher under authoritarian or politically repressive regimes.

To return to the context of Nazi-occupied Europe and to the postwar literary and cinematic representations of the period, some of the most powerful of these works dramatize the grimmest acts of political complicity brought about by arguably "innocent" or at least "mundane" motives or circumstances. A recent example occurs in Bernhard Schlink's novel *The Reader* (1998). During the postwar trial for complicity in the Holocaust of his former lover Hanna Schmitz, the narrator realizes to his consternation and horror that during the war Hanna had passed up an innocuous bureaucratic promotion at Siemens in order to take a job as a guard in one of the satellite labor camps of Auschwitz. Hanna did so in order to hide her illiteracy—a source of deep and abiding shame—that would have been revealed had she accepted the promotion. At the camp, she had become complicitous in the deaths of hundreds of women for the same reason. For the reader and certainly the narrator of Schlink's novel, the urge to forgive Hanna for her all-too-human failing and an apparent lack of harmful intentions seems reasonable. But as Christopher Kutz warns in his own remarks on *The Reader*, forgiveness itself can be a "dangerous and complicitous urge."[10]

In *The Assault* (1982), Dutch novelist Harry Mulisch describes an equally troubling act of complicity with Nazi murderousness. When the collaborationist chief of police is assassinated by the Resistance on a residential street in Harlem, the parents and brother of young Anton Steenwijk are brutally murdered and their house burned down by the Nazis because the dead policeman's body is found in front of their residence. Neither the parents nor Anton's brother had anything to do with the assassination. The novel follows Anton's escape, survival of the war, and coming to adulthood in postwar Holland. It also traces the incident's effect on his life and, eventually, his efforts to understand the murder of his family and why the neighbors, the Kortewegs, had dragged the policeman's corpse in front of Anton's house. Years later, Anton learns from Karin Korteweg, who had helped her father move the body, that her father was attempting to save his pet lizards, who would have perished had his home been burned instead of the Steenwijk's.

Such a petty motive for complicity in the murder of three human beings appears both abject and cowardly on the face of it. But as the novel shows, Korteweg's subsequent actions and further revelations concerning his motives make his complicity all the more complex and disturbing and, on one score at least, almost laudable.

Karin explains to Anton that after her mother's death, her father had come to love the lizards more than anything else, that they meant "something about eternity and immortality" to him. They had become, simply, "his only reason for living."[11] But following the murder of Anton's family, he had removed them from their cages and stomped them to death in despair. The reader also learns that Korteweg had chosen the Steenwijk residence rather than neighbors on the other side because the latter were hiding a family of Jews, something no one else in the neighborhood knew. Korteweg had wished to protect them. For Anton at least, this revelation confirms that Korteweg had been "a good man" after all. After his meeting with Karin and his final understanding of everything that had happened on the night of his family's death, Anton wonders, "Was everyone both guilty and not guilty? Was guilt innocent, and innocence guilt?"[12] One is not obliged to accept the extreme moral relativism implicit in Anton's questions to appreciate the tragic ambiguities of Korteweg's action and of the situation itself.

Those familiar with French postwar cinematic representations of the Occupation—especially Louis Malle's masterpieces *Lacombe Lucien* (1974) and *Au revoir les enfants* (1987)—are also aware of the extent to which complicity with Nazi murderousness could be the tragic and ironic result of chance or, equally ironically, of concern for someone else's safety. In *Lacombe Lucien*, the young peasant boy Lucien Lacombe falls in with a band of French Fascists and thugs working as German police who catch him out after curfew because of a flat tire on his bike. He soon not only adopts his fellow policemen's political prejudices and racism, but he also joins in their acts of extortion, torture, and murder. In *Au revoir les enfants*, young Julien Quentin accidentally betrays his Jewish friend Jean Kippelstein, who is being hidden by the priests in the Catholic school both boys attend. When the Gestapo chief comes into the boys' classroom looking for the Jewish students, Julien exposes his friend by turning to look at Jean, apparently out of fear for his safety. Jean is led away by the Nazis at the end of the film, and the voice-over informs the spectator that he later dies at Auschwitz.[13]

These examples of complicity with political evil are, of course, fictional. But in Malle's films and Mulisch's novel, they are drawn from historical events and very real circumstances. With the exception of Lucien Lacombe, these cases reflect neither a willful desire to participate in political evil nor an overt espousal of its aims and ambitions. But even when these aims and ambitions are openly embraced, they may not be truly understood by the complicitous individual. Lucien has no real political understanding of the war, of why he should hate the Jews, of why he should torture and kill Resistance members. In fact, before happenstance throws him in with the "German police," he attempts to sign up for the Resistance and is rejected.

But Lucien is an ignorant peasant boy. What of educated, cultured individuals and of intellectuals in particular? Should one assume that because they are informed and discerning they are fully cognizant of the implications of their political involvements and complicity with political evil? Sadly, the record of the twentieth century proves that a large—indeed shocking—number of intellectuals, artists, and scholars were complicitous with oppressive, authoritarian, racist, and antidemocratic regimes. The record also suggests that the intellectual and artistic talents of these individuals, rather than aiding their understanding of the brutal realities of these regimes, often blinded them to the most fundamental features of the politics and ideologies they embraced. Despite their culture and intelligence, many of these individuals revealed themselves ultimately to be the victims of what Mark Lilla has characterized as their own "reckless minds."[14]

Especially since the Martin Heidegger and Paul de Man affairs of the late 1980s, any number of studies have focused on intellectual and artistic complicity with Nazism, Italian Fascism, and Vichy, and have examined the misguided allegiances of some of the twentieth century's most important artistic and intellectual figures. For example, in a study of what she labels "aesthetic fascism" in Italy and France from the interwar years through the end of World War II, Mary Ann Frese Witt explores the relationship between the politics and aesthetics of a number of important Fascist or *fascisant* writers and playwrights including Gabrielle D'Annunzio, Luigi Pirandello, Henry de Montherlant, and Jean Anouilh. Pirandello's case is especially interesting in that, as Witt points out, while he was not unaware of Fascist violence and even joined the party after the murder of Italian Socialist leader Giacomo Matteotti, he confused his own aesthetics with Fascism and saw as the essence of both "the incessant and ever-renewed conflict between life and form."[15] His support for the regime derived, then, from an abstract and idealized (mis)understanding of Fascism that allowed him to ignore or dismiss the brutal core of Mussolini's movement—the true basis of its power and dynamism.

Complicity of this sort was not restricted to Italy or France. Richard Wolin has argued in *Heidegger's Children* that Martin Heidegger's scandalous complicity with Nazism derived at least in part from a failure to grasp the brutal, petty reality of the movement combined with a tendency to interpret its essence in relation to the exalted categories of Heidegger's own existential philosophy. Wolin also cites a comment by Heidegger's pupil Karl Löwith to the effect that Heidegger was blinded simply by his own class background: Heidegger "failed to notice the destructive radicalism of the [Nazi] movement and the petty bourgeois character of all its 'strength-through-joy' institutions, because he was a radical petty bourgeois himself." Even after the war and the horrors of the Holocaust, Heidegger did not grasp the wellsprings of the regime's murderousness. He attributed the "genocidal politics of the Nazis . . . to the evils of 'technology,' the distortions of the 'modern world-picture,' the post-Cartesian 'will to will,' or the 'forgetting of Being.'" As Wolin puts it, Heidegger's "metapolitical" explanations stressed everything but the obvious.[16]

The involvements of Pirandello with Italian Fascism and Heidegger with Nazism bring us, broadly speaking, to the central concern of this book: the complicity of writers and intellectuals in reactionary antidemocratic and racist politics. However, the geographical context is neither Italy nor Germany but France, and the time frame to be treated is not just the interwar years and the period of Nazi hegemony in Europe between 1940 and 1945 (1944 in France) but the 1990s as well.

Some readers will find the linkage of the two time periods initially puzzling, if not implausible. After all, in historical and political terms, the France of Philippe Pétain and of collaboration with the Nazis would appear to have absolutely nothing in common with the Fifth Republican France of the Socialist François Mitterrand and the Gaullist Jacques Chirac. However, that linkage is necessary and indeed crucial to understanding the intellectual commitments of the figures discussed from the 1990s as well as the implications of those commitments, because the history and especially the memory of Vichy, Nazism, and the Holocaust provided a constant frame of reference through which contemporary crises were interpreted.

Conversely, in discussing the complicity and collaborationism of three writers from the so-called Dark Years of the German Occupation, it is important to stress that our ability to interpret their involvements has been enhanced by the availability of new and richly documented research as well as by original sources not previously available. It has also been enhanced by new and richer perspectives on the period generated in large part by a strong, and some would argue obsessive, fascination with the World War II period in France and elsewhere throughout the 1990s. Specifically, the preeminence of the so-called Vichy Syndrome, to be discussed shortly, not only dramatically recast our understanding of the period as well as the wages of complicity with Nazism and Vichy in particular but also made the Occupation very much a part of *l'actualité*—of the present—during the past decade. In different forms and different contexts, the three collaborationist writers to be discussed here are part of this "presence" of the Vichy past and have therefore left their marks on contemporary French cultural politics. And in one of the three cases, that of Henry de Montherlant, this "presence" has also been felt in important intellectual debates in the United States as well. Those who followed the de Man affair will recall that several of the most visible figures who sought to defend de Man against charges of pro-Nazism and anti-Semitism—Jacques Derrida and J. Hillis Miller among them—did so by arguing that because de Man had been highly critical of Montherlant's collaborationist book *Le solstice de Juin* in a November 1942 review in the Belgian collaborationist newspaper *Le Soir*, he could not possibly share Montherlant's collaborationist views. They claimed that de Man's criticism of *Le solstice* proved that he was at least implicitly *résistant*. However, the fact is that de Man in his review did *not* criticize Montherlant's politics but rather his excessive individualism and his presumption as an artist to speak of politics. Under any circumstances, Montherlant's "case" as well as his collaborationism and complicity with Vichy and Nazism are much more complex than the simplistic discussions during the de Man affair acknowledge.[17]

It is important at this juncture to make clear the ways in which words including *commitment* (or "engagement"), *collaboration*, and, most importantly, *complicity* will be used in the chapters that follow. *Commitment* implies a conscious and articulated support of a political, ideological, or national cause. *Collaboration*, as applied to the context of Vichy France, generally implies overt or at least tacit support of the regime of Philippe Pétain but also, and more importantly, an attitude favorable to the presence and politics of the Nazis. *Collaboration* covers a wide range of activities and degrees of support, and therefore the collaborationism of particular individuals is often debatable, depending on one's perspective. Perhaps the best definition of *collaboration* in France during World War II is the one offered by Philippe Burrin: "accommodation raised to the level of politics."[18]

Complicity, as I will use the word in this book, is as varied in its applications — that is, the forms and degrees of involvement it assumes — as is *collaboration*. But *complicity* also embraces individual motives as well as the often unforeseen and negative *political* implications and consequences of one's choices and beliefs, political and otherwise. Motives can embrace political perspectives and prejudices as well as religious beliefs. In the case of Henry de Montherlant, they can also embrace chivalric ideals and psychosexual motivations. Equally important, they also involve the vision of history — often flawed or skewed — of the writer, intellectual, or historian in question.

As for unforeseen implications and consequences, by this I mean the largely unintentional or unintended results of one's actions or positions, the kind of "blind spots" explored in the novels of Harry Mulisch and Bernhard Schlink, the films of Louis Malle, and the examples of mundane day-to-day complicity described by Christopher Kutz. Pacifism and a particularly archaic form of Christian religiosity, although not necessarily condemnable in the abstract, lead to complicity with Nazi murderousness and war making. In the 1990s, a belief in a nation's right to sovereignty, or in the need to resist American hegemony and to rekindle French grandeur, or, finally, in a duty to the memory of Communism's victims led to sup-

port of authoritarian, ethnocentric, and antidemocratic regimes as well as dangerous historical "revisionisms" with disturbing implications for the present.

The first three chapters of this study examine the careers, writings, and—most
centrally—the political complicity with Vichy and Nazism of three writers known
at the time primarily for their novels and essays. The first of these is the aforementioned Henry de Montherlant, a veteran of World War I and a leading member in
France of what the historian Robert Wohl has labeled the "Generation of 1914."[19]
As chapter 1 demonstrates, Montherlant's complicity, especially with Nazism, derived less from a direct sympathy with or embrace of Nazism's political and racist
doctrines than from a combination of the writer's obsession with virility and force,
his sexual proclivities, his skewed and simplistic vision of history, and the inadequacy and indeed bankruptcy of his personal, "heroic" ethics. That is, Montherlant's complicity with Nazism and Vichy derived in the main from a troubling mix
of largely *apolitical* penchants and perspectives that made him susceptible in several
ways and for a number of reasons to the "new European" masters. While Montherlant was neither a political "innocent" nor ignorant of many of the implications of
his complicity, his obsession with indulging in his own pleasures, his misplaced confidence in his own vision of history, and his arrogant faith in his own ethics blinded
him to the full implications of the historical convulsions occurring around him.

Chapter 2 covers the writer Alphonse de Châteaubriant. Châteaubriant made his
literary mark before World War I and during the interwar years as a Breton regional
novelist who won important literary prizes both before and after the Great War. By
the 1930s, his desire to write regionalist fictions celebrating the virtues of rural life
and tradition became increasingly submerged under the weight of an apocalyptic
Christian mysticism. That mysticism shaped and eventually grossly distorted his understanding of history and politics and clearly eroded what critical intelligence he
had. It also led in the mid-1930s to a fatal error in political judgment. In 1936,
Châteaubriant traveled to Nazi Germany, where he became a "convert" to Nazism.
The evidence of this "conversion" can be found in *La gerbe des forces*, a book published on his return to France that dealt with his journey to the German Reich. In
the book Châteaubriant revealed his greatest discovery, that Adolf Hitler was nothing less than the new incarnation of Christ.

After the French defeat of June 1940 and the occupation of much of France by
the Germans, Châteaubriant became one of Paris's most vocal collaborators and an
incessant champion of Hitler's "New Europe." Châteaubriant's fanaticism led in
the postwar years to his dismissal as France's most distasteful and mindless pro-Nazi
zealot and as a writer of no talent or interest. But Châteaubriant is noteworthy to the

extent that his complicity—and in his case, his direct *engagement*—with Nazism derived, like Montherlant's, from arguably apolitical concerns. Both his apocalyptic
and millenarian Christian mysticism and his obsessive desire to return to a premodern medieval Europe led him to embrace an ideology and a politics whose historical mission and aims were, he believed, divinely inspired. Even after the war, the
power of the writer's perverted religiosity prevented him from understanding the
reality of Nazism.

Chapter 3 is devoted to the Provençal novelist Jean Giono. A respected "classic"
whose works continue to receive a good deal of scholarly attention, especially in
France, Giono began his career as a writer in the late 1920s and early 1930s with the
publication of novels that celebrated the beauty and power of nature in his native
Provence as well as the virtues, purity, and hardships of peasant life. As a regionalist novelist, he was more talented and certainly more poetically gifted than
Châteaubriant. A veteran of the trenches during World War I who gave up a career
as a bank clerk to become a writer, Giono had also become by the mid-1930s an outspoken proponent of integral pacifism as well as a kind of prophet of an antimodern
"return to the soil." His opposition to the outbreak of war was thus "preordained,"
and to a significant degree he held the French Third Republic accountable for the
outbreak of hostilities. Given these perspectives, his complicity with Vichy and
sympathy for the Germans was predictable. But as much as he was motivated by certain cultural and ideological affinities with Vichy, he was also motivated by his vision of the role of the writer in society. To the degree that war and especially what
might be described as "Third Republican modernity" threatened the writer's function (the "poet," in Giono's view), it threatened his very existence as well. In this
sense, his complicity was at least as "existential" and "aesthetic" in its motivation as
it was political.

Why choose Henry de Montherlant, Alphonse de Châteaubriant, and Jean
Giono in studying political complicity with Vichy and with Nazism in Occupied
France? All three collaborated—to varying degrees, in various ways, and, most in-
terestingly, for a variety of reasons and motives. What is most interesting, however,
is the *range* of beliefs, prejudices, and penchants that influenced their political
choices and contributed to their complicity with the antidemocratic and authoritarian politics and practices of Vichy and the Third Reich. A consideration of these
motives and beliefs, as well as their practical consequences, also reveals these figures
in their flawed humanity. My intention is neither to excuse nor exonerate but to
make their complicity more readily comprehensible by recognizing the flaws, errors, and blind spots of these figures and how these led to the choices they made and
the historical perspectives they adopted.

Although Montherlant, Châteaubriant, and Giono collaborated to one degree or another with Vichy and Nazism, none was considered to belong to the generation of Fascist and anti-Semitic writers and intellectuals who largely shaped extreme right-wing sensibilities in France during the interwar years and the Occupation. Therefore, with the occasional exception of Montherlant, all have been more or less ignored in a number of important recent works on French literary and cultural Fascism. Members of the "Fascist generation"—primarily Pierre Drieu La Rochelle, Robert Brasillach, and, for his pro-Nazism and anti-Semitism, Louis-Ferdinand Céline, as well as figures such as Lucien Rebatet, Thierry Maulnier, and Paul Morand—have been the objects of much critical attention in France and in the United States. Alice Kaplan's *Reproductions of Banality* (1986) and David Carroll's *French Literary Fascism* (1995) deal broadly with the topic of literary and cultural Fascism and the writers just mentioned, and Kaplan has devoted to Brasillach a book-length study, *The Collaborator: The Trial and Execution of Robert Brasillach* (2000). Drieu, for his part, was the subject of a Sorbonne colloquium in 1993 and has been the focus of a major monograph by Jacques Lecarme, *Drieu La Rochelle, ou le bal des maudits* (2001). Earlier, Rima Drell Reck had written a study of Drieu's art criticism and its relation to his fiction in the United States. Even Lucien Rebatet receives chapters in Carroll's and Kaplan's books and has been the subject of a recent book in France by Robert Belot (1994). Céline scholarship is a publishing industry unto itself. In treating the cases of Montherlant, Châteaubriant, and Giono, then, one of the purposes of this study will be to situate them, at least in general terms, in relation to the tradition of French literary Fascism.

The second part of this book examines three very different figures in the 1990s and looks at their respective roles in relation to three controversial events and debates of the past decade. The individuals in question are not novelists or *littéraires*— the category of writers who largely controlled the intellectual discourses of the 1930s and the Occupation—but rather philosophers, "public intellectuals," and historians. Although there were engagé novelists in the 1990s who were outspoken and indeed influential in their views (the case of Pascal Bruckner, a successful novelist and *philosophe*, comes to mind), the intellectual and political discourse of the decade itself was dominated by philosophers and historians (as well as sociologists such as Pierre Bourdieu) including André Glucksmann, Bernard-Henri Lévy, Étienne Balibar, Tzvetan Todorov, François Furet, Henry Rousso, and others. So the study of political complicity during the 1990s would seem to offer the richest possibilities in looking at the actions and choices of individuals from these categories.

Chapter 4 deals with philosopher and "public intellectual" Alain Finkielkraut's early and outspoken support for Croatian independence during the violent breakup of the former Yugoslavia in the early 1990s. Finkielkraut expressed his support for Croatia in books and pamphlets including *Comment peut-on être Croate?* (1992) and *Le crime d'être né: L'Europe, les nations, la guerre* (1994); in numerous articles, interviews, and editorials; and in more recent works including *L'Ingratitude* (1999) and *L'Imparfait du présent* (2002).

Finkielkraut's support for Croatia and the regime of Franjo Tudjman is laudable to the extent that it was timely and needed in the face of brutal acts of Serb aggression including, for example, the destruction of the town of Vukovar and the grim beginnings of ethnic cleansing. However, obscured in the story of Croatian martyrdom are the nationalist and xenophobic origins of Tudjman's governing party, which proudly embraced the traditions and symbols of the Croatian Ustaša movement. During World War II, the Ustaša had fervently embraced Nazism, anti-Semitism, and Italian Fascism. Former Ustaša members contributed to Tudjman's party and had returned from exile with Tudjman's rise to power. In political speeches, Tudjman had expressed satisfaction that his wife was neither Serbian nor Jewish, and in his autobiography he made statements that bordered on denying the Holocaust.

In embracing the Croatian cause, Finkielkraut made himself de facto complicitous with the darker side of Croatian nationalism, although no one would suggest that he was sympathetic to its ethnocentrism and racism. But in his more recent writings on Croatia, Finkielkraut has shown a troubling tendency to excuse and exonerate. In *L'Imparfait du présent* he denounces the efforts of the International Criminal Tribunal to arrest and try Croatians accused of ethnic cleansing. For Finkielkraut, this would be tantamount to asserting that "all cats are gray" in the night "of history,"[20] that is, that the crucial distinction between victim and perpetrator is being lost. But in insisting on an absolute distinction between these two categories, one ends up with a Manichaean view of history and rigid categories of guilt and innocence that do not always conform to historical reality.

Chapter 5 of this study is also devoted to French intellectual reactions to events in the Balkans. Several years after Finkielkraut announced his support for Croatia, during the 1999 NATO bombing campaign against Serbia intended to stop Serb abuses against ethnic Albanians in Kosovo, the philosopher and "mediologist" Régis Debray set off a firestorm of controversy by publishing an open letter in *Le Monde* concerning the conflict. Debray's letter denounced the Allied bombardments and protested the persecution of the Serbs. Debray also presented Slobodan Milosevic as a latter-day Charles de Gaulle. Finally, he insisted that Serb crimes against Kosovar Albanians were largely trumped up and that Serb security forces were actually watching out for the security of the majority ethnic Albanian population.

For some, Debray's letter smacked simply of Parisian intellectual grandstanding and sensationalism. But its import was in fact much more serious in that it deliberately recast the role of persecutor and persecuted in the conflict and came dangerously close to whitewashing the crimes of the Serbs. Debray's explicit support for— his complicity with—Milosevic's Serbia shocked many. Some of his friends and fellow intellectuals went so far as to break off relations with him over the incident, or at least claimed to publicly. It was, it seemed, difficult if not impossible to reconcile Debray's pro-Serb stance with his long career, first as a leftist revolutionary, then as an advisor to French President François Mitterrand, and finally as a fierce defender of French "National Republicanism."

Chapter 6 is devoted to a final incident of complicity with antidemocratic and racist politics, this time in the context of one of the historical controversies that raged in France during the 1990s and in many ways characterized the decade. In fall 1997, while the trial in Bordeaux for crimes against humanity of former Vichy functionary Maurice Papon riveted national attention on the Vichy past, the Éditions Robert Laffont published an encyclopedic, multiauthored account of Communism's crimes worldwide, the *Livre noir du communisme*, or *Black Book of Communism*. The work of six distinguished historians, the volume was edited by Stéphane Courtois, director of the review *Communisme* who was chosen to oversee the *Livre noir* project after the untimely death of François Furet, who had originally agreed to direct it.

When the *Livre noir* appeared, it immediately generated tremendous public debate. The parameters and ramifications of that debate, largely generated by Stéphane Courtois's controversial introduction, will be discussed in detail in chapter 6. In his introduction, Courtois chose not to summarize the findings of the other contributors. Instead, in his self-assigned role as "memory militant" for Communism's victims, he turned his introduction into a polemic that both distorted the actual findings of his coauthors and put those findings to a purpose for which they were not intended: a comparison of the crimes of Communism to Nazism. Moreover, basing his comparison on moral and legal arguments, Courtois determined that Communism's crimes were not equal to those of the Nazis but were in fact worse. He concluded by calling, in effect, for a Nuremberg tribunal for the crimes of Communism.

On the face of it, Courtois's demand that Communism's victims be acknowledged and the criminality of Communist regimes exposed is laudable and, in his stated view in the book, in keeping with the duty and responsibility of the contemporary historian. But in comparing Communist crimes to those of the Nazis, Courtois's aims and ends become murkier and the implications of his reasoning and arguments much more troubling. Shortly after the *Livre noir* appeared, the distinguished Holocaust historian Annette Wieviorka blasted Courtois for attempting in effect to erase Nazism's criminality by putting Communism's criminality in its place. For Wieviorka, this amounted to Holocaust denialism on Courtois's part.

So, what links to each other Finkielkraut and his complicity with Croatian nationalism, Debray and his complicity with Serbia's brutal hegemony in Kosovo, and Courtois and his complicity with a dangerous historical revision? First, they are connected by the paradoxical nature of their respective positions. With the possible exception of Debray's support for the Serbs in Kosovo, the three positions taken certainly have their merits: they can be considered reasonable and even just causes. In the face of Serbian hegemony in the early 1990s, Croatia's bid for independence had much to recommend it. And in a decade committed to remembering the victims of Nazism and Vichy, remembering Communism's innumerable victims seemed not only appropriate but necessary as well. Even in the case of Kosovo, one could argue that the Serbs were not the only guilty parties and that, under any circumstances, NATO's overwhelming military superiority, its destruction of civilian targets— whether inadvertent or not—and its unwillingness to endanger its own troops by placing them on the ground cast it in the role of bully and the Serb civilians, at least, in the role of victim. Be that as it may, all three commitments also implicated their authors in intellectual positions and political ends hardly in keeping with democratic principles. At the risk of oversimplifying, both the "good" and the "bad" sides of these commitments will be examined in the chapters that follow.

Second, all three men justified and contextualized their choices through explicit or implicit comparisons to World War II, Nazism, and the memory of Vichy and the Occupation. As we shall see, Finkielkraut compared Croatia to the smaller countries gobbled up by Hitler's Reich during World War II, which of necessity cast Serbia in the role of a latter-day Nazi Germany. The "duty to memory" to the victims of Nazism therefore dictated resistance to Serb aggression. Similarly, for Courtois, the full horror of Communist crimes could only be appreciated through moral and legal comparisons with those of the Nazis. Finally, Debray relied on the same historical context to justify his position but reversed the terms of comparison by casting Milosevic in the role of de Gaulle, the very symbol of Resistance to Vichy and Nazism.

In order to appreciate how the memory of World War II, Nazism, and Vichy became such a powerful hermeneutic device or "interpretive magnet" in the 1990s, it is important to stress again the extraordinary weight or *presence* of that memory in French political and cultural life in the 1990s. This "presence" was evident not only in the trials for crimes against humanity of former Vichy henchmen and civil servants such as Paul Touvier in 1994 and Maurice Papon in 1997–1998 but also in the

scandal surrounding the role of former Vichy chief of police René Bousquet in negotiating with the Nazis the deportations of Jews from France in spring 1942. A successful postwar businessman and friend of President François Mitterrand, Bousquet
would also have stood trial for crimes against humanity—indeed, his would have
been by far the most important trial—had he not been gunned down by a crazed
publicity seeker in July 1993.

Added to these trials and other controversies associated with French complicity
in the Nazi genocide of the Jews was the scandal surrounding 1994 revelations concerning the extent and duration of François Mitterrand's service to Vichy and his
prewar right-wing and anti-Semitic sympathies. Although all of this was not news to
many historians (as well as to some on the extreme Right who had been trying to use
Mitterrand's Vichy past to damage him politically for years), the fact that Mitterrand
had won the regime's highest service award, the *Francisque*, and had been close to
Bousquet for years left many of the French in shock. In political and judicial terms,
not only did the Vichy past appear to be "a past that would not pass" (to paraphrase
the title of a book by Henry Rousso and Éric Conan),[21] but it seemed capable of unsettling comfortable political and cultural certainties that many took for granted in
postwar France. For a good number of those shaken by revelations concerning
Mitterrand's Vichy and right-wing past, the most difficult pill to swallow was that
Mitterrand was the very symbol of the resurgence of the French Left in the postwar
years and an authentic Resistance hero to boot. How could this man *also* have been
the very opposite of everything he supposedly embodied? Given its power to haunt
and unsettle, Vichy managed to resonate as a kind of malignant presence. The title
of the April 1992 issue of the distinguished review *Esprit* seemed to sum up a concern lurking in the French national conscience: "What to do with Vichy?"—and
this question was asked even before the worst of the "eruptions of memory" had
occurred.

Apart from the Mitterrand scandal and the trials for crimes against humanity, the
constant presence on the political scene of the extreme right wing and xenophobic
National Front and its leader Jean-Marie Le Pen stirred troubled memories of and
encouraged enumerable comparisons with Vichy and Nazism. At each election, the
visibility of National Front campaign posters showing blond-haired, blue-eyed
"French" people encouraged these memories and comparisons, as did Le Pen's own
disdainful dismissal of the Holocaust as a "detail of history." All of this, of course, hit
a high watermark not in the 1990s but in spring 2002, when Le Pen made it to the
second and final round of the presidential elections.

French domestic politics were not the only politics colored by the presence of
Vichy. Alain Finkielkraut was by no means alone in seeing Serb aggression as a kind

of renascent Nazism. In his 1994 book *Ce fascisme qui vient . . .* (This fascism that is coming . . .), Jacques Julliard compared the European situation at that moment to the Europe of Munich.

As if political scandals and controversial trials were not enough, films and novels dramatizing the Vichy past seemed to appear at an ever-increasing rate in the 1990s. Major directors in France devoted their talents to making films about the Occupation. Claude Chabrol made two compelling films about the Vichy past: the documentary *The Eye of Vichy*, and *A Story of Women*, the powerful fictionalized portrayal of an abortionist executed by the Pétain regime. Claude Berri adapted *Uranus*, Marcel Aymé's bitter novel of the hypocrisies of the Occupation and the Liberation for the screen, and also made a hagiographic film of the Resistance, *Lucie Aubrac*, centering on the heroism of Lucie and Raymond Aubrac. Less well-known filmmakers produced works dealing with the period as well.

Among France's most visible novelists, Vichy, Nazism, and the Holocaust were also popular subjects. Jorge Semprun and Patrick Modiano devoted major works to the period—both Semprun's *L'Écriture ou la vie* and Modiano's *Dora Bruder* are now widely recognized as masterpieces—and visible younger novelists such as Marc Lambron, Lydie Salvaire, and Pierre Assouline have chosen the period as the backdrop for their works as well.

In dealing with popular novels and films, it is of course important to distinguish between those works that are simply intended to cater to current interests and fads and those that seek to reflect seriously on important cultural issues of the present. Each work has to be weighed on its own merits. But the sheer number and range of fictional works dealing with the Vichy past that appeared in the 1990s confirm the powerful hold of that past on the French collective imagination. Moreover, the complex human dramas played out in many of these works confirm the extent to which the Occupation served as a crucial historical *and* moral reference point, despite the fifty years that had elapsed since the Liberation.

Given these circumstances, it is very understandable that Finkielkraut, Debray, and Courtois should interpret current issues and debates in relation to the Vichy and Nazi pasts. Moreover, for the purposes of attracting public attention to their positions as well as swaying the public to their views, what better strategy than to cast their arguments against a historical backdrop with which the public was very familiar and with which it was very much engaged?

The danger is, of course, that historical comparisons can be profoundly misleading, both to the person who makes the comparison and to those one seeks to persuade in making that comparison. In the cases discussed here, the comparisons made imposed particular interpretations that in turn de-emphasized and even obscured the more troubling dimensions of the cause espoused or the position taken. In effect, Finkielkraut, Debray, and Courtois became complicitous in large part *through* the history they invoked in order to illuminate, and *not* to obscure, the present. Finally, like Montherlant, Châteaubriant, and Giono before them, because their political involvements did not, generally speaking, derive *directly* from the political, historical, and ideological issues at hand but were rather *refracted* through the memory of World War II, one can speak of all of these examples of complicity with antidemocratic politics as essentially oblique in nature.

Exploring political complicity in this fashion and in these contexts raises a number of sensitive issues and potential problems that should be mentioned at the outset. First, it is a dangerous temptation in dealing with a subject such as this to slip into facile judgments and condemnations of others' complicity with political evil, especially when one is safely insulated from that evil. In America—even after 9/11 and with the threat of terror supposedly ever present—it is hard to imagine living in Occupied France under the domination of the Nazis and, toward the end of the Occupation, in a state of virtual civil war.

But this concern assumed a more dramatic and concrete form in France in the 1990s, and with specific reference to the Dark Years themselves. For example, within the context of fulfilling the "duty to memory" to the victims of Nazism and Vichy, many have questioned the wisdom of sitting in judgment of the perpetrators fifty years after the fact, both without any real knowledge or understanding of the historical circumstances of the time and without risking anything oneself in condemning these perpetrators. To take an obvious judicial example, during the 1997–1998 trial for crimes against humanity of Maurice Papon, a number of commentators and observers expressed serious doubts about the justice of a trial in which members of the jury, none of whom had ever had to experience the horrors of Nazi Occupation and were never forced to make difficult political choices in dire circumstances, sat in judgment of a man who had. At least judges and jurors during the postwar Purge trials in France had experienced firsthand the deprivations, brutalities, and fears of the Dark Years, and were thus better equipped to understand and judge complicity with political oppression.

Writing about the political complicity of intellectuals is of course not at all the same thing as being a juror in a trial for crimes against humanity, but the same problem of summary (and ill-informed) judgments can arise in this context as well. At the height of the scandal surrounding Yale critic Paul de Man's collaborationist past, Frank Kermode challenged those who were quick to condemn de Man by arguing that had the Nazis succeeded in invading Britain early in the war, many aspiring young intellectuals and writers in Britain would probably also have embraced col-laboration with the Nazis in order to get ahead. Kermode's point, at least indirectly, was that some of those damning de Man might well have acted as he had if they had faced similar circumstances and pressures.

If summary condemnations of political complicity are a danger to historical understanding—and in the Papon trial—to justice itself, so too, some argue, is the opposite danger of explaining complicity away and indeed justifying it in a pur-ported effort to understand its subtleties. The resulting exoneration or whitewashing of the complicitous individual may not be deliberate, but in discussions of the po-litical complicity of intellectuals and artists, it is often linked to an impulse to sal-vage a reputation or at least artistic or intellectual achievements. To return to the de Man affair, some of de Man's more ardent defenders attempted to deny his anti-Semitic and pro-Nazi articles by recontextualizing them in such a way as to make them appear innocuous or even subtly *résistant*. This strategy was necessary because de Man's critics had insisted on an inescapable linkage between his collabora-tionism and deconstruction itself. In order to protect deconstruction, it became necessary to whitewash de Man's wartime past.

In his recent book on Drieu La Rochelle, Jacques Lecarme borders on apology—and certainly splits some dubious intellectual hairs—in defending the writer's lit-erary achievement by insisting that Drieu was only *truly* anti-Semitic in his jour-nalism, not in his fiction. So, was Drieu *the man* anti-Semitic or not? Lecarme also attempts to attenuate the anti-Semitism evident in at least one of Drieu's nov-els, *Gilles*, by arguing that it is nothing compared to the anti-Semitism of Hem-ingway's *The Sun Also Rises*. Here, the French writer's racism is effaced in the com-parison (shades of Stéphane Courtois, according to Annette Wieviorka, as we shall see), but at the cost of accusing Hemingway of racism. In both instances, Lecarme's effort to defend the writer he admires makes him culpable of a kind of literary negationism.[22]

But by no means do all efforts to comprehend and explain the subtleties of po-litical complicity amount to apology. In the preface to *Ordinary Men*, a book that explores in harrowing detail the murder of Jews in Occupied Poland by Reserve Police Battalion 101 of the German Order Police, Christopher Browning rejects this linkage explicitly. Browning even goes so far as to insist that one must recognize one's own capacity for murder in order to understand it, but that understanding it does not mean to excuse it: "I must recognize that in the same situation [that of the members of Battalion 101] I could have been either a killer or an evader—both were human—if I want to explain the behavior of both as best I can. This recognition does indeed mean an attempt to empathize. What I do not accept, however, are the old clichés that to explain is to excuse, to understand is to forgive. Explaining is not excusing, and understanding is not forgiving."[23]

Browning is of course speaking of very extreme circumstances and situations, and none of the cases of political complicity I will be dealing with here are as brutal, direct, or lethal. But especially in the first three chapters, it must be kept in mind that exploring the range of motivations and contributing factors that account for the political complicity with Nazism and Vichy of Henry de Montherlant, Jean Giono, and especially Alphonse de Châteaubriant is in no way intended to make their complicity any less repellent. That being said, as Browning observes, historical understanding also requires "the rejection of demonization,"[24] and that must be kept in mind as well.

If it is necessary to avoid the twin dangers of demonization and apology, as a contributing factor to these two tendencies it is also essential to avoid an assumption of the absolute inseparability of the personal and political and of the intellectual and aesthetic. Seyla Benhabib has asserted in a recent essay that this tendency constitutes nothing less than "the principle challenge to philosophy in contemporary culture" since it leads to what Paul Ricoeur has called the "hermeneutics of suspicion"—the idea that "every grand theory and noble sentiment hides a base motive." For Benhabib, the price of indulging in a hermeneutics of suspicion in assessing the work and politics of great thinkers is that it is tantamount to a refusal "to take philosophy and ideas seriously." One ends up conflating "the biographical with the theoretical, the personal with the political," and dismissing the "latter in the name of the former."[25]

Benhabib may well be oversimplifying matters in her comments on the hermeneutics of suspicion here. Nevertheless, in a study of the complicity of French writers and intellectuals in the 1940s and 1990s, it is important to avoid overly generalized and yet constraining accounts of the relationship among the personal, the political, and the intellectual or artistic that binds and even fuses these elements completely. An example of this danger occurs precisely in one of the books Benhabib criticizes in her essay, Mark Lilla's *The Restless Mind*. In the afterword to *The Restless Mind*, Lilla argues that the same force or "striving" that draws individuals to philosophy draws them to politics and, in the cases Lilla discusses, to tyranny. That force is *eros*, and it is the essential unity of one's *eros*, coupled with an inability to master or channel it properly, that accounts for the political complicity of major intellectual figures with antidemocratic, racist, and totalitarian regimes. *Eros*, in short, explains these figures' "intellectual philotyranny."[26]

Eros as Lilla defines it is too vague and imprecise a concept to account for the instances of political complicity to be discussed here. (It does not even account for the subtle readings of the political complicity of the likes of Heidegger, Schmitt, Foucault, and others that Lilla offers in his own book.) Moreover, it tends to dehistoricize and decontextualize complicity while working off of a series of apparently obvious but anachronistic assumptions. In his own critique of *The Restless Mind*, Allan Stoekl points out, for example, that whereas in the posttotalitarian world of today democracy may appear to be—and be championed as—the best and *only* legitimate political system, in France in the 1930s and in Germany after 1933 this view was not necessarily self-evident. The Nazis were elected democratically and to some, at least initially, appeared a welcome relief from the chaos and death throes of the Weimar Republic. Similarly, for many even on the Left in France, the fragility of Léon Blum's Popular Front government, and especially its ineffectuality in dealing with the threat of Fascism, most notably during the Spanish Civil War, caused many French citizens to despair of the Third Republic itself.[27] According to film critics, the great Poetic Realist films featuring the solitary tragic figure of Jean Gabin provide eloquent and moving testimony to this despair.

There are a number of other issues that will need to be addressed in relation to the studies of political complicity in the chapters that follow. Among these are the terribly vexed issue of the uniqueness of the Holocaust, which arises in the *Black Book* controversy and the "fading" of the Vichy and Nazi past as a historical and moral touchstone in the wake of 9/11 and, most recently, the war in Iraq. To a significant extent, these events, and others, effected a seismic shift in France's intellectual field, the implications of which are still being played out.

CHAPTER ONE

Henry de Montherlant

Deception and the Wages of Ambivalence

For the general reader inside and outside France, Henry de Montherlant is most widely recognized today as the author of a number of austere and arguably tragic dramatic masterpieces produced primarily in the postwar period and into the 1960s.[1] Works including *Le Maître de Santiago, Malatesta, Port-Royal, Le Cardinal d'Espagne,* and *La Ville dont le prince est un enfant* were regularly and widely performed, especially on the Parisian stage of the 1940s and 1950s. These plays remain staples of the Comédie-Française along with the works of Molière, Pierre Corneille, Alfred de Musset, Paul Claudel, and other great French dramatists.

Less well known is Montherlant's career as a novelist. During the interwar years, Montherlant first achieved literary fame with a series of largely autobiographical novels, beginning with *Le songe* and *Les bestiaires,* both published following World War I in the early 1920s.[2] These works were followed in the 1930s with the prize-winning novel *Les célibataires* and the *succès de scandale* of the quartet of novels known collectively as *Les jeunes filles* (The young girls). Following a long hiatus from fiction writing to devote himself to drama, Montherlant resumed his career as a novelist in the decade leading up to his suicide in 1972. During the 1960s and early 1970s, he published critically acclaimed fiction including *Le chaos et la nuit, Les garçons,* and *Un assassin est mon maître.*

But while Montherlant's plays and novels have earned him the reputation of a twentieth-century "classic," much of his work now suffers, unfortunately, from benign and not-so-benign neglect on the part of most literary critics. (An arrogant and haughty figure, Montherlant offended many and was once described by the great Yale critic Henri Peyre as "a very great writer, a very bad man.")[3] Be that as it may,

Montherlant, his career, and his work remain of keen interest to intellectual and cultural historians dealing with such topics as the relations between politics and aesthetics (Fascism, in Montherlant's case), the politics of gender, and more traditional "historical" topics including the concept of "literary generations" and the politics and culture of the Occupation period. In her classic book *The Second Sex*, for example, Simone de Beauvoir devotes an entire chapter to the novelist and playwright, whom she considered an exemplary misogynist. Beauvoir also discusses Montherlant in a series of articles published in *Les Temps modernes* in the 1950s on the subject of "right-wing thought today."[4] As all of these works clearly indicate, Beauvoir's distaste for Montherlant knew no bounds.

More recently, Robert Wohl, as noted in the Introduction, has studied Montherlant along with other literary figures and veterans—including Pierre Drieu La Rochelle in France and Ernst Junger in Germany—as exemplifying the disaffected but grandeur-haunted writers of the post–World War I generation.[5]

But for the most part, the most recent historical and critical interest in Montherlant concerns a later period in the writer's life, particularly the beginnings of his dramatic career during the Occupation. Mary Ann Frese Witt has explored Montherlant's major dramas, especially *La reine morte*, as examples of what she labels modern tragedies "informed by aesthetic fascism."[6] Kenneth Krauss is interested in the same works as revelatory of Montherlant's pederastic proclivities and the resulting political implications in Nazi-occupied Paris.

The works of Beauvoir, Wohl, Witt, Krauss, and others all contribute to piecing together the puzzle of Montherlant's collaborationism during World War II as well as the contours of and reasons for his complicity with Vichy and especially Nazism. Montherlant's complicity derived from personal—sexual—motivations as well as the complex of attitudes and characteristics related to the writer's pederasty. But his complicity with Nazism in particular also derived from deep-seated conflicts in his own character between the contradictory imperatives of what I describe as "force" and "charity." It was also the consequence of the dramatic failure and inadequacy of Montherlant's vision of history, summed up in the notion of *alternance* (alternation), and of his heroic ideal, expressed in the notion of *service inutile* (futile service).

Before addressing these topics directly, it is helpful to situate Montherlant in the political and cultural climate of Nazi-occupied France and to offer a dramatic, if personal and partisan, snapshot of the period itself.

One of the richest and most compelling contemporary accounts of life in German-occupied France is Jean Guéhenno's wartime diary, published as *Journal des années noires* in 1947. Guéhenno, a *lycée* professor, writer, and politically committed editor of the left-wing reviews *Europe* and *Vendredi* before the war, remained in his teaching post after the disastrous defeat of June 1940 and quickly joined the Resistance. He was a founding member of the clandestine Comité National des Écrivains (CNE) that, among other activities, drew up the blacklists of collaborationist writers near the end of the Occupation. Guéhenno also published a section of his wartime journal with the underground *Éditions de Minuit* under the pseudonym "Cévennes," the name of a mountainous area in southwestern France.

The *Journal des années noires* chronicles the hardships of daily life in Paris during 1940–1944 and reports on Nazi brutalities as well as numerous acts of French cowardice and courage. Guéhenno also follows the ebb and flow of Germany's military victories and defeats and describes them with dread and hope, depending on the outcome. He is merciless in his depictions of Vichy's political leaders and their capitulation before the Germans. For example, in the first journal entry, dated 17 June 1940, Guéhenno describes Philippe Pétain's radio address to the nation in which Pétain announces that he had asked for an armistice from the Germans:

> There, it's finished. An old man who no longer even possesses the voice of a man, who speaks like an old woman, tells us at 12:30 today that last night he asked for peace.
>
> I think of our youth. It was painful to see them go off to war. But is it less painful to force them to live in a dishonored country?[7]

For Guéhenno, Pétain and his subordinates are not the legitimate leaders of the nation. "The government of Vichy," he writes on 25 October 1940, "most assuredly does not represent France." A sort of national "fainting spell" has allowed Vichy's rulers to take power. But "they are nothing, they represent nothing. Everything that they will decide is destined in advance to disappear into the void." Vichy, in effect, is simply "one of two complicitous tyrannies under whose surveillance we live."[8]

If Guéhenno is brutally harsh and indeed openly disdainful of Vichy's leaders, he is at least as ferocious in his denunciations of France's collaborationist writers and intellectuals, and especially those of the newly Nazified Paris. For Guéhenno, culture embodies both a "tradition and hope [in the future],"[9] and because literature is an integral part of culture, those writers and literary figures who accommodate themselves to the German presence are guilty not only of betraying the nation but of betraying literature itself:

> Literature. Nothing is nobler in its expression, when it is the flower of freedom, but nothing is more ignoble than when literature is the means of ignoring freedom, of avoiding freedom's risks, when literature is pure entertainment and nothing more than the spectacle of a voluntary servitude. What should one think of French writers who,

to be sure of not displeasing the occupying authority, decide to write about everything else except the one thing that all the French are thinking about, and who, through their own cowardice, lend their support to the plan of this same occupying authority to make it appear that everything in France continues as before?[10]

The pages of Guéhenno's *Journal des années noires* are in fact full of acerbic portraits of collaborationist writers, astute analyses of their most abject works, and occasionally, in spite of their politics, praise for the literary qualities of what they write. Guéhenno knew personally many of these writers, so his commentaries often entail assessments of character and discussions of intellectual limitations. They also, on occasion, include revealing conversations with them.

Of all the collaborationist writers Guéhenno discusses, perhaps none receives more extended, if episodic, treatment than Henry de Montherlant. Guéhenno comments on Montherlant's most significant publications during the early years of the Occupation, including his articles in the *Nouvelle Revue Française* and especially the collection of essays titled *Le solstice de Juin*, to be discussed in detail shortly. Guéhenno also reports on displays of the writer's work in bookshops and even describes a chance encounter with Montherlant in 1941.

Although Guéhenno occasionally praises Montherlant's literary talent, he is primarily interested in him as a figure who embodies what is most typical of France's literary collaborators: their vanity. Like other "men of letters" who publish in the *Nouvelle Revue Française*—including Paul Valéry, André Gide, and Jean Giono—Montherlant is "incapable of living out of sight for long." He would, like the others, "sell his soul in order that his name *appear*."[11] In the same vein, Guéhenno later speculates that Montherlant's main failing is "that he can never keep quiet." This, ultimately, makes him "ridiculous."[12]

But the critique of Montherlant in the pages of the *Journal des années noires* goes beyond general references to the vanity of the writer. Guéhenno speculates occasionally on other, more personal reasons that help explain the writer's complicity with Vichy and especially the Germans. A "sociological" reason is the writer's pederasty. And, Guéhenno affirms rather crudely, like other pederasts, Montherlant's "joy [with the arrival of the Germans] is like that of the inhabitants of a small town brothel when a regiment passes through."[13] On a more cerebral note, Guéhenno also attributes Montherlant's collaborationism and complicity with the occupiers to the inadequacies of his philosophy of history, as expressed in the principle of *alternance*, and of his chivalric ideal. We shall return to all of these issues later in the chapter.

A perfect embodiment of so much that dishonors France and French culture, Montherlant is the target of numerous insults in the *Journal des années noires*.

Guéhenno characterizes him as "a perfect charlatan," a "pederastic Don Juan," a "fifty-year-old spoiled child," a "gifted rhetorician who can always come up with good reasons for his acts of treason," and "a young imbecilic centaur, more horse than man. He has to paw the ground and prance. Either in the mud or the shit. This splatters others, but he creates a halo around himself."[14] Guéhenno describes a chance encounter with Montherlant at the Gallimard publishing house during which Montherlant's physical vanity, opera star persona, and exclusive interest in his own pleasure and well-being are echoed in his complete indifference to the historical humiliation through which France is living. When Guéhenno asserts that the poison in the air is due to the presence of the occupant, Montherlant responds, "I much prefer *feldgrau* poison to that of the sacristy."[15]

Given the climate of the times in which the *Journal des années noires* was written, Guéhenno's pro-Resistance sympathies, and the immediacy with which events and people are reported and described in the journal's pages, it is not surprising that Guéhenno's portrayal of Montherlant is almost entirely negative and completely caricatural. In lumping Montherlant together with other literary collaborators and stressing the vanity, superficiality, and even abjectness of them all, Guéhenno ignores those attributes of the writer that distinguished him in a positive way from figures such as Robert Brasillach, Pierre Drieu La Rochelle, and Louis-Ferdinand Céline. Specifically, Montherlant was not an anti-Semite or, at least in the prewar years, merely a knee-jerk reactionary motivated by a hatred of Communism or an adulation of such figures as Hitler, Mussolini, and, within France, the Communist-turned-Fascist leader Jacques Doriot. Indeed, before the war Montherlant had taken positions distinctly opposed to the aims of Fascist dictatorships. For example, he had opposed Mussolini's invasion of Abyssinia.

These and other complexities concerning Montherlant confirm that to understand his collaboration and his intellectual, personal, and political complicity with Vichy and Nazism, it is necessary to look more closely at his wartime activities and trajectory as well as his prewar literary and political itinerary.

In 1948, Montherlant wrote a *Mémoire*, or "statement of accounts," in which he attempted to explain and justify his actions during the Occupation period. In the foreword to the *Mémoire*, he notes that an earlier, less detailed version of the document was prepared to accompany his official dossier as it passed through the various Purge committees established following the Liberation. Montherlant had been accused by the Comité National des Écrivains, among other Resistance groups, of publishing a number of pro-German texts, including especially the aforementioned 1941 book *Le solstice de juin* as well as a number of essays, articles, and interviews, most of which had originally appeared in the collaborationist press between 1940 and 1942.

With one exception, the Purge committees found Montherlant innocent of all charges. The exception was the Comité National d'Épuration, composed of five of the writer's peers. On 29 October 1946, that committee found Montherlant guilty as charged and forbade him to publish or lecture publicly in France for one year. However, as Serge Added notes, the sentence was applied retroactively. It was considered to have gone into effect on 1 October 1944, more than two years prior to the sentencing date. As a result, it had no tangible impact on the writer's life or literary career.[16] Montherlant states in the foreword to the *Mémoire* that the conviction was one of "pure form," especially since only two of the five committee members were present and involved in sentencing him. He claims that his condemnation had little if anything to do with what he had or had not done during the Occupation. The Paris literary community had always disliked him, he asserts, and they simply took advantage of the historical moment to pounce on him. Before the war, he states, one critic had observed that if someone "throws out the name Montherlant," immediately "all sorts of foolish assertions pour forth." Montherlant concludes: "If it was like that in serene times, what will happen, what did happen, in a volatile moment like the present? It has been less a question of misunderstanding what I have written than of deliberately misunderstanding it."[17] He does not seem to notice that his claim to being persecuted by the Parisian intelligentsia as a whole does not square with his earlier assertion that his conviction was one of "pure form" largely because *only two colleagues* found him guilty of collaboration.

Montherlant concludes the foreword by insisting that his victimization in post-Liberation France was not merely the result of professional animosities but also a symptom of the climate of the times themselves. And, he continues, he was not alone in his persecution. In the postwar period, "every Frenchman is an accused" and "criminal dossiers" are opened for everything. In melodramatic fashion, Montherlant here echoes the view of many on the postwar Right in France in insinuating that the Purge was a sham because it targeted the innocent as well as the guilty in placing everyone under suspicion. Moreover, in concluding the foreword to the *Mémoire* by insisting that he was accused unjustly and that this was a fate shared by all the French, Montherlant is clearly attempting to stir the reader's sympathy and promote for himself a sense of solidarity and even complicity.

In the *Mémoire* itself, these somewhat histrionic protestations of the writer's innocence and denunciations of the postwar period give way to a more sober, detailed, and supposedly objective account of Montherlant's activities during the Occupation as well and his prewar political commitments. The image Montherlant seeks to create of himself in the pre-Occupation itinerary is that of a dedicated patriot deeply concerned with the security of his country. A volunteer soldier during World War I, Montherlant states that he was seriously wounded at the front and that the wound he received required medical attention until 1936. He also asserts that he emerged from that war convinced that nothing had been resolved and that another war between France and Germany was inevitable. This concern, he writes, is evident in his first book, *La relève du matin* (1920), and continues as a major theme in his other works published throughout the interwar period. Unlike other French writers who refused to "face up to reality," Montherlant was willing to play the role of Cassandra during the 1920s and 1930s, repeatedly calling on France to develop "a taste for force and courage" in order to confront its traditional German enemy.[18]

As to his politics between the wars, Montherlant claims to have been essentially apolitical. By this he does not mean that he had no political opinions but that he shared sympathies with both the Right and the Left. This attitude was consonant with his philosophy of *alternance*, according to which ultimately all doctrines— political, religious, and otherwise—are equally valid and deserving of respect. In addition, the wisdom of *alternance* requires that one embrace alternately or successively these opposing doctrines and beliefs in order to lead a richer life. Montherlant points out that during the 1930s, therefore, he contributed to the Communist newspapers *Commune* and *Ce soir*, the left-wing weeklies *Vendredi* and *Marianne* (he was a war correspondent of sorts for the latter at the moment of France's defeat in 1940), and also the right-wing reviews *Candide* and the *Revue des deux mondes*. Solicited by the Left to speak on behalf of the Spanish Republic, he was also invited to the Nazi Congress in Nuremberg in 1929. (Although he did not make the journey, he was praised for supposedly having done so in the collaborationist press in 1942, a fact he fails to mention in his *Mémoire*.) Invited to speak at a meeting of the extreme-right *Rive Gauche* group in November 1938, Montherlant states that he surprised his audience by expressing his opposition to the Munich Accords. When he reiterated this view in *L'Équinoxe de Septembre* (1938), he stresses that the Communists alone praised him.

Taken at face value, this account of the writer's political activities during the interwar years might well lead one to conclude that before France's defeat in 1940 Montherlant was, as he claims, a patriotic, if outspoken, citizen unlikely to betray his country in a moment of crisis. However, closer inspection of the facts, as well as the faultiness of the writer's logic in specific instances, puts this inference in doubt. First, Montherlant's service during World War I in no way precluded collaboration during the Occupation. Philippe Pétain himself was, of course, the "hero of Verdun" and France's greatest military hero of World War I. French Fascists such as Joseph Darnand, head of the Milice, Vichy's paramilitary police force, and Marcel Bucard, leader of the Fascist group the Francistes during the 1930s and the Occupation, were decorated veterans of the trenches as well. And Pierre Sipriot's biography of Montherlant reveals that he had hardly been the heroic and patriotic soldier he claimed to be. Montherlant had volunteered during World War I essentially as a means of advancing his literary ambitions. He had attempted to use family connections to secure military honors that he had not earned, and, in letters to his grandmother, Marguerite de Riancey, he openly flaunted his lack of patriotic sentiment. In one of these letters, written after the war in February 1919, Montherlant states that "the ones I pity are the *true believers*, those who are truly interested in social issues, who truly want what is good for France, etc. For my part, I am concerned only with myself and those I love." And, he concludes, "*I am a kind of social eunuch.*"[19]

Nevertheless, Montherlant was right about the fact that being a "war hero" would advance his literary career. Sipriot's biography also shows the extent to which writers, politicians, and military leaders were willing to help the young veteran because of his service. Along with the likes of Pierre Drieu La Rochelle, Montherlant did in fact launch his literary career through celebrations of his wartime experience. This was, of course, quite typical of his generation in France and elsewhere.

On another level, Montherlant's call for France to develop an ethic of "force" and "courage" did not necessarily lead to a staunch and unerring patriotism. Instead, it pushed him toward pro-Nazi, anti-French, and, for all intents and purposes, treasonous positions during the Occupation.

Finally, in one instance at least, Montherlant's account of his journalistic career before the war is misleading in that it fails to mention his contribution to the pro-Fascist—and not merely right-wing—weekly *Je Suis Partout* in March 1938. This brief essay, a response to a query concerning French youth of the day, is hardly openly Fascistic, but its Social Darwinism ("If a less accomplished humanity is devoured by a more accomplished humanity, is there really anything to complain about in that?"), elitism, emphasis on youth, and expression of faith in the sanctity of violence and death ("It is good, it is salutary, to feel that tomorrow one will kill or be killed.") are certainly reminiscent of the writings of the weekly's more openly Fascist and pro-Nazi contributors.[20]

The second and lengthiest section of the *Mémoire*, focusing on the Occupation itself, deals with three main topics: Montherlant's relations with Vichy, his dealings with the German authorities, and his interpretation of *Le solstice* and other supposedly incriminating writings on which the charges of collaboration were based. Montherlant's strategy in all of these areas is ultimately to deny any guilt and to claim, despite all appearances, that he was at least a spiritual *résistant* before the idea had even occurred to the majority of his countrymen.

An early supporter of Vichy, Montherlant states that he had become disillusioned with the Pétain government by December 1940. A two-day visit to Vichy had convinced him of the pettiness of the regime as well as its incapacity to rejuvenate a moribund nation. Subsequently, he claims, he refused to write a monograph in praise of Pétain's politics for the publisher Grasset, and in *Le solstice* and elsewhere he openly criticized Vichy's organization for war veterans, the *Légion*, as well as its cult of youth and the vulgarity of its propaganda. As to his occasional praise of Pétain in *Le solstice*, which was published in October 1941, Montherlant asserts that he left these compliments in the text out of personal gratitude to Pétain for releasing, at Montherlant's request, a schoolteacher jailed for statements critical of Pétain.

In discussing his relations with the Germans, Montherlant notes that unlike other well-known writers accused of collaboration, Drieu La Rochelle and Brasillach among them, he refused on two occasions, in 1941 and 1942, to attend the Nazi-sponsored European Writers Congress in Weimar. Similarly, he declined to contribute to the German-language Parisian daily *Pariser Zeitung* or to write the text for a photo album of the work of Arno Breker, the Nazis' favorite sculptor, whose exhibition in Occupied Paris beginning in May 1942 was a major cultural event. When *Le solstice* was published, Montherlant states, he refused to autograph copies on sale at the pro-German Rive Gauche bookstore on the Place de la Sorbonne, a bookstore Jean Guéhenno's *lycée* students derisively referred to as the "Rive gauche du Rhin" (left bank of the Rhine).

The German response to the writer's recalcitrant attitude, according to Montherlant, was increasing impatience that eventually yielded to suspicion and hostility. Several of Montherlant's articles for the Parisian press were censored by the German authorities, and in March 1944 the Gestapo searched his residence and questioned him concerning possible ties to the Resistance. For those suspicious of his account of the Gestapo raid, Montherlant provides the name of a witness, attached to the German embassy at the time, who would be willing to testify to the truth of his claims.

How precise and thorough is Montherlant's account of his dealings with and attitudes toward Vichy and the Germans during the Occupation? Although some of the details he offers concerning his involvements are accurate, others are highly misleading. There are gaps in his story as well. For example, Montherlant's *Mémoire* understates his initial enthusiasm for Vichy and describes his one trip there in negative terms. In his correspondence with Roger Peyrefitte published in 1983, he offers a very different view of his journey and also provides the reason for undertaking it.

At the outset of the Occupation, Montherlant had been picked up by the police in Marseille for pederastic activities and the corruption of a minor. In October 1940, he had written to Peyrefitte—a fellow pederast and confidant—and explained that "I would like to rub up against Vichy in order to give myself the assurance that I'm on their good side before I start prowling again." Later, he would give a very positive assessment of the Vichy regime itself in a letter to Peyrefitte dated December 1940: "I leave Vichy drunk with enthusiasm for what I've seen there: high morale, order, and an atmosphere devoid of petty interests. Truly the New Regime has won me over."[21] And yet late 1940 is precisely the period when, in his *Mémoire*, Montherlant claims to have lost faith in the regime. As the historian Philippe Burrin observes, Montherlant may not have liked what Burrin calls Vichy's "churchiness," but he was certainly an admirer of its authoritarianism and elitism.[22]

Montherlant's account of his dealings with and attitudes toward the Germans and the details he offers of his life in Occupied Paris suffer less from inaccuracies than from a number of important omissions and misrepresentations. For example, even before returning to Paris from the south of France in May 1941, in December 1940 Montherlant had delivered in Limoges an address on the freedom of the artist. As Pierre Sipriot notes, the first two rows of the audience were filled with German officers. Montherlant cited Hitler at length on the value of art even in troubled times, such as were currently present, when art would seem to have little importance. Montherlant also praised Hitler as an "authentic man of action." The lecture was later published in its entirety in *Le solstice* in 1941, but when *Le solstice* was included after the war in the 1963 Pléiade edition of Montherlant's essays, the references to Hitler had been removed along with other compromising passages. The Pléiade edition was published some fifteen years after the *Mémoire* was written, but the *Mémoire* itself provides no details of the lecture, the audience, or the references to Hitler.

Although it is true that Montherlant, once back in Paris, declined invitations to a Nazi-sponsored writers' conference, the clandestine newspaper *Les Lettres Françaises* reported in April 1943 that he had in fact actively solicited the invitation of 1942 from the Germans but had declined it after learning of initial Russian victories on the Eastern Front.[23] As to his refusal to sign copies of *Le solstice* at the Rive Gauche bookstore, apparently this did not mean that he was averse to having the bookstore celebrate his life and work. In November 1941, a month *after* the publication of *Le solstice*, a window of the bookstore displayed photographs and other memorabilia from the writer's youth as well as pages from his earliest literary efforts. On the night of 20–21 November, the bookstore windows were blown out by the Resistance and the Montherlant memorabilia was destroyed. Speaking of the bombing and especially the destruction of the memorabilia in his *Journal des années noires,* Guéhenno remarks ironically, "What an irremediable loss!"[24] Finally, although Montherlant claimed, accurately enough, that he did not contribute to the *Pariser Zeitung,* he did publish a tribute to his German friend and translator Karl-Heinz Bremer, killed on the Russian front, in the German-language *Deutschland Frankreich.*[25] The tribute appeared in 1943. Earlier, in 1942, he had published "Fragments of a War Journal" in the same publication.

Montherlant was not accused by the Purge committees of fraternizing with the enemy, but in the *Mémoire* he chooses nevertheless to downplay personal and social contacts with the Germans. Pierre Assouline, among others, has pointed out that Montherlant frequented the German Institute in the company of André Thérive, Jacques Chardonne, and Drieu La Rochelle, all well-known pro-Nazi writers.[26] Moreover, in one of his articles published in the collaborationist press during the Occupation, Montherlant speaks of social evenings spent in the company of Nazis such as Karl Epting before the war. These were the very contacts with the Germans that led Louis-Ferdinand Céline—hiding in exile for several years after the war—to announce to his lawyer that Montherlant had been "a thousand times more of a collaborator" than he himself had been.[27]

If the inaccuracies and omissions in Montherlant's account of his wartime activities as well as his attitudes toward Vichy and the Nazis suggest an effort to whitewash a past more compromising than some have subsequently assumed, his readings or, more precisely, misreadings of *Le solstice* and other writings published during the Occupation only serve to confirm this impression. Despite Montherlant's claims to the contrary, these texts reveal not only the nature and extent of his collaborationism but also the Fascistic impulses and anti-French sentiments that motivated him, in part, to compromise himself.

Montherlant's defense of *Le solstice* as a book undeserving of the charges leveled against it begins with the assertion that the book was initially censored by the Germans and that the issue of the *Nouvelle Revue Française* containing the title essay of the collection was suppressed as well. In fact, according to Gérard Loiseaux, the book was censored not by the Nazis but by Vichy, and Montherlant's German friends Karl Epting and Karl-Heinz Bremer eventually had the censure lifted. Just the same, Montherlant claims that the German authorities continued to object to both pro-British statements made in the text and calls for France to regenerate itself. Criticisms of Petain's *Légion* were also not well received by the Germans or by Vichy itself, according to Loiseaux.[28]

Also supposedly shocking to the Germans was an essay titled "La sympathie" in which the writer expressed solidarity with Parisian workers after attending a ceremony at the *Mur des Fédérés* in 1936 during the Popular Front period. The text, Montherlant claims, is openly favorable to Léon Blum's prewar leftist and anti-Fascist Popular Front government and therefore supports "the ideas being fought against" by the Nazis.[29] "La sympathie" appeared, moreover, at a time when a German victory seemed assured.

A close reading of the essay confirms that it does not, in fact, conform in many details to the description provided in the *Mémoire*. First, there is no explicit or implicit statement of support for the Blum government. Second, while Montherlant does indeed express sympathy for the workers' demands for better pay and living conditions, his sense of solidarity is attenuated by his belief in his own social and natural superiority. When one of the workers addresses him as "comrade" and uses the polite form "vous" rather than the familiar "tu" form one would expect with the use of "comrade," Montherlant reflects: "This 'comrade' linked to 'vous' was most profound. The 'vous' recognized the fatal inequality of conditions within society as within nature herself; the 'comrade' joined to 'vous' indicated that with a little intelligence, good will and generosity, camaraderie could exist beyond this inequality."[30] Camaraderie between the two men can exist, then, as long as it is founded on a recognition of social and natural differences existing between individuals, differences that can never and should never be challenged. It is hard to imagine why social conservatism and natural elitism of this sort would offend the Nazis.

In another brief essay in *Le solstice* titled "Vingt lignes sur l'héroïsme" that, Montherlant speculates, must have gone unnoticed by the Nazis, the author claims to express very subversive ideas on the nature of heroism. Asked to compose these lines by the Vichy Ministry of Youth, Montherlant offered the following in the pages of *Le solstice*: "Civic heroism. Its multiple forms. I am nevertheless drawn to only one of these. That of the individual who through fidelity to his ideas, his beliefs, or his style of life, accepts, in the France of 1941, to remain isolated; or that of the group which for the same reason, accepts its status as a minority."[31]

In the *Mémoire*, Montherlant provides the following gloss on this passage: "I wrote these lines in March 1941 and since the armistice, I had resided exclusively in the Free Zone. The only group which, in France and most particularly in the only France I knew at the time, that of the Free Zone, was a minority, what did it consist of, if not those who resisted the politics of Vichy?"[32]

It is hard to imagine that during a period *preceding* the publication of Montherlant's most procollaborationist and indeed pro-Fascist writings (the most incriminating pieces in the collaborationist press were published from August 1941 to January 1943), he was busy writing subtle apologies for the Resistance. A more plausible interpretation of the passage is that the group in question consisted of Montherlant, Peyrefitte, and their circle of prepubescent male lovers, a group Montherlant referred to fondly as a "chivalric order." (The initial essay in *Le solstice*, "Les chevaleries," is, in fact, a veiled and highly embellished description of the group.) During the Occupation, both Montherlant and Peyrefitte were arrested for pederastic activities, and their aforementioned correspondence contains numerous references to their persecution at the hands of the Vichy authorities. It is this group, then, "isolated" in the France of 1941 but faithful nevertheless to a "style of life," to which the passage on heroism most likely refers.

If the texts that Montherlant would have the reader believe are subversive do not stand up to close inspection, many of the other essays in the collection do not even allow for alternative readings of this sort. They are overtly procollaborationist, anti-French, and ultimately pro-Nazi. Montherlant admits in the *Mémoire* that he strongly supported the signing of the armistice in 1940, and in *Le solstice* he calls for France, like a vanquished athlete, to sit down at the table with its conqueror and help celebrate the victory. As painful as the debacle of 1940 was to the French, the metaphor of the athletic competition employed by Montherlant is largely innocuous and in no way denigrates the loser—although it does help to explain his political complicity, as will be demonstrated. This cannot be said, however, of Montherlant's choice of metaphors in other essays. In "Les chenilles," he implicitly compares the defeated French to the caterpillars on which he urinated to entertain himself during pauses at the front in 1940, where he served as a war correspondent. He states that "I liked to contemplate them, while they convulsed interminably in bouts of agony; these creatures usually so nonchalant, at present tied in knots, exhibiting in their contortions a white belly I didn't know they possessed; stretching their heads towards the sun in a movement both pathetic and ludicrous."[33] Montherlant proceeds to acknowledge that he permitted those who withstood the onslaught to survive out of a sense of "fair play." "Les chenilles" not only suggests a darker side to Montherlant's analogy between sport and war but casts the French people in a most abject and humiliating role. It also justifies Thierry Maulnier's criticism of *Le solstice*, expressed at the time, that Montherlant's descriptions of his country's defeat are recounted with an "insulting verve."[34]

The title essay of *Le solstice*, which deals directly with France's military defeat, also denigrates the French while singing the praises of its conquerors. Montherlant dismisses the French army as an army composed of "skinny officers wearing glasses," "overweight bourgeois," and "hysterical women." The society that spawned these pathetic men is described as a "hollow sham" where all is "facade" and "superficiality."[35] The German soldiers are, by contrast, "large schoolboys" with muscular, naked legs, playing harmonicas as they advance. These "invaders from

Clovis's kingdom" possess all the vitality and joy of youth and easily overrun their French counterparts.[36]

The oppositions that Montherlant establishes in these descriptions are consistent with the rhetoric of prewar Fascism in France and the most fervent collaborators during the Occupation. Fascism's and Nazism's appeal resided precisely in their "spirit of joy" and exaltation of youth, vitality, and virility. The democracies, and specifically the French Third Republic, were, by contrast, considered exhausted, decadent societies corrupted by bourgeois values as well as an indifference to physical well-being. Montherlant taps into this rhetoric in *Le solstice* and exploits it to create an enthusiastic epic of the Nazi victory, which he likens, finally, to the victory of Pan over "the Galilean," to paganism's conquest of Christianity. He blames the latter, in fact, for developing among the French "a taste for weakness" and making them "anemic." That he wishes to identify himself with the powerful "pagan" victors is evident in his appropriation of the swastika to his own principle of *alternance:* "The victory of the solar wheel [the swastika] is not only the victory of the sun, of pagan life. It is also the victory of the solar principle that nourishes me, that I have celebrated and that I feel governs all my life."[37] Given these views, it is not surprising that Montherlant wrote a letter of congratulations to the outspoken Fascist collaborator Lucien Rebatet praising him for the success of his 1942 book *Les décombres.* A bestseller during the Occupation, *Les décombres* is described by Rebatet's biographer Robert Belot as "embodying in every detail the collaborationist aberration. Its author celebrates the martial and military values of Fascism but also demonstrates, under the complicitous eye of the Occupier, a neurotic complacency in underscoring the signs of national 'degeneration' while elevating submission [to the Nazis] to the status of a virtue."[38]

If Montherlant's reading in the *Mémoire* of *Le solstice* is selective and gives a false impression of the work as a whole, his discussion of his contributions to the collaborationist press is at least equally evasive and misleading. Montherlant's major journalistic contributions during the Occupation were written for the collaborationist political and cultural weekly newspaper *La Gerbe.* (*La Gerbe,* along with its founder and éminence grise, Alphonse de Châteaubriant, will be discussed in detail in chapter 2.) While Montherlant's contributions to *La Gerbe* were not his only journalistic publications during the Occupation, they are by far the most significant and the most revealing of these pieces.

In the *Mémoire* Montherlant describes *La Gerbe* as the "most literary" of the Occupation weeklies and acknowledges having published one article and one interview there during the war. He denies any deep ideological connection with *La Gerbe* and its publisher, and he insists that the journal's indifference to him is evident in the fact that the editors of *La Gerbe* chose not to review *Le solstice* when it appeared. Referring to the one article he acknowledges having contributed to the weekly that, he claims, appeared in 1942 and that deals with the wisdom of the Persian moralists, Montherlant offers the following interpretation: "It is impossible to imagine anything more contrary to National Socialism than Persian morality and civilization of the Middle Ages, which are proposed as models here?"[39] As for the interview he gave to *La Gerbe*, which, he acknowledges, offended some at the time, Montherlant argues that *La Gerbe* cut the section expressing anticollaborationist sentiments and that this section was later censored by Vichy when Montherlant tried to publish it in a review in the Unoccupied Zone. Finally, Montherlant claims to have quit writing for *La Gerbe* and the wartime Parisian press more generally at the end of 1942. After the German invasion of the Unoccupied Zone in November 1942, any "collaboration" with that press would have been, according to Montherlant, "indecent."[40]

On all counts, these statements are misleading or false. First, although *La Gerbe* had "literary" pretensions and published such items as fiction and theater reviews, it was in fact primarily a *political* weekly and strongly pro-Nazi and anti-Semitic in its editorial outlook. Second, Montherlant's contributions to the weekly were not purely "literary" in nature. Third, *La Gerbe* was hardly indifferent to Montherlant. In October 1940, Alphonse de Châteaubriant personally wrote to Montherlant inviting him to consider *La Gerbe* as "a field of expression for your views." In his letter Châteaubriant also clearly articulates the weekly's ideological stance, which, he obviously believes, Montherlant shares in many ways.[41] As for the *Le Gerbe*'s choosing not to review *Le solstice*, such a review might well have seemed redundant, since several of the essays in the book—"Lettre à Radio-Jeunesse" and "La Friture," for example—had already appeared in Châteaubriant's weekly. Finally, reviews of other works by and about Montherlant appeared regularly in *La Gerbe*, as did essays in praise of the writer. On 23 April 1942, for example, he is described as a writer whose works paved the way for the "European renewal." The essay concludes: "If Montherlant does not himself become the man of the New France, the men who wish to build this France should fortify their spirits through contact with him and his work."[42]

Despite the "indecency" of writing for the collaborationist press after the invasion of the Free Zone, Montherlant published in *La Gerbe* well beyond the end of 1942. The post-1942 articles include more or less innocuous items such as the aforementioned meditation on the lessons of the Persian poets—which appeared in June 1943, not in 1942 as Montherlant claims in the *Mémoire*—as well as statements given especially in the context of interviews. The last of these, an interview with Christian

Michelfelder concerning Montherlant's play *Fils de personne*, was published on 16 December 1943.

Montherlant's statements in *La Gerbe* are generally consistent in tone and degree with the collaborationist rhetoric of *Le solstice*, but two items in particular surpass the most procollaborationist essays in the 1941 collection in their disdain for the French, their admiration for the Germans, and their Fascistic tone. In an essay titled "Le goût d'attaquer," published on 28 August 1941, Montherlant describes an evening before the war spent with Karl Epting, then director of the German student house in Paris, at a boxing competition between French and German students. Montherlant notes that the French students failed to win a single bout and then offers the following explanation of their humiliating defeat: "They thought it [the competition] was a joke. They refused to train. Then there were Marcelle and Germaine, those perfect emptiers [*videuses*] of men, and the long besotting in the cafes. As to 'national prestige,' they couldn't give a damn." It is no wonder, he concludes, that "la 'doulce' France," whose youth was raised on "a hatred of force" and a love of a soft, decadent existence should be crushed in war by their virile enemies.[43]

Montherlant's obvious disdain for the French boxers is no more pronounced here than is his disdain for the caterpillars of "Les chenilles," and the "lesson" of "Le goût d'attaquer" is quite similar to that of the title essay of *Le solstice*. In the article in *La Gerbe*, however, Montherlant openly flaunts his personal connections with the Nazis and embraces a misogyny strongly reminiscent not only of French Fascists such as Drieu La Rochelle but even of the Freikorps soldiers so vividly described by Klaus Theweleit in his celebrated study *Male Fantasies*.[44] Women drain men of their vitality and force and, in so doing, threaten their very existence. It is the Frenchman's willingness to have commerce with them that has undermined the nation and brought about its destruction.

The second item, an interview with Michel B. de la Mort—the same interview that, in the *Mémoire*, Montherlant claims was truncated by the weekly without his prior knowledge or permission—was published on 8 January 1942. In the interview, Montherlant is asked to offer a postscript to *Le solstice*. He takes the opportunity to present a new characterization of the conflict raging in Europe: "The struggle against the average Europeans (of course, this means the lower Europeans) has commenced. The struggle between the heroic elite of the new European civilization and the lower Europeans: the struggle of the heroes against the slaves." And, he adds, "Let us note quickly that the heroic values [of this new elite] do not coincide necessarily with moral values: these heroes are not all just men."[45]

For Montherlant, the heroic elite struggling to create a new European civilization are, to all appearances, the Nazis and those who measure up to them, while the "slaves" are those who resist them. The Nietzschean language not only confirms the extent of his admiration of these new masters but also suggests his readiness to acknowledge in them a superior race. Montherlant's use of the term "lower Europeans" for Germany's enemies reinforces the racist slant of the description, because it suggests an opposition between the northern European Aryan Germans and the darker southern races they dominate.

Montherlant insists that this new elite must not be confused with moral elites of the past, those who would, for example, be wedded to Christian values and virtues. Although he fails to identify the heroic virtues that motivate this new elite, he does specify that the new heroes are by no means all "just" men. Given the context of his Occupation writings, one would assume that heroic virtues consist primarily of the force and virility of the conqueror. In the new European civilization, these virtues take precedence over "moral values" and "justice," which have weakened France and Christian Europe in the past. In condemning justice and championing force, Montherlant condones, if indirectly, the brutality of the Nazi New Order.

The most striking passage in the interview, however, concerns the responsibility of the heroic individual in the current situation: "When certain communities will have shown that their nature is that of the slave, the heroes belonging to these communities will know, when necessary, to detach themselves and join up elsewhere."[46] Although the "communities" in question remain unidentified, Montherlant's intention seems clear. If France fails to measure up to the "new European civilization," if it proves to be a nation of "slaves," then its heroic individuals, clearly including the writer himself, must cast their lot elsewhere. The obvious choice, given the "values" Montherlant is extolling, would appear to be Hitler's Reich.

Montherlant's *Mémoire* concludes with an apology to the reader for the "dryness" of the text, a shortcoming he justifies on the grounds that his purpose has been to remain objective and to present all of the essential facts of the case. The "statement of accounts" and the political itinerary it seeks to establish, however, fail to hold up. Behind Montherlant's facts and the textual interpretations he offers are other facts, other interpretations, that point to an itinerary whose contours are very different from the one Montherlant proposes in the *Mémoire*. Hardly the intellectual resister of the first hour he claimed to be, the image of the writer that emerges is at best that of a deceptive opportunist and at worse a self-styled "hero" who condemns and belittles his country and announces his readiness, indeed his obligation, to make common cause with the heroic elite of the Nazis' "New Europe."

It is tempting to conclude, on the basis of the wartime essays and journalism examined here, that Montherlant was simply another "integral" Fascist[47] whose reactionary views led logically to collaboration after June 1940. His own evasiveness and distortions in the *Mémoire* only serve to reinforce this impression. Nevertheless, the particulars of Montherlant's case are not that simple, his itinerary not that direct. Although the conclusion of the essay "La sympathie" reaffirms social and natural hierarchies, Montherlant's sympathy for the plight of workers in 1936 should alert us to other aspects of his character that his Fascistic impulses can neither explain nor accommodate. Montherlant frequently compares these impulses to Christian charity and a concern for the downtrodden. They appear alongside more properly Fascistic exaltations of youth, virility, and misogyny in his work, especially his fiction, throughout the prewar period and into the Occupation itself. As one might expect, the marriage of the two extremes is not a happy one, and they confront each other in Montherlant's most accomplished artistic achievement during the Occupation, the 1942 tragedy *La reine morte*. The history of these extremes—the history of "charity" and "force"—and their confrontation in *La reine morte* are important in understanding the nature of Montherlant's collaborationism and his complicity with Vichy and Nazism during the Occupation.

As noted earlier, Montherlant established his reputation as a novelist during the 1920s with the publication of two autobiographical novels, *Le songe* (1922) and *Les bestiaires* (1926). The hero of both novels is Alban de Bricoule, an arrogant young aristocrat intent on testing his strength and courage in life-and-death situations. *Le songe*, dealing with Alban's experiences as a soldier during World War I, focuses on the theme of male camaraderie—*l'ordre mâle*—at the front, but it also examines Alban's love affair with Dominique Soubrier, a young athlete whose discipline and independence appeal to him. The relationship, although unconsummated, thrives until Dominique, overwhelmed by her love for Alban, begins to forsake her independence in an effort to secure a stronger commitment from him. Alban, horrified by her passion, sentimentality, and, in his view, loss of dignity, begins to detach himself. His affection for her remains, the narrator informs us, but "the highest part of his being was drawing back from the young woman, drawing back out of a superior disesteem."[48] At the end of the novel, Bricoule abandons Dominique and happily returns to the "masculine order" and violence of the front. It is this life of unbridled force that, after all, appeals most to him: "Something inside of him cried out that the life of the predator coincided best with his nature, that he would be happier tomorrow fighting—unjustly this time—against innocent Arabs [in the colonies] than he would ever be happy sitting in town."[49]

Les bestiaires deals with the prewar apprenticeship of an adolescent Alban in the bullfighting rings of Spain. This novel also focuses on the "masculine order" of courage, violence, and death, this time in a struggle against beasts instead of other men. And, as in *Le songe*, this masculine order is set in opposition to a feminine world of sexual passion and sentimentality. Bricoule's romantic interest in *Les bestiaires* is the haughty Soledad, who refuses to give herself to Alban until he has conquered the fiercest of bulls, the "Bad Angel." Testing his courage, resolve, and strength to the limit, Alban vanquishes the beast but then rejects Soledad, realizing that to involve himself with a woman would be to betray all that he has accomplished in the masculine order. The novel closes with Alban exulting in his victory over the "Bad Angel" and celebrating the rites of the ancient god Mithras, whose bull-killing exploits he has imitated so well.

Despite major differences in historical setting and geographical locale, the thematics and plot structures of the Alban de Bricoule novels are remarkably similar. The young hero must prove himself in the masculine world of violence and death, and his superiority is ultimately a function of his physical prowess in dominating man and beast. He reaches maturity when he understands that his true nature coincides with that of the predator and that the exercise of force is good in itself and needs no justification. In *Le songe*, Alban longs to fight and dominate the Arabs after the war, even though he understands that such a course of action is unjustified. But no matter. The apotheosis he seeks, the god he wished to become, is, like Mithras, a divinity whose sole qualification is his capacity to dominate and destroy.

The apotheosis of sorts that Alban achieves at the end of both novels is also, obviously, accomplished at the expense of women. Dominique and Soledad are both sacrificed to the hero's quest to attain a virile ideal, and each ultimately embodies the negative principle itself. In *The Second Sex*, Simone de Beauvoir argues that in Montherlant's work, woman is "night," "disorder," and "immanence."[50] In *Le songe* and *Les bestiaires*, women fail to escape these categories. Dominique is proud, autonomous, and essentially virile at the outset, but as she succumbs to her feminine passion for Alban, she becomes despicable and is compared to those women who cling to their lovers' arms and resemble "invertebrate creatures . . . large snails in disguise."[51] The image of the snail ("slug" is another possible translation) suggests not only proximity to filth but the formless abjectness of subhuman existence.

Soledad hardly fares better. She, too, is stripped of her humanity in being reduced to the status of a mere obstacle in the hero's quest for transcendence. Her refusal to give herself to Alban is intended not to spur him on but to remind him of his weakness. In fact, according to Beauvoir, Montherlant's women do not wish their men to succeed—to surpass themselves. They wish instead to close men in, to limit them. A woman "does not feel the *élan* of [the male's] transcendence, she has no sense of his grandeur."[52]

Although Alban's mistresses are the targets of hostility in *Le songe* and *Les besti-aires*, other women in different roles also come under fire in Montherlant's early works. In the play *L'exil* (1914) and the semifictional tribute to sports *Les olympiques* (1924), it is the mother who impedes her son's self-fulfillment, in the first instance by preventing him from joining *l'ordre mâle* (the male order) at the front and, in the second, by refusing to allow him to test himself on another masculine proving ground, the soccer field.

But as Beauvoir points out, the mother is also guilty of another, more profound sin, that of being responsible for her son's birth. The godlike, masculine heroes Montherlant's protagonists seek to become resent owing their existence to *anyone*, because a true divinity is self-created: "A god is no engendered being; his body, if he has one, is a will cast in firm and disciplined muscles, not a mass of flesh vulgarly subject to life and death: he holds his mother responsible for this perishable flesh, contingent, vulnerable, and disowned by himself."[53]

As Alice Kaplan explains in *Reproductions of Banality*, this need for self-gener-ation, this desire to eliminate entirely the role of the female in the process of pro-creation, is frequently a part of what she labels "fascist fantasy narratives." In Marinetti's epic *Mafarka*, for instance, the hero's greatest accomplishment is the en-gineering and construction of his son, Gazouramah.[54] Although Montherlant does not share the futurists' fascination with modern technology, he does share their dream of an ideal race of men completely independent of female intervention.

Despite the obvious Fascistic overtones of Montherlant's early fiction—the fas-cination with violence and death, the idealization of the virile male, and the hatred and fear of women—the works in question are devoid of any overtly social or politi-cal context. By the early 1930s, however, this had changed. Montherlant was ready to engage explicitly with social and political issues for the first time in his fiction. The result is *La rose de sable*, a contemporary novel set in French North Africa and completed in 1932.

For those accustomed to the celebration of force and violence in *Le songe* and *Les bestiaires*, *La rose de sable* comes as a complete surprise, both in terms of the hu-man values it celebrates and, ultimately, the political views it espouses. Summing up the novel three years after its completion, Montherlant described it as a work "whose central fire is charity" and whose aim was to criticize "the colonial princi-ple" and to speak out for the downtrodden and exploited Arabs.[55]

Despite the length of *La rose de sable*, its plot is quite simple. Michel Raimond describes the plot as follows: "A young lieutenant, enamored of patriotic and colo-nialist principles, gradually discovers the Arab world, comes to question the legitimacy of the French presence, contests the value of military operations, and decides not to participate in what his heart and mind condemn."[56] The young lieutenant, Auligny, also discovers in the desert the love of an Arab girl, Ram. It is the tenderness he feels for her that initially awakens in him a realization of the sufferings of the Arabs and the cruelty of the French and leads him, finally, to abandon his post. In every important way, La rose de sable breaks with Montherlant's earlier fiction. The exaltation of force, violence, and virility—the "Nietzschean Mask" as Raimond describes it—drops away and is replaced by sympathy, selflessness, and charity, none of which had appeared in Montherlant's earlier works. Woman is no longer an obstacle to overcome but a catalyst that allows man to form a more equitable and generous vision of the world.

Two factors are responsible for the complete reversal in Montherlant's perspective. The first, described in the foreword to the 1936 collection of essays, Service inutile, concerns a change in attitude toward violence itself: "At war, in the stadium, I had witnessed only violence between equals: healthy violence. In North Africa, I saw violence exercised by the strong, the European, against the weaker native: I think that that experience disgusted me with violence for life. And I started to love the vanquished."[57] The second concerns Montherlant's discovery in 1928 of Sainte-Beuve's history of Jansenism, Port-Royal. Montherlant was profoundly impressed with this most austere form of Christianity and the virtues it espoused. Although he could not share the Christians' faith, "I shared to a large degree their sentiments; I remained outside religion but I respected it."[58]

Having spent the first two years of the 1930s in North Africa writing La rose de sable, Montherlant returned to France in April 1932, intending to publish the completed manuscript. Shortly after his arrival, however, he changed his mind, reasoning that the "debilitated" state of the nation would make the publication of a novel critical of France and French colonialism untimely and ultimately damaging to national morale.

In 1932, Montherlant published in the pages of the newspaper La Liberté his impression of the nation he found on his return from North Africa: "Our nation is subverted from within, attacked from without. The Foreigner is in our home, by subterranean infiltration. I see the national spirit weakened or indecisive, the total absence of public spirit, a conformism of disorder which possesses all the stupidity that it tries to attribute to a conformism of order. No indignation, no strong reaction from anyone: France is a soft cheese which one can enter and cut up as one pleases. I've been reproached at times for not having enough love, but I have indignation, which is a form of love." Montherlant concludes by noting that the country's elite, unlike its German counterpart, had done nothing to bring about the nation's renewal: "While Germany's elite has saved it from the consequences of its defeat, France's elite has greatly contributed to the sabotage of our victory."[59]

Once again, there is a complete reversal in Montherlant's perspective. The sympathy for the native, for the "other," in *La rose de sable* is replaced by a paranoid denunciation of the outsider, who has insidiously invaded *la patrie* (the fatherland) and is contributing to its destruction. Weakness, disorder, and indifference prevail in a country gone soft, a country whose elite does not measure up to the German elite across the Rhine.

The article in *La Liberté* is significant not only because it reaffirms a reactionary, Fascistic ethic in which force and toughness are at least implicitly championed but because it inserts that ethic into a context that is openly ideological. A fierce and indignant nationalism and a call for order are now linked to the manly virtues espoused in *Le songe* and *Les bestiares*. The whole passage smacks of the critique of French decadence found in *Le solstice* and other wartime writings. All that is missing is the misogyny of the Alban de Bricoule novels, but this returns with a vengeance in Montherlant's succès de scandale of the mid-1930s, the four novels known collectively as *Les jeunes filles*.

The individual titles of the quartet of novels—*Les jeunes filles* (The young girls) (1936), *Pitié pour les femmes* (Pity for women) (1936), *Le démon du bien* (The demon of goodness) (1937), and *Les lépreuses* (The leprous ones) (1939)—reveal a strong animosity toward women that the novels' contents bear out. The haughty, condescending tone of the first two titles gives way in the final volume title to an image intended to evoke corruption, contamination, and horror. The plots of the novels follow the "amorous" adventures of the writer-hero Pierre Costals and, in the process, present a unilateral condemnation of women and their corrupting influence on men and on contemporary French society. Costals is involved with three women: Thérèse Pantevin, a hysterical religious fanatic who confuses her love for Christ with her passion for Costals; Andrée Haquebaut, a frustrated provincial intellectual who cannot accept Costal's sexual indifference to her; and Solange Dandillot, a wealthy bourgeoise who alone appeals to Costals because she is the most "natural." Considered together, the three women sum up and express for Montherlant the vices not only of the female sex but of a French society that has been softened and degraded by the enervating influence of women. Women are no longer simply a threat to the individual, as they are in the Alban de Bricoule novels, but also to the fabric of the culture itself. According to Henri Perruchot, the debilitating vices embodied in women include sentimentality, gregariousness, and "irréalisme"—an incapacity to see and accept things as they really are.[60] They also comprise a sterile intellectualism and strong religious sentiments, both of which weaken the spirit and the will. Many of these elements reappear, of course, in Montherlant's attacks on French decadence during the Occupation.

On a personal level, Montherlant exorcises his own demon of goodness by attributing charitable urges associated with religious sentiments to the women whom the novels condemn. Thérèse Pantevin, whose single-minded religiosity resembles the devotion of the Jansenists themselves, slowly loses her mind and is dismissed by Costals. The respect for Christian sentiments, which Montherlant claims to have discovered in the late 1920s and which inspired the writing of *La rose de sable*, is suppressed in *Les jeunes filles*.

The only woman who escapes a complete condemnation in the novels is Solange Dandillot, and the reasons she is exceptional are most revealing. The narrator describes her as being completely "natural," by which he means that she is entirely inconsistent and whimsical. She lacks both a strong will and the intellect to provide a coherence to her character, and this is precisely why Costals is so taken with her: "I can't stand women who possess their own will and that's why you're made for me for all eternity."[61] Of necessity, Solange seeks authority and direction outside herself, so she is drawn to the Right. As the narrator informs us, she has even belonged to "a group of the extreme-Right," but he refuses to identify the group out of a sense of delicacy, since Solange has previously slept with one of the group's members.[62]

Although Costals ultimately rejects her, Solange does represent the only female "type" that the fictional writer, and possibly his real-life creator, finds acceptable. Devoid of a will and an identity of her own, she seeks to be dominated by a strong male and finds security in an authoritarian political order. She is the object of Costals's lust but never achieves the status of an independent partner in their lovemaking, because that would imply a form of equality that Costals cannot abide. He decides to leave her definitively when she seeks to tie him down in a stultifying, bourgeois marriage. Acceptance of the marriage would acknowledge her dignity, her humanity, which Costals is unwilling to do, and it would also entail a concession, disastrous in its consequences, to a decadent French society destitute of redeeming, manly virtues. In breaking with Solange (and the other women who pursue him), Costals — and Montherlant through him — announces his liberation from a culture gone soft and reaffirms his commitment to the phallocentric and Nietzschean values of Montherlant's early fiction. These values are now moored to a cultural critique that is profoundly reactionary in its essence. *Les jeunes filles*, therefore, sets the stage for the most overtly procollaborationist and Fascistic Occupation writings to come.

If *Le solstice* and the articles in *La Gerbe* were all that Montherlant produced during the Occupation, it would be easy to conclude that the struggle between force and charity, so evident in the writer's prewar itinerary, had concluded with the defeat of the latter and resulted in an outright and unequivocal commitment to the former—and to an overt sympathy for Nazism and, to a lesser degree, to Vichy as a result. The presence of the dramatic masterpiece *La reine morte*, however, renders such a conclusion simplistic and premature.[63] Produced in December 1942, after the publication of Montherlant's most politically compromising essays and articles, the play stages a "return of the repressed" (charity) and dramatizes the direct confrontation with its opposite (force) in Montherlantian thematics. The struggle is played out in an explicitly political context. Thus, the drama would appear to provide a crucial piece of evidence in establishing the contours of Montherlant's wartime politics and their relation to his prewar itinerary.

Taking place in Portugal "in bygone times," *La reine morte* examines the political and human crises surrounding the marriage of Don Pedro, a Portuguese prince. King Ferrante, the prince's father and the play's protagonist, wishes his son to marry the Infanta of Navarre, a proud, arrogant, and strong woman who cares nothing for human emotions and was, in her own terms, "raised to rule others."[64] Such a marriage, in the king's view, would not only benefit Portugal directly by furnishing it with a powerful ally in Navarre but would also provide a strong partner for his son, who lacks strength and the will to rule. When Ferrante demands of Pedro that he marry the infanta, the prince refuses, confessing his love for another woman, Inès de Castro. Illegitimate and a foreigner, Inès is the infanta's opposite in every way. She has no interest in politics and is a creature of remarkable generosity and kindness. In her own words, "To love, that's all I know how to do."[65]

When Ferrante learns from Inès at the end of the first act that she and Pedro have been secretly married for a year, he imprisons his son and tries to persuade Inès to accept a divorce, with the understanding that she can continue to be his mistress. Although he wants to break up the marriage, Ferrante is nevertheless drawn to Inès and wishes to protect her in a political situation in which she is the most vulnerable player. Inès refuses, and the infanta, impatient by nature, leaves Portugal and returns home.

In the final act of the play, Inès, who has become increasingly close to Ferrante during the course of the story, confesses that she is carrying Pedro's child, a son. Ferrante, seeing all of his political plans come to ruin, orders Inès's execution. Torn apart by the political and personal quandaries surrounding Pedro's marriage, Ferrante witnesses the dissolution of his own identity ("I have melted away like the wind in the desert")[66] and dies in his throne room. Pedro enters, accompanied by courtiers bearing the body of Inès. Pedro places a crown on her body, and all present kneel around her, ignoring the prostrate form of the dead king.

Given the action of the play, the characters presented, and, most importantly, the historical moment the play was staged, *La reine morte* lends itself to a variety of political readings. It could be argued, for example, that the infanta represents the virile German conqueror who is ultimately rejected by a French nation seduced by the charms of the gentle and feminine—and therefore decadent—Inès, an illegitimate intruder. Generally speaking, such a reading would be consistent not only with Montherlant's most evidently pro-Nazi writings in *Le solstice* and *La Gerbe* but with his 1932 attack on the decadence of the French nation in *La Liberté*.

Another scenario, proposed by Simone de Beauvoir in *The Second Sex*, also paints *La reine morte* as a pro-Fascist drama in which Ferrante is first compared to a German official "bustling about the German Embassy for reasons of state." Beauvoir then argues that the Portuguese king has "not far to go" before becoming "a Himmler." She writes that "One kills women, kills Jews, kills effeminate men and Christians under Jewish influence, one kills all one has interest or pleasure in killing in the name of these lofty ideals." As for Inès, Beauvoir simply imagines her at Buchenwald.[67]

More recent interpretations of *La reine morte* also entail political readings of the play, although the points of focus as well as the nature of the analyses presented vary considerably. For Mary Ann Frese Witt, Montherlant's drama is also a "fascist tragedy" that consistently denigrates women. Witt notes, for instance, that the original subtitle of the play was "How to Kill Women," a subtitle that Montherlant later—fortunately—dropped. But for Witt, as opposed to Beauvoir, the essentially Fascist inspiration of the work can best be detected not by comparing characters to Nazis or in likening them to death camp victims but by demonstrating that the play revolves around the conflict between "masculinity" and "femininity" or "grandeur" and "mediocrity." Fascist grandeur, in this scheme, is essentially an "irrational drive toward totalizing purity," and it simply cannot tolerate, and must sacrifice, the "cluster of impulses represented by 'woman'—happiness, compromise, mediocrity, weakness."[68] According to Witt, this same conflict lies at the heart of the dramatic works of all those she labels "aesthetic fascists" in France as well as in Italy. In France, the list includes Drieu La Rochelle, Robert Brasillach, and Jean Anouilh along with Montherlant. In Italy, the "aesthetic facists" are Gabriele D'Annuzio and Luigi Pirandello.

If Witt's interpretation of *La reine morte* is structured, fundamentally, around gender politics, so too is Kenneth Krauss's reading of the play, although his approach and conclusions are quite different. Relying heavily on the Montherlant-Peyrefitte correspondence and the former's voracious pederasty before, during, and after the war, Krauss argues that the play is in essence a subtle exposure of—and apology for—the playwright's pederasty. Why else, in the play, does Ferrante, as he himself asserts, lose interest in his own son Pedro at the age of fourteen, precisely when the boy hits puberty? And why else, at the end of *La reine morte*, does Ferrante embrace a page boy, Dino del Moro, before dying in the hope that the boy can "save" him? And in the play's final scene, why does Pedro place the crown on the *body* of the dead Inès rather than on her head, if not to celebrate the unborn *boy* within her? Krauss concludes from the evidence accumulated that the play is really about pedophilia and affirms that for Montherlant pedophilia had become "more than just his sexuality: It became his identity, his cause, *and his politics.*"[69]

All of these readings have their virtues, but they have shortcoming as well. It is always risky to impose an explicitly historical reading on a work of art, and doing so in the case of *La reine morte* is no exception. First, to cast the infanta in the role of a conquering and virile Germany and Inès in the role of a decadent and feminized France raises the dangerous possibility—in Occupied Paris, at least—that the play could be interpreted as favoring the Resistance. It is the infanta, after all, who abandons her "conquest" and leaves the field to Inès.

Simone de Beauvoir's historical analogies pose problems of a different sort. First, the Portuguese king in Montherlant's play hardly resembles a cold-blooded Nazi executioner, especially where Inès is concerned. In the second act, Ferrante refuses to execute Inès even though his councilors make a good case for such an option; he relents and orders her death *only* when he has lost his grip on the kingdom and on himself. Second, if one were to compare Ferrante accurately to a historical figure from the war, the most likely choice would be Pétain himself. Like Pétain, Ferrante is old. He attempts ultimately to root out "softness" and "decadence" in forcing his son to marry the virile infanta. And he seeks to establish his country in a kind of "New Europe" by linking it through marriage to the hegemony of Navarre. Finally, leading the sheltered and comfortable life that she does, Inès hardly resembles a death camp victim.

In eschewing historical analogies and centering her analysis instead on a "tragic *agon*" that opposes grandeur and mediocrity, Witt encounters still other difficulties. In reducing the play essentially to an allegorical struggle between grandeur and mediocrity or femininity, Witt risks diminishing the richness of Montherlant's characterization in the play. All the characters in *La reine morte* are fully drawn, and all "step outside" the values they supposedly embody at some point or another in the drama. In stressing Montherlant's "aesthetic fascism," Witt suggests that, from his perspective, Ferrante's striving for purity and grandeur is inherently superior to Inès's femininity and her—and Prince Pedro's—mediocrity. Again, as the play confirms, the author's preferences and predilections are not so clear-cut. Finally, if one follows the Hegelian model for tragedy, the tragic struggle is essentially between good and good, and tragic loss occurs when either or both antagonists are destroyed. By contrast, the Fascistic hierarchy of values supposedly operative in *La reine morte* would essentially cast the struggle of grandeur and mediocrity as being one between good and bad. For Hegel at least, this is not tragedy but melodrama.

At first glance, the same types of criticisms leveled at Witt's "binary" approach to *La reine morte* could apply to a reading of the play as essentially a conflict between force and charity. However, the difference in the latter case is that Montherlant expressed sympathy for *both* drives and recognized as well that they readily coexist and confront each other within the individual. This fundamental duality explains the contradictions and even the self-destructiveness of some of the characters in the play and makes it possible to present the clash of force and charity through the characters in a sympathetic and even tragic light.

In Montherlant's aesthetics, then, force and charity both have their place. Moreover, his appreciation of their tragically destructive power when confronting each other—discovered, so to speak, in the writing of *La reine morte*—inspired many of the great theatrical works of the postwar period including *Le maître de Santiago*, *Port-Royal*, and *Le Cardinal d'Espagne* as well as novels such as *Le chaos et la nuit*, written in the decade before Montherlant's suicide in 1971.

But returning now to the Occupation and Montherlant's relations with Nazism and Vichy, what does Montherlant's ambivalent relationship to force and charity tell us about his politics and, ultimately, the nature of his complicity? The earlier discussion of his writings and activities during—and even prior to—the war in relation to his postwar *Mémoire* confirms that he entertained a strong and at the very least episodic "sympathy" for Fascism and Fascist ideals, and even for the seductions of Hitler's "New Europe." It also confirms that despite his occasional protestations to the contrary, Montherlant had no qualms about doing his part to foster the illusion that French culture continued business as usual during the war—despite the German presence—by writing for the collaborationist press, giving talks, publishing books, and producing plays for the stage. And for these activities, as Julian Jackson observes, Montherlant was handsomely rewarded. He made 3,000 francs for one radio talk and received more than 140,000 francs for his journalistic writing during the war.[70]

Nevertheless, the "ambivalence" of Montherlant's Fascism, counterbalanced as it apparently was by his sympathy for charity as displayed in *La reine morte*, certainly contributed to his refusal—or his inability—to embrace Fascism wholeheartedly and continuously. Unlike Drieu La Rochelle, for example, who joined Jacques Doriot's Fascist Parti Populaire Français in the 1930s and, after a period of disaffection, reaffirmed his support during the Occupation (along with Brasillach and others,

Drieu also traveled to one of the writers' conference in Weimar during the Occupation), Montherlant never joined a political party during the 1930s or the Dark Years. He also never assumed a leadership role in the collaborationist cultural hierarchy by, for example, editing a prestigious literary review, as Drieu did at the *Nouvelle Revue Française.*

After the war, Montherlant's seemingly equivocal relation to Fascism and what might be described as the "politics of force" led some to conclude that his wartime politics and collaborationism were not that egregious. While Simone de Beauvoir certainly did not share this perspective, as her reading of *La reine morte* confirms — nor, for that matter, did the German writer Klaus Mann, who concluded that Montherlant "had probably always been a fascist" and remained a "cantor of the bullring, inclined at the same time to aestheticism and sadism"[71] — for many, including Jean Paulhan, the éminence grise of the *Nouvelle Revue Française* and a noted literary *résistant*, the worst that could be said of Montherlant was that "he had failed to live up to his own exalted morality."[72] Jacqueline Verdès-Leroux, in her excellent study of the literary politics of the period, concludes similarly that Montherlant was "in fact hardly guilty" of collaborationism and that he was unjustly victimized by the "vengeful and systematic and often stupid ill will of the left-wing press after the war."[73] Verdès-Leroux's statements concerning Montherlant's postwar victimization are — perhaps surprisingly — reminiscent of his own self-serving views as expressed in the preface to the *Mémoire.*

Finally, the fact that Montherlant's most visible and evidently pro-Fascist and collaborationist text, *Le solstice*, appeared in late 1941 made it possible for still others to conclude that Montherlant's collaborationism had tapered off and even perhaps reversed itself by the end of the war. This view was apparently one that the writer himself encouraged in private, or at least when he was not proclaiming his complete innocence, as in the *Mémoire.* Albert J. Guerard wrote shortly after the war that a friend of Montherlant told Guerard that at the moment of the Liberation, Montherlant had "considered the F.F.I. capture of Paris magnificent" and that "he would regret for the rest of his life being on the wrong side of the barricades."[74]

Whatever the case, unlike his more completely "committed" fellow collaborationists, many of whom paid for their opinions and actions with their lives, Montherlant got off very lightly after the war. Evidently, the "ambivalence" of his Fascism, the presence of charitable urges that prevented him from identifying completely and unequivocally with the "politics of force," served him well.

While the politics of force and charity contribute significantly to understanding the nature and vicissitudes of Montherlant's wartime collaborationism as well as postwar perceptions of it, does the evocation of these contradictory impulses in the writer's life and work account entirely for his ambivalent complicity with Nazism and Vichy? If one accepts Kenneth Krauss's reading of *La reine morte*—that is, as a revelation of and defense of the writer's pedophilia and the expression of only true *politics* that he espoused—then one needs to view Montherlant's complicity in a different light. According to this perspective, any political involvement by the writer, any act of collaboration or statement of support for Nazism and Vichy, was ultimately merely a means to what would be for most an "unpolitical" end. And that end was the freedom to roam the streets and movie houses in search of adolescent boys with whom the writer could have sex. In one of the more disturbing passages in Sipriot's biography of the writer, Sipriot notes that one of the ways that the war itself affected Montherlant's "hunting" was that it provided him with an image of himself in these forays as a "war pilot" swooping down on his young prey. The fact that the French military and civilian population had recently suffered terribly in attacks from German dive-bombers did not seem to have given him pause in using this imagery. In and of itself, this reinforces the notion that Montherlant was fundamentally indifferent to anything but his own sexual gratification.

Discussing Montherlant's pederasty also raises, of course, the broader issue of the gay community's reaction to the invader. The British historian Richard Cobb, among others, has argued that the Nazi cult of virility and masculine beauty led many gays to be sympathetic to the presence of the occupier. This was clearly the case for Jean Cocteau and Robert Brasillach, and of Jean Genet as well. According to Edmund White, Genet was in fact "delighted" by the German victory, although he apparently took as much pleasure in Hitler's defeat of the French army—who were "cowards" in Genet's view—as he did in the arrival in Paris of the Nazis.[75]

But while Montherlant shared the Nazi's cult of virility and force, Krauss argues that he should not be included among the Nazis' *homosexual* admirers, because Montherlant explicitly rejected the notion that he was homosexual—adult males, and even postpubescent adolescents, apparently held no interest for Montherlant and in fact repulsed him. Whatever the case—whether or not Montherlant was purely and simply a pedophile or could also be described as a homosexual—ultimately has little bearing on his attraction to Nazism's cult of masculinity and virility. The masculinity or virility of his sexual partner was not so much the issue as his *own virility* and the dominant, hypermasculine role he assigned himself. That was all that mattered.

If Montherlant's sexuality fills in one more piece of the complex puzzle of the writer's complicity with Vichy and especially Nazism, two final—and crucial—pieces remain to be examined. These are the writer's personal ethics and his philosophy of history as expressed in the principle of *alternance*.

In 1936, Montherlant published *Service inutile*, intended to sum up not only the writer's personal code of ethics but also what he considered to be the only wise and reasonable way to live nobly in an absurd and meaningless world. "The soul says 'service,'" he wrote, "and the complete intelligence says 'futile.'"[76] One must act nobly, must serve, understanding all the while that this service will not change things—that it will not make the world a better place.

Paradoxical in its essence, "futile service" nevertheless allows for—and even mandates—a form of exaltation of the self that approximates both a disabused Christian charity and a quixotic chivalrousness, both of which appealed to Montherlant (as so many of his prewar works confirm). It also encourages, in its various forms of expression, both the warrior ethic associated with force and the generosity and gentleness associated with charity. In this regard, it is interesting to note that in a number of his writings, the figure of the *moine-soldat* (monk-soldier) held a particular and abiding fascination for Montherlant, as did the Samurai warrior, who shows up in *Le solstice* and other of his wartime writings. Finally, in its austere nobility, the principle of futile service appealed to a subsequent, if in some instances more idealistic, generation of writers including Albert Camus, whose own invocation of the myth of Sisyphus as a model for conduct in an absurd world is clearly reminiscent of the Montherlantian model.

At the same time, however, it is also clear that the notion of futile service is profoundly nihilistic. It insists upon an ideal of service while simultaneously affirming that no principle, value, or, for that matter, political belief or ideology is worthy of that service. Indeed, all such beliefs or creeds are, implicitly at least, delusions. The "knight of nothingness"—to use another of Montherlant's famous expressions—fights for his cause, all the while knowing that what he is fighting for is not worthy of his efforts.[77]

To return to the historical context of the Occupation, it seems apparent that this "detached" form of commitment also colored Montherlant's complicity with Vichy and the Nazis. It allowed him to convince himself, at least, that he maintained his own "freedom" during the war, despite compromising involvements and pronouncements, and to claim after the Liberation that he had not collaborated.

At the conclusion of *Le solstice*, Montherlant exposes the ultimate vacuity of his ethics in admitting his fundamental *indifference* to the terrible events that had recently occurred as well as to the ideologies and beliefs—good and bad, demo-cratic and Fascistic—that motivated them: "In truth, events have never really engaged me. I have only appreciated them for the ways they have illuminated my being in passing through me like rays of light. Let events be as they will be and let the world adjust to them. Everything will happen as it does in spite of us, so let's not worry about it. What do men want? To be slaves. And they will be, to one master or another."[78]

Affirming as it does the ultimate futility of all beliefs and ideals, political, religious, and otherwise, futile service—despite its pretensions to the contrary—also finally strips action, and certainly historical action, of any real or lasting meaning. The same, of course, can be said of history itself, and this allows Montherlant, as his prewar political itinerary suggests, to shuttle more easily between opposing political positions and perspectives and, apparently, to slip comfortably into collaborationism following the defeat of 1940. But as these changing positions also suggest, Montherlant's vision of history is not purely and simply nihilistic, or at least static. There is for the writer a logic and a meaning or significance of sorts to history's ebb and flow, and this is summed up in the principle of *alternance*.

In Montherlant's 1948 *Mémoire*, it is fascinating to discover that despite the political trouble the writer made for himself in linking Nazism's ascendancy to a turn of the wheel of history, to the "victory of the solar principle" over "the Galilean" in *Le Solstice*, he was nevertheless willing in the postwar period to invoke the same "turning," the same *alternance*, to account for Nazism's defeat. In the notes to the *Mémoire*, he points out that the first American units entered the city of Cherbourg, the first major French city to fall to the Allies, on the June solstice of 1944—clearly, another "turning of the wheel." And for good measure, Montherlant continues, the Popular Front, the antithesis of Nazism, had come to power in June 1936, precisely four years before the French defeat in 1940. The writer concludes, in reference to the American arrival in Cherbourg: "Is it not extraordinary, and inebriating for the imagination, that in June 1940, I foresaw this *half-turn* of the wheel?"[79]

What is in fact "extraordinary" is that three years after the war's conclusion, and given the terrible destruction—the horrors of the Nazi death camps, for example, had long been known in France—Montherlant could continue to see history itself as a kind of cosmic abstraction, fully and completely immune to any human influence or manipulation and also impervious to human comprehension except in the futility of its perpetual rotations on its own axis. That Montherlant had learned nothing from the turmoil of recent history—that he could not distinguish between Nazism, its minions, and its opponents in any meaningful way—is also reflected in his continuing insistence in the *Mémoire* that war is essentially sport. War's adversaries are, *au fond* (at the bottom), athletic competitors, and they must, above all, observe the rule of "fair play"—Montherlant uses the English expression again for emphasis.[80] While imagery of this sort was offensive to many in France after the national humiliation of the 1940 defeat, by 1948 it was nothing short of obscene.

Not content, finally, to reaffirm his own infallibility where history and war are concerned, Montherlant also takes the opportunity in the *Mémoire* to offer his view of the role *"les clercs"* — the intellectuals — should play in contemporary society: "If the intellectuals have a role to play in this world, it is to make ponderation win out occasionally over absurdity, barbarism, and the vulgarity of thoughtless impulses." They should, he continues, attempt to "discredit hate, *limit* war to combat, prevent it from infiltrating itself into all the soul's reactions, into all parts of the social body — in all of life itself — where it poisons everything." He concludes that "therein lies civilization."[81] For Montherlant in 1940, to "discredit hate," to "limit war" and thereby to promote "civilization," meant encouraging France not only to accept its defeat but to embrace it, to become complicit with Nazism and, to all appearances, to deny the meaning and implications of these actions after the Liberation. It is therefore not surprising that Montherlant, despite his noble pretensions, came to be viewed by many in the postwar years not as a voice of conscience to whom the nation should listen — as he hoped — but, in the words of Jean Paulhan, as "a traitor of little interest."[82]

CHAPTER TWO

Alphonse de Châteaubriant

Apocalypse, Nazism, and Millenarianism

Of the many writers and intellectuals who supported Vichy and especially the Nazis during the Occupation, perhaps the least controversial, that is, the most universally vilified following the Liberation, was the novelist, essayist, and journalist Alphonse de Châteaubriant. Founder, director, and editorialist of the archcollaborationist weekly newspaper *La Gerbe* during the war, Châteaubriant lived in exile during the postwar years, was condemned of treason in absentia in 1948, and died abroad in the early 1950s. Although his son Robert and his publisher Grasset attempted to rehabilitate him in the 1950s by publishing expurgated versions of his prewar works as well as posthumous writings, few, if any, in the immediate postwar period attempted to defend his reputation or save him from ignominy. No credible claims were put forward that he was a misguided patriot, nor did leading writers join together to demand a pardon for him on the basis of his literary talent, as they did for Robert Brasillach. Of course, Châteaubriant had chosen to flee France and was therefore not facing imminent execution, as was Brasillach. Finally, neither Châteaubriant nor his work attracted the sympathy or support of the postwar generation of right-wing writers known as the Hussards. The Hussards—Antoine Blondin, Jacques Laurent, and, most notably, Roger Nimier—spent a good deal of time and energy defending and attempting to rehabilitate other pro-Nazi and collaborationist writers including Drieu La Rochelle, Céline, Brasillach, and Paul Morand (also living in exile), but they were largely if not entirely indifferent to Châteaubriant.[1]

The only literary figure of any prominence during the postwar years who tried at least to understand and account for Châteaubriant's political choices was Jean Paulhan. Paulhan had been a founding member of the Comité National des Écrivains

(CNE) but had left the group in protest over its blacklists of collaborationist writers, among them Châteaubriant. In a series of letters to the committee members collected in De la paille et du grain (1948), Paulhan insisted that a writer had "the perfect right to make a mistake." After all, the writer "is not a priest, nor a magus. And he is obliged every day to express his opinion on a thousand subjects which he has not had the time to study."[2] In making his political choices, the writer cannot foresee the consequences of the choices or the actions of the cause he embraces. As an example, Paulhan argued provocatively but accurately that in choosing collaborationism and in embracing Nazism to one degree or another, "neither Drieu, nor Montherlant nor [André] Thérive could foresee . . . the horror of the concentration camps or the gas chambers."[3]

Despite his sympathy for politically misguided writers as well as a pronounced distaste for postwar France's self-avowed "patriotic" intellectuals, all Paulhan was able to muster on Châteaubriant's behalf was a sympathetic reading of his character. Like his friend Romain Rolland, who had earlier been condemned for his pacifism during World War I, Châteaubriant was "among those writers who at every instant engage their very souls in all their actions." He and Rolland were "warm and noble, given to grandiloquence." They were also both prone to adopting heretical views, and both cherished "the German soul." Finally, Paulhan noted parenthetically, both were victims of their own "confused minds."[4]

But if Paulhan was willing to characterize both men personally in similar, and in fact generous, terms, he was unwilling to do the same where their political choices and commitments were concerned. Rolland was famous for his pronouncements in Au dessus de la mêlée, written in Switzerland during World War I, denouncing the French cause as no different from and in fact equally as murderous as the German cause. For this, Rolland had been roundly denounced in France by the nationalist Right and others and was branded a traitor. For Paulhan, the issue was not that Rolland had betrayed France but that he had betrayed the cause of France in condemning it along with the German war effort. Rolland had not betrayed France, Paulhan continued, because he had not embraced the cause of her enemy. By contrast, Alphonse de Châteaubriant had betrayed both the French cause and the nation itself in his actions leading up to and during the Occupation. In publishing his pro-Nazi book La gerbe des forces in 1937, he had betrayed the French cause. And in welcoming the invader in summer 1940 and working for him afterward, he had quickly become a traitor tout court.

It is a measure of the depth of Châteaubriant's ignominy following the Liberation that for simply comparing the characters of Châteaubriant and Rolland and mentioning their friendship, Paulhan himself came under intense criticism from his former colleagues on the CNE as well as others. Some saw this as part of a broader strategy on Paulhan's part to exonerate even the likes of Philippe Pétain and Joseph Darnand, the leader of the Vichy's paramilitary and Fascist police force, the Milice.[5] While this was certainly not Paulhan's intention, what seems clear is that for most in the postwar period, Châteaubriant belonged right alongside the very figureheads and symbols of the most extreme forms of collaboration with the Nazis. He enjoys a place of honor in the pantheon—or, more accurately, the rogues' gallery—of collaborators that even the likes of Robert Brasillach, the martyr of literary collaboration, does not enjoy.

Partially as a result of his status as the pariah among pariahs, Châteaubriant has until recently eluded serious and thorough study as an exemplary case of literary collaborationism in France. Despite, or perhaps because of, his pro-Hitler zealotry, he has generally been overlooked in recent U.S. studies of literary Fascism in France.[6] Unlike other literary Fascists who considered themselves to be fierce *French* nationalists pursuing a strong and virile France, Châteaubriant was interested in this only to the extent that it would occur as a by-product of France's embracing a supporting but subservient role in a rejuvenated, *Nazified* Europe.

But if Châteaubriant's monomaniacal adulation of Hitler and Nazism explains his lack of treatment in studies of French literary and cultural Fascism, the very fact that he has been all but ignored in these discussions leaves unanswered some interesting and important historical and literary-historical questions. In historical terms, if Châteaubriant's collaborationism and his Hitler idolatry cannot be explained through recourse to what might be described as a French Fascist template or paradigm, what factors or beliefs account for and explain his complicity with Nazism? From a literary-historical perspective, if Châteaubriant is not a *literary* Fascist, which (if any) characteristics of his literary production help explain his political choices?

In her excellent study *Alphonse de Châteaubriant: Catholic Collaborator* (2002), Kay Chadwick addresses the first of these questions. But her take on the writer as essentially the victim of his own Christian "idealism" and on his collaborationism as a deliberate and *fully conscious* choice leads her to ignore an important and indeed crucial dimension of Châteaubriant's misguided Christian religiosity—his millenarianism. Chadwick's perceptions also lead her to attribute the writer's postwar revisionism to personal failings, including cowardice and opportunism, whereas I believe history's destruction of his apocalyptic longings explains this revisionism at least as well, if not better. But before drawing final conclusions concerning the range of factors and beliefs—religious, political, and even possibly aesthetic—that account for Châteaubriant's complicity with Nazism as well as his postwar literary and political status, it is necessary to examine in detail his political itinerary along with his literary production and legacy. Although the writer was born in 1877 and his major literary works were written before 1930, an appropriate starting point for the discussion is the mid-1930s, at the moment of Châteaubriant's turn to Nazism.

In 1936, Châteaubriant undertook an extended journey to Nazi Germany. Following a briefer "initiatory" trip the previous year, the writer's 1936 journey to Hitler's Reich lasted most of the summer and fall and included visits to Heidelberg and Cologne as well as excursions to the Black Forest, which Châteaubriant had already come to love. During his 1936 stay, he also made a pilgrimage to Bayreuth to see a performance of *Lohengrin* and to attend a reception hosted by Winifred Wagner.[7]

But Châteaubriant's 1936 visit to Nazi Germany was not merely touristic or "high-cultural" in its objectives, nor was it undertaken purely for pleasure. On a "pilgrimage" to Offenburg, Châteaubriant spoke to a group of nine thousand Hitlerjungend. He then made a "second pilgrimage," this one to Nuremberg and the annual Nazi Party rally, where he was a guest of honor. He was also invited to the opening ceremonies of Hitler's Summer Olympics, intended to demonstrate the superiority of the Aryan race and soon to be immortalized, of course, in Leni Reifenstahl's famous propaganda film.

Châteaubriant's stated purpose in making the journey and in choosing his stops along the way was, as he put it, to "know" and "understand" the "New Germany" and, more generally, to discover "the secret of German thought." But his investigation was motivated by much more than intellectual curiosity. He was also driven by "an ardent necessity, that of discovering in a people of the present a little more than simply reasons to despair of man."[8] In Germany he hoped to discover not only a new vitality that would offer hope for Europe's and the West's future but "a humanity more worthy of Christ."[9] For the Breton writer, the two ambitions were ultimately synonymous. And as Châteaubriant's subsequent writings and career would make abundantly clear, he found what he was looking for.

Back in France, in early 1937 Châteaubriant published with Bernard Grasset a book-length meditation on his journey and its lessons titled *La gerbe des forces*. The global and indeed cosmic pretensions—and apocalyptic tone—of the work are evident from the outset. "Men of demagogic democracy" have destroyed "the marvelous forces of Unanimity in order to exhaust themselves in the dead-end anarchies of small, individual wills."[10] The Bolshevik Revolution, with its promise of change, is in fact no revolution at all. Rather, it is the organization "of the last stage of the evolution of bourgeois society."[11] Châteaubriant describes Bolshevism itself as a cultural, social, and spiritual disease—and a subtle poison. It "is the slope down which humanity is sliding as a result of two phenomena which have presented themselves, the decomposition of the life of a culture and the decadence of the religious spirit." Bolshevism, as Châteaubriant would later write in his *Cahiers* in July 1942, represents "the dissociation of ancient forms and of their vital force," and it affects humanity like a "vapor" that penetrates one's clothes and one's body "down to the deepest internal organs." Unbeknownst to those it has infected, it "obliterates consciences and disbands ancient nobilities." It is not a vision of the world but "a state of the world, a despairing state."[12]

No hope for resistance to this dreaded contagion will be forthcoming from the French nation. As described in both *La gerbe des forces* and *Cahiers* from the same period, France, and certainly the France of the Third Republic and the Popular Front, is nothing more than "a great desert" inhabited by individuals whose obsessive rationalism blinds them to all but the most mechanistic and material aspects of reality. These individuals suffer from a kind of "intellectualism" comprised of "superficial activities" that form the identity of the "superficial man" from the moment of his birth to the instant of his death. The spiritual dimension is completely lacking in the Frenchman. He reasons, "but he does not *see*."[13]

If the French as a people are in dire straits, the bourgeoisie is in a worse condition still. In the pages of *La gerbe des forces*, Châteaubriant describes the bourgeois as a "[p]oor, outdated soul that drags about amidst the shocks of all the events that a hell he has spawned has unleashed in the guts of life!"[14] And if France's dominant class is helpless and rudderless, then it follows that, in political terms, the nation itself can be nothing more than the unwitting pawn of global forces it does not understand but that condemn it nevertheless to a state of continual decline.

But happily, Châteaubriant affirms, there is Germany and the German people. Salvation will come from Germany, and specifically from Hitler's Reich. It is around the Third Reich, as Châteaubriant will later write in 1942, that the disparate and disconnected "vertebrae" of Europe's spine will reassemble themselves "in a heroic endeavor."[15] The salvation Châteaubriant envisages is not merely historical in nature. A response to historical developments, the Nazi revolution is nevertheless outside and beyond history. It is undertaken "in absolute justice, outside the categories created by the defeats or the victories of history."[16] And it is the "German expression" of a "Universal necessity." Wholly biblical in dimensions and inspiration, it constitutes nothing less than "the human apparition of the renewal of God's work."[17] The National Socialist man is the new monk-soldier, inspired by eternal Christian truths, "old truths that have always been the mothers of the world."[18]

Hitler is, for Châteaubriant, the new Christ. Rooted in and an emanation of the German soil, Hitler exudes "a veritable perfume of aristocracy." But the secret of his being and his power lies elsewhere. "Hitler is good, immensely good. Look at him surrounded by children."[19] "If Hitler has one hand which salutes, which reaches out to the masses in a fashion with which we are familiar, his other hand, invisibly, does not cease to fade faithfully into the hand of the One who is called God."[20] Already Germany's savior, Hitler is destined to become the savior of France and the world as well. He is the "great poet" who alone knows how to read "in the secrets of the essences of things," how to join men together, how to lead a great people to the fulfillment of its destiny in troubled times.[21] And Châteaubriant will be Hitler's apologist and prophet.

Upon publication, *La gerbe des forces* was generally greeted with stupefaction, or worse.[22] In a letter to Guillaume de Tarde, Jean Paulhan wrote that its author was "half mad."[23] Others concluded that Paulhan's description of the writer included one adjective too many. Even on the Right and extreme Right, the reactions were no different. Reviewing the book in July 1937 in the pages of *L'Action Française*, Robert Brasillach, no stranger to Nazi Germany himself and a fellow admirer of Hitler, dismissed *La gerbe des forces* as a "frightening example" of "a failure of intelligence."[24] (Brasillach's review, as Jacques Lecarme has written recently, is nothing less than a series of "delicious pulverizations of Alphonse de Châteaubriant," truly too Hitlerian even for Brasillach.)[25] André Thérive described the book as a "tissue of asinine assertions and gobbledygook" and then went a step further. *La gerbe des forces* contained "sentences that smell of the traitor."[26] But, as Kay Chadwick reports, *La gerbe des forces* proved persuasive in at least one interesting—and troubling—case. A few years after its publication, *La gerbe des forces* had a "significant influence on Cardinal Baudrillart, rector of the *Institut catholique* in Paris and a man who might be considered the foremost Catholic academic administrator in France at the time, convincing him of the validity of Germany's 'mission.'"[27]

Despite the severe criticisms of both the book and its author, *La gerbe des forces* and Châteaubriant went on to play a prominent role in the cultural politics of Occupied Paris. In *Miroir des livres nouveaux, 1941–1942*, the official "best hits list" of collaborationist texts, *La gerbe des forces* was praised as a "prophetic work" and as one of the most "nourishing reads available."[28]

As for its author, Châteaubriant quickly established himself as one of the nouveaux monsieurs of a Nazified Paris. In September 1940 he founded the Groupe Collaboration, whose major activities, according to Bertram Gordon, included holding public discussions on collaborationist themes, showing films produced in Axis countries, and sponsoring lectures by visiting Germans.[29] Although not a political party, the Groupe Collaboration recruited actively well into the Occupation and managed to continue to grow through 1943 when collaborationist political parties were losing strength. In fact, after the German defeat at Stalingrad, the group successfully recruited from among a French bourgeoisie increasingly frightened by the threat of Communism at home and abroad. By the end of the year, the Groupe Collaboration claimed a membership of one hundred thousand. Although the group sponsored a militantly Fascistic youth organization, the Jeunesse de l'Europe Nouvelle, by and large its own members were not similarly inclined. According to Gordon, the group "satisfied the voyeurs rather than the participants in the wartime French fascist experience." And few of its members paid much attention to the "mystical eulogies of Hitler that poured forth from the pen" of Châteaubriant himself.[30]

Founding the Groupe Collaboration was by no means Châteaubriant's only or most important activity undertaken to forward the cause of collaboration with the Nazi occupant. In *Catholic Collaborator*, Kay Chadwick offers a full laundry list of these activities. The list is impressive:

> [Châteaubriant] served on the central and honorary committees of a range of wartime organizations, such as the *Légion des volontaires français contre le bolshevisme*, set up in July 1941 and whose troops fought in Russia for the German cause; Marcel Déat's *Front révolutionnaire nationale*, founded in September 1942 with a view to unifying the collaborationist camp; and the *Cercle Européen*, also known as the *Cercle de collaboration économique Européenne*. He was a member of the *Institut d'études des questions juives* which organized the exhibition "Le Juif et la France" staged in Paris in September 1941; and he openly condoned the anti-Semitic *Comité pour l'épuration de la race Française*. He sympathized with Joseph Darnand's *Milice Française*, created in January 1943 to guarantee internal order.[31]

The Milice was the Fascistic paramilitary organization that persecuted Jews; fought the Resistance, often at the side of the Germans; and included among its members Paul Touvier, tried and convicted of crimes against humanity in 1994.[32]

Chadwick's list of Châteaubriant's collaborationist and pro-Nazi activities does not stop there. She notes as well that Châteaubriant "knew and socialized with influential Germans in Paris, including Otto Abetz, the Reich's ambassador to France, and Karl Epting, director of the *Institut allemand* [German Institute] in Paris."[33] (Epting was Montherlant's companion at the prewar boxing competition described in chapter 1.) Châteaubriant also spoke on the Nazi-operated Radio-Paris and served on the translation committee of the German Institute.

But all of these activities pale in comparison with Châteaubriant's major contribution to the cause of collaboration and in the service of Hitler's "New Europe": the directorship of the weekly Parisian newspaper *La Gerbe*. In his classic study *Vichy France: Old Guard and New Order*, Robert Paxton observes that *La Gerbe* was "created out of whole cloth" by the German embassy and its ambassador, Otto Abetz, in the weeks following the armistice. It was the only French newspaper actually created by the Germans, and its purpose was to advance the political and cultural aims of the Nazis.[34]

In Occupied Paris, *La Gerbe* quickly became, in the words of Lucien Rebatet (who wrote for *Je Suis Partout*, the principal rival of *La Gerbe*), "the self-righteous, pretentious organ" of the highbrow collaborationist milieu.[35] *La Gerbe* was ably managed at the outset by Marc Augier, a veteran of the prewar French youth hostel movement, who, following his stint at *La Gerbe*, became the editor of the Anti-Bolshevik Legion's newspaper, *La France Combattante*, and served on the Eastern Front alongside the Germans. The newspaper was also managed by a shrewd young German embassy official and former Berlin sportswriter, Eitel Moellhausen, who contributed to the weekly using the pen name "Aimé Cassar." Under the leadership of these men, *La Gerbe* quickly turned a profit. Within three months of the publication of the first issue in July 1940, it expanded from four to ten pages and sold more than 100,000 copies. By 1943, its circulation had reached 140,000.[36]

Conceived to replace the prewar right-wing weeklies *Candide* and *Gringoire* and to provide tangible evidence that French culture was continuing business as usual under the Germans, *La Gerbe* attracted not only outspokenly pro-Nazi literati such as Drieu La Rochelle, Céline, and Brasillach (despite his earlier criticism of *La gerbe des forces* and its author, and after his departure from *Je Suis Partout*)[37] but also more "soft-core" literary collaborators, including Henry de Montherlant and Jean Giono.[38] In addition, *La Gerbe* attracted writers whose politics as well as contributions to the newspaper were somewhat more ambiguous. Among them was Marcel Aymé, praised in the pages of *La Gerbe* for his "Frenchness," for being a "man of the soil," and for his characterization of humble people in works such as the prewar novel *La table aux crevés*. Another was the playwright Jean Anouilh, who wrote articles on the life and craft of the theater and whose plays, especially the 1944 *Antigone*, were praised in the pages of the newspaper. One of the more interesting of these contributors to *La Gerbe* was Colette, who in November 1942 wrote an article titled "My Poor Burgundy" in praise of her region. Although by no means pro-German, the article does fall neatly into the propaganda mold of Pétain's National Revolution, celebrating regionalism, the "return to the soil," the virtues of family life, and the pronounced paternalism of the father. As Anne-Marie Thiesse observes, such ruralism and regionalism were of no interest to the Nazis, but they were of a piece with Châteaubriant's own novelistic inspiration as well as his vision of France itself.[39]

According to Lucien Combelle, André Gide's former personal secretary and briefly editor of *La Gerbe* (by his own account, Combelle was fired by Châteaubriant for angering the Germans over a censorship issue), many of the figures who wrote for the newspaper showed up for parties at the journal's offices on the Rue Chauchat. On these occasions, Châteaubriant always dressed carefully and immaculately to look the part of a Breton sage, complete with flowing white beard. He sported a large cape and a knobby cane and was invariably accompanied by his cocker spaniel, Myrta. Combelle called him *"le Burgrave"* because of his beard or described him as a "monumental Huron from the Vendée marshes."[40]

As for Châteaubriant's wartime political views, these had, if possible, become more extreme than they were in 1937, when he published *La gerbe des forces* and had, as Combelle wryly observed, "made the gift of his person to Nazi Germany."[41] (Combelle's tongue-in-cheek reference is to Pétain's famous statement in his 1940 armistice speech that he was making "the gift of his person to France.") After the French defeat of 1940, Châteaubriant could still be characterized as "a Hitlericized mystico-Breton novelist," to use Combelle's colorful description of him.[42] The front page of *La Gerbe* became Châteaubriant's personal soapbox. He "crushed" it, according to Pascal Ory, under the weight of editorials, each of which was characterized by "an apocalyptic style, bristling with capital letters and exclamation points, and weighed down with historical and biblical references, alternating between prophecies and objurgations."[43] This assessment is quite accurate. A sampling of the titles of his editorials demonstrates his continuing focus on Nazism and its struggle for "Europe," his fetishistic fascination with the person of Hitler, his penchant for apocalyptic pronouncements and perspectives, and his taste for biblical and medieval imagery and history and their applications to the present. These titles include "National Socialism and Us"; "For the West"; "Revelation of the Present"; "The Supreme Solution"; "Prophetic Writings"; "Europe's Last Chance"; "The Monster and His Lie"; "Europe!"; "Life or Death"; and "Joan of Arc."[44]

As for the actual content of the editorials, a few examples are telling. On 19 February 1942, Châteaubriant published an article on the Allied and Axis struggle in the Far East and specifically the battle of Singapore. The Manichaean and apocalyptic implications of the conflict are underscored in the writer's overheated prose: "So the two worlds confront each other: the somber, materialist world of yesterday, resolved to continue in its own fashion, unconscious of the judgment that condemns it to plunge further into a [process of] dehumanization always closer to death, and the other world which, struggling under the paw of Satan, forces itself to rescue the poor human substance from the yoke of the ultimate consequences of its blindness, and to awaken in that human substance the flames of love, of disinterest, of loyalty, of a generative order, of indispensable hierarchies, of the sense of grandeur and the de-sire for the future."[45]

Toward the end of the war, similar cosmic and Manichaean clashes haunt Châteaubriant's vision and his prose, except that now, with Nazi defeats and Soviet victories mounting, the writer returns to a favorite theme, the biblical evil of Bol-shevism: "The frightful evil progresses every day. This Bolshevism, intrenched in human consciences and on the map [of the world], which so many men and so many nations completely fail to understand, and which represents all that is terrible in our universe at this hour because it is an arch-secular presence, because it is the convulsion and agony of the world, because it is the world after the departure of Psy-che, because after Psyche there is nothing, because Bolshevism is the organization of a humanity that, because of the depredations suffered through centuries, has lost contact with the principle of its own force."[46]

As for France, Châteaubriant was of course staunchly collaborationist from the outset, and the same hyperbolic and grandiose prose characterizes his calls early in the conflict for unqualified cooperation with Nazi Germany. Collaboration alone will not allow France to recover its lost grandeur, as the writer asserts in an editorial from October 1941: "We wish for it—collaboration—because we sense that a human endeavor without precedent is shaping itself irresistibly in aspirations and wills; and we want a collaboration that is active, resolute, total, not just to save France—that would not be enough—but to return France to its greatness."[47]

As the end of the war grew near and the Nazi defeat appeared inevitable, Châteaubriant, in one of his last editorials in *La Gerbe*, bitterly reproaches France for betraying Nazi Germany and the sole hope for humanity that it represented:

> In the great decadence of peoples, when everything was sinking because the flame of faith had been extinguished, one people alone was young, strong, healthy, pregnant with accomplishments to come, was inventive and powerful in the art of recreating the flower of life. . . . This people loved France, admired France, accepted the prestige of France, offered its force to France.
>
> France declared war on this people!
>
> And today [France] looks on without pity and even without hope—that's the least that one can say—as worlds pounce on this people, in the hope of destroying its life, which risked being too beautiful in a world that was too old![48]

Constant in his adulation of Hitler throughout the war, Châteaubriant praises the Nazi leader as a "whirlwind stronger than death" and as a model for *French* writ-ers and writing in the future: "Reread the speech of the Fuhrer Adolph Hitler, for example, and you see materialize before your very eyes the fundamental premises of the language of the future. Observe how his words express action, how they are adapted to all the internal and external peripeteia of the great storm, how not a single useless word slips in."[49]

In his *Cahiers* entries dating from the Occupation, and not just in his editorials appearing in *La Gerbe*, Châteaubriant also continued to hammer away at these familiar themes. He denounces French decadence in overtly biblical terms. The French earth "is soaked with the blood of the just: Cain has become a film maker, a politician, a journalist, and he has killed Abel for the second time."[50] He argues as well that France needs absolutely to embrace Hitler's "New Europe." In fact, according to Châteaubriant, there can no longer be a "great Frenchman" who does not incorporate a "great European" within himself.[51] And Europe itself cannot survive without Nazi Germany, which, in the current circumstances, is the only bulwark against "the great invasions that are coming."[52] In a different venue (a speech at the Salle Pleyel on 14 November 1942), Châteaubriant asserts that the French nation's only hope lies more than ever in embracing Nazi Germany, "which knows better what France wants than she does herself."[53]

Châteaubriant's adoration—in the Christian as well as the lay sense of the word—of Hitler and Nazi Germany also finds expression in the *Cahiers* and is, as always, inseparable from his religiosity. In a November 1942 entry, he writes that he embraced National Socialism because "I am a Christian."[54] In justifying Nazi (and Vichy) tyranny in the name of Christianity, Châteaubriant asserts elsewhere that nothing is "less Christian" than "a man who 'has rights.' "[55]

Ironically, it was fellow collaborationist writer and pro-Nazi zealot Lucien Rebatet who, after the war, best summed up Châteaubriant's muddled wartime thinking, editorial ruminations in *La Gerbe*, and the intellectual incoherence and lack of integrity of the newspaper. In *Les mémoires d'un fasciste*, Rebatet dismissed Châteaubriant's editorials in *La Gerbe* as "soothsaying and homilies that are as confused as they are pompous." The newspaper itself reflected its director's "confused morals" and revealed, ultimately, the "mind of a madman."[56]

Rebatet was not wrong, certainly where the intellectual rigor of *La Gerbe* was concerned. Despite the writers it attracted, the newspaper remained intellectually flabby and ideologically incoherent throughout its four-year existence. It embraced Georges Montandon's racist eugenics at the same time that it endorsed Charles Maurras's cultural anti-Semitism. It lauded Nazism's Fascist "New Europe" and praised Vichy's "return to the soil" even though the two were in many ways incompatible. Its editorials confused historical epochs and religious and political figures and credos in praising Joan of Arc as a heroine of the "New Europe" and Hitler as a

Christian savior. Not long before the Liberation, *La Gerbe* published editorials and petitions denouncing the so-called terrorism of British and Allied bombing. To the end, however, it continued to attract big-name contributors.

With the Liberation, *La Gerbe*'s offices on the Rue Chauchat were searched by the police and then taken over by the Resistance newspaper *Action.* According to David Price-Jones, the collaborationist newspaper's files were dumped in the street. Châteaubriant, along with other archcollaborators, was forced to flee France. Earlier, in the Tyrol in January 1944, he had lamented the impending destruction of the Nazi dream and the "New Man" it had promised. If, he wrote, in compensation for the destruction and ruin of war "a new man, a man of the light, a man, for example, devoid of this brutal automatism that men receive from machines," had emerged, the game would have been worth the effort. Unfortunately, this had not occurred. Instead, the world was left with "the empty machine of man."[57]

But for Châteaubriant, this was not the worst of it. One night he was startled by noises that made his cottage on the edge of the forest tremble. Stepping outdoors, he heard in the distance the rumble of Allied bombers. In his *Cahiers* he recalls that one of these bombers had been brought down a few nights earlier near Dusseldorf. To his consternation, the aviator turned out to be a woman, "a young woman with a made-up face, with blue eye shadow, with fingernails lacquered and caked with cinnabar." For Châteaubriant, the message is clear. The Allied victory will bring "painted cadavres," proof for him that "the reign of the Beast" is at hand. The Allied warriors are the Devil's henchmen ("lowly officers of the Beast"), and the noise that made his cottage tremble was nothing less than the noise announcing the arrival of the Apocalypse.[58]

Along with Pétain, Laval, Céline, and many others, Châteaubriant found himself in the fall and spring of 1944–1945 at the castle of Sigmaringen. There, he became a character—or more accurately, a caricature of himself—in Céline's novel *Castle to Castle.* In one of the finer comic scenes, Céline witnesses an exchange between Otto Abetz, the former German ambassador in Paris, and Châteaubriant, accompanied by his dog and still dressed as a Breton country nobleman but now sporting a Tyrolean hat and carrying an ice ax. Still optimistic about a German victory because the Nazis and their collaborationist allies have the "quality of soul"—and "the soul, that's our weapon"—Châteaubriant announces that he is on his way to the mountains to locate a spot where, with a few trusted friends, he plans to build a bomb that will allow Christianity at last to triumph: "a bomb of concentration! Of faith! . . . a terrible moral bomb!" Abetz then proposes to Châteaubriant to think along different lines and to focus his attention on a massive Nazi victory celebration in Paris— by now, of course, a totally delusional notion. Abetz disagrees with the musical arrangement Châteaubriant proposes, the "Ride of the Valkyries," for the celebration. Contradicted in his enthusiasm, Châteaubriant becomes enraged. In typical Célinian fashion, the scene ends with Châteaubriant hurling crockery at Abetz across the latter's desk. The reader is never told whether Châteaubriant succeeds in exploding his moral bomb.[59]

To the end of the war, Châteaubriant kept the faith, remaining firm in his collaborationism and his support of Nazism and its providential mission. Before leaving France in summer 1944, he had signed a petition calling for Pétain to dismiss Laval in favor of a head of government "fully committed to the German war effort."[60]

In January 1945, in the newspaper *La France*, published by the French government in exile in Sigmaringen, Châteaubriant insists that Germany — "this immense school of human thought" — could not really be vanquished because, in effect, God is watching over it. But, he wonders, revealing his own uncertainty, what if God "got distracted" for a time and Germany was destroyed and sank in the "Ocean of History" like Atlantis? Then, too late, Europe will discover that *it* was Germany, that all it could ever aspire to was incorporated in the Nazi dream, and therefore nothing will remain of Europe after Germany's disappearance. In the meantime, Châteaubriant asserts, the face of the German soldier reveals that while he might suffer military defeat, he can never truly be beaten, and indeed it is his victorious opponent who will turn out to be the loser: "When a country is about to suffer defeat, this can be seen in the man of this country, on the face of this man worn out by combat. But one only has to look at him, this German man, who has never been as clear in his relentless stoicism and in his quiet force. You may be able to crush him, but you cannot beat him. Because *he* is not the beaten man of the present. It is obvious that the reverse is the case."[61]

In the final days of the war, as Allied troops moved through Germany, Châteaubriant fled to Austria for good. There, he lived safely and comfortably in Kitzbühel under the alias Dr. Alfred Wolf. In 1948, he was tried in absentia before the *Haute cour de justice* in France for his wartime activities. He was condemned to death and to *indignité nationale* (national unworthiness).[62] From exile, he greeted news of his condemnation with apparent indifference, writing in his *Cahiers* in a section titled "The Bouquet of My Joy" that he now saw things from "a higher plane" and through a filter of "forgetfulness."[63]

But Châteaubriant's self-described detachment did not prevent him from continuing to comment on European and global developments or, for that matter, from insisting that he had been prescient in his earlier political choices and understanding and that he had always acted in the best interests of France. As Kay Chadwick observes, for Châteaubriant to justify these claims, he needed to indulge in some remarkable and profoundly dishonest and self-serving historical revisionism.[64] This he did on a number of fronts in his *Cahiers.*

Obviously, the first stumbling block to Châteaubriant's justification of his earlier views was his unqualified and uncritical support at the time for Nazi Germany and its leader as ahistorical and "Christianizing" forces upon which Europe's salvation depended. In defending the validity of his initial commitment, Châteaubriant deployed several strategies. First, he argued that *over time* the Nazis and their leader had betrayed their own transcendent mission by forsaking their "European" calling. Drunk with their military victories, they sank into an abject and extreme nationalism comparable to that of their Soviet enemies. And without explicitly contradicting his earlier claims for a Nazi elite, Châteaubriant argued that "National Socialist formations were constituted, above all, by popular elements" that lacked vision.[65] So much for the providential mission of the German people as a whole.

The horror of the Nazi death camps was a much more difficult issue to deal with. Here, Châteaubriant chose to spread the blame to all of humanity, deny the *specificity* and uniqueness of the Nazi crimes, and, finally, shift the focus away from concrete historical events and toward the global and indeed cosmic sweep of seismic, metaphysical happenings. In the *Cahiers,* he writes: "We have not really understood the terrible, universal implications of the examples of inhumanity offered by the German camps. Political phariseeism and the illusions of nationalisms wish only to recognize German crimes at issue here, and to foist off onto Germany what had been a premonitory symptom in Germany, after it had been a premonitory symptom in Russia, in Spain, and other places as well, of the mental disorganization of humanity, destined to become increasingly accentuated, to become more and more generalized, until the point when hell will be realized by a humanity among which will fade, until they disappear, the last traces of God."[66]

It is not difficult to detect in this passage the strategy later used by many revisionists and even Holocaust deniers of challenging the uniqueness of the Holocaust by merging it with other crimes and claiming *universal* culpability for it. In his insistence that earlier, comparable exterminations, and specifically Soviet crimes, preceded the Nazi genocide, Châteaubriant anticipates the strategy deployed by Ernst Nolte during the Historians' Debate of the 1980s. For Nolte, the Soviet mass murders served to explain and even "justify" the Nazi crime, beecause supposedly Hitler conceived the later as a kind of preemptive strike and an act of "self-defense." (These issues will be discussed in greater detail in chapter 6.)

As for Châteaubriant's collaborationism and his welcoming of the German occupant to France, he continued to justify his position and his patriotism as well, although in the postwar years he was willing to concede that Germany exploited

France during the Occupation, something he had not admitted earlier. But on the basic issue of the Nazi presence on French soil, this continued in his mind to be a wise and expedient choice, because "we needed them essentially [as a bulwark] against Soviet Russia."[67] Had Germany won the war, France would have enjoyed an equal partnership with Hitler's Reich in the "New Europe."

In the postwar years, Châteaubriant applauded Winston Churchill's calls for a Franco-German reconciliation, ignoring not only the difference between Churchill's perspective and his own but the events that dictated Churchill's postwar outlook. As Chadwick observes, Franco-German reconciliation as well as postwar efforts to create a united Europe were still, in Châteaubriant's view, pretexts for creating a racist—a "truly biological"—United States of Europe. But wily to the end, Châteaubriant denied that his calls for a new "biological" Europe meant that he was now or ever had been an anti-Semite. In a final piece of historical revisionism, Châteaubriant asserted that he never considered the Jews to have been among the causes of "the decadence of our civilization." For Chadwick, this statement "stands as a blatant and outrageous reinterpretation of his wartime persona."[68]

Châteaubriant died in 1951. His posthumous legacy has been ably traced by Chadwick.[69] Shortly after the writer's death, Grasset began to publish his unpublished works. The editor in charge was Robert de Châteaubriant, Alphonse's youngest son. The titles of these works, *Lettre à la chétienté mourante* and *Itinéraire vers la lumière divine*, are indicative of the extent to which Châteaubriant was now being presented as a man of primarily if not exclusively religious and spiritual concerns. The publication of these works was followed by the republication of his prewar novels in an effort to rehabilitate the writer as an important literary figure. In the mid-1970s, during the *mode rétro*—France's perverse fascination with the 1940s, Vichy, and Nazism in particular—L.-A. Maugendre's biography *Alphonse de Châteaubriant, 1877–1951* appeared. The book downplayed or distorted its subject's political commitments and offered stunning examples of historical revisionism, oversimplification, and ideological bias. These include the claim that during the Popular Front period, "In Paris, as in Madrid, the Comintern was pulling the strings."[70] Maugendre also asserted that during the Occupation, *La Gerbe* attempted to distance itself from anti-Semitism.[71] There are many other examples of distortions and inaccuracies along these lines in Maugendre's biography.

In 1981, the Club Châteaubriant was formed to protect and promote its subject's memory, revise his postwar conviction, and announce his prescience in denouncing Bolshevism and calling for collaboration with Nazi Germany. Not surprisingly, it was a mouthpiece for the views of Jean-Marie Le Pen's National Front and the Nouvelle Droite (New Right). According to Chadwick, it numbered seventy-three members, most of whom were old enough to remember the Occupation and cling nostalgically to their own dubious past political commitments. In 1987, in an effort to further his father's political rehabilitation, Robert de Châteaubriant and the re- actionary Nouvelles Éditions Latines published *Procès posthume d'un visionnaire,* an expurgated collection of Châteaubriant's political writings. The book accentu- ates Châteaubriant's postwar disappointment with Hitler and highlights the writer's denunciations of the dangers of Bolshevism. According to Chadwick, all of this was undertaken by Robert de Châteaubriant in order to make a case for the author of *La gerbe des forces* as, ultimately, a "lucid political historian."[72] Needless to say, few if any take this claim seriously.

Alphonse de Châteaubriant is not generally included under the rubric of French Fascism because, among other reasons, his total subservience to Hitler and Ger- many precluded even the possibility of a fierce *French* nationalism on the writer's part. It is also implausible to classify Châteaubriant as a Fascist literary modernist with the likes of Drieu, Brasillach, and even Montherlant, because he was anything but experimental in his writing and eschewed completely any engagement with ur- ban and technological modernity in his fiction. He also ignored or dismissed the profound dislocations of modern life and the impact of history on the individual. In the case of his first novel, *Monsieur des Lourdines,* this can be attributed in part to the fact that the novel was written before the terrible trauma of World War I, but this is not the case with his subsequent fiction. Resolutely antimodern and antimod- ernist even in his later works, Châteaubriant never figured as a significant or con- temporary literary presence to be reckoned with during the interwar years and the Occupation.

It is therefore not entirely surprising that recent accounts of Fascist and, more broadly, literary modernism ignore Châteaubriant or dismiss his work as insignifi- cant and anachronistic. Studies appearing in the United States such as David Car- roll's *French Literary Fascism* do not discuss the writer and his work at all. In France, works such as Jacqueline Verdès-Leroux's *Refus et violences* insist on Châteaubri- ant's total lack of literary talent. According to Verdès-Leroux, Châteaubriant's oeuvre, including the award-winning novels *Monsieur des Lourdines* and *La brière,* "demands oblivion for itself." She justifies this assertion by pointing out that these novels rep- resent "a phony rural and noble world . . . described in a heavy and worn-out style which is often ridiculous."[73]

Nevertheless, given that literary Fascism and literary collaborationism in France are often examined and discussed together because of their historical coincidence during the Occupation, and also given that there are certainly shared literary affinities between Châteaubriant's novels and, for example, the "Fascist fairy tales" of Robert Brasillach, the complete omission of the Châteaubriant's oeuvre is somewhat surprising. Be that as it may, his novels do provide insights into his political and social views and therefore enrich our understanding of the motivations and contours of his complicity with Nazism.

In general terms, it is frankly difficult to disagree entirely with Jacqueline Verdès-Lerroux's negative assessment of the literary merits of Châteaubriant's novels. The central characters of these works are largely one-dimensional figures lacking in complexity and nuance. They are also frequently either royalist and Catholic landed gentry spouting the wisdom of faith and hierarchy or obedient servants or wily peasants attempting to save their traditions and their land from the encroachments of modernity. The plot of each novel usually leads to a moralizing, edifying conclusion that affirms or reaffirms the traditional, conservative, and reactionary values exemplified by the protagonists. The central character in *Monsieur des Lourdines*—the 1911 Goncourt Prize winner later under Vichy made into a successful movie directed by Pierre de Hérain, Pétain's stepson[74]—is Timothée de Lourdines, an aging country squire of a piece with the Breton land and culture from which he springs. Early in the novel, Châteaubriant informs the reader: "Impossible to encounter a man better suited to his habitat than this small country gentleman was to his ancient castle. Both came from the same soil and both were almost the same color."[75] Echoes of Balzac's insistence on identity of character with their milieu are obvious here, and, as Chadwick points out, Barrès's more ideologically loaded attachment of men to their native and national habitat is also evident.[76]

Lourdines's peaceful and isolated existence is interrupted by a letter demanding payment for bad debts accumulated by his wayward son, Anthime, in Paris. The debt is enormous, and to clear it Lourdines will be forced to mortgage the estate on which he lives. The estate serves as a microcosmic and completely hierarchical and paternalistic world that assigns each person a place as well as an identity and role in life. Such is the shock of the debt and its destructive implications for everyone's future that Madame des Lourdines succumbs to the blow. Her son returns as she is dying, and his appearance in the novel confirms that he bears the worst traces of the rootless, cosmopolitan, and decadent world of Parisian sophistication. Chadwick notes, for example, that he arrives with his Russian greyhound, as out of place in the Breton countryside as his master now is. The dog is, moreover, "the symbol of [Anthime's] hedonistic life in Paris."[77]

Giving in, finally, to the pressures of Anthime's money lender, Muller—a name both "foreign" and Jewish, possessed by a man whose role in the novel is purely destructive—Lourdines decides to settle the debt. Learning that his inheritance is mostly gone, Anthime first contemplates suicide but then, overwhelmed by his father's generosity and love of the land, renounces his evil city ways and remains with Lourdines at novel's end. Anthime's "conversion" occurs while listening to his father's sublime, ethereal violin playing.

La brière, winner of the 1923 Grand Prix de l'Académie Française, once again pits regional and rustic virtues against big-city corruption, this time in a struggle between large capital interests from outside the area and the inhabitants of the Brière region, whose marshes are threatened with industrialization. The novel was inspired by a real court case, and despite Verdès-Leroux's allusions to the artificiality of Châteaubriant's novels, in this instance at least the novelist made a serious effort at authenticity in his depictions. Told of the trial by a relative, Châteaubriant moved to the region from Paris and remained there for a year, studying the customs, the people, and the natural environment. The son and grandson of painters, Châteaubriant also drew his aesthetic inspiration for the novel from the works of Dürer the elder, which he attempted to incorporate in his characterization.[78]

In order to save the domain of his people, the hero of La brière, the wily old Briéron, Aoustin, must find the royal decree that many years before had ceded the lands to the local inhabitants. As a subsidiary to the main action of the novel, Aoustin must also try to prevent the marriage of his daughter to someone from another region, which is an egregious violation of Briéron custom. (He has already condemned his son for the same reason.) Both of these concerns, moreover, go to the very heart of his being. As a contemporary commentator on the novel and its central character observed in 1923, Aoustin is "the fanatic of his country and his race." He is "the integral individual, the product of his milieu and his climate."[79] And his children's romantic and sexual involvements constitute for Aoustin both a "national" concern, in that anyone not of the region is considered by him to be a "foreigner," as well as a "racial" concern. Chadwick notes that Aoustin shares "Barrès's Darwinian vision that 'racial pollution must be resisted at all costs lest the fit be made unfit.' He is proud of the previous racial purity of his family."[80] In its public and "domestic" politics, then, this "masterpiece inspired by land in which it is rooted" champions the same sharply reactionary views as Châteaubriant's earlier novel.[81]

In La réponse du seigneur, the conflict between city and country, modernity and tradition, is somewhat muted in a text whose principal aim would appear to be to link Châteaubriant's reactionary social vision with his understanding of Christian spirituality. The novel follows the apprenticeship of a young, city-dwelling law student who, while on vacation in the countryside, learns true wisdom at the feet of an aging Breton nobleman, Monsieur de Mauvert. Not surprisingly, Mauvert's wisdom consists of a quasi-mystic adoration of the land and an intense spirituality that reconfirms God's place at the center of human existence. But Mauvert's "spirituality" is also grounded in a belief in the absolute necessity of hierarchy and of accepting one's place within it. He waxes nostalgic for the Middle Ages, when everyone served according to the hierarchy, everyone knew his or her place, and commanding and obeying were part of "the same great act."

Pascal Ory astutely observes that *La réponse du seigneur*, originally published in 1933 — the year of Hitler's rise to power — marks an important change from the writer's earlier work. The novel demonstrates the "emptiness" of a *disappointed* Christian, now nourished by Nietzsche and haunted by megalomaniacal and prophetic tendencies. In this sense, according to Ory, *La réponse du seigneur*, more than the earlier novels just described, clearly prepares the way for Châteaubriant's "conversion" to Nazism and announces the perversion of his own Christianity in the process. It does not, however, reflect any *literary* development or improvement on Châteaubriant's part. Quite the reverse. To the degree that the earlier works merit at least some attention as authentic regionalist fiction, *La réponse du seigneur* constitutes more of a hodgepodge whereby these same "rustic virtues" are increasingly conflated with a misguided and egomaniacal religiosity.[82]

If these remarks tend to suggest that Châteaubriant's oeuvre is ultimately of little real or lasting literary interest — at best, perhaps, the work of a successful, if minor, regional and regionalist novelist — it is important to stress that the recent scrutiny accorded figures such as Brasillach, Rebatet, and perhaps Drieu has decidedly *not* restored their credentials as literary talents of the first order or established or reestablished the "canonicity" of their works. In fact, the recent interest in French literary Fascism and collaborationism has tended instead to debunk the notion, fostered especially in the immediate postwar period by the Right, that "good writing" by the likes of Brasillach and Drieu was being unjustly ignored because of their "bad politics." In the case of Brasillach, the efforts of Maurice Bardèche and others to create the myth of a brilliant young *poète maudit* (accursed poet) and one of the greatest writers of his generation, executed unjustly in his prime in 1945, has been challenged most recently by Alice Kaplan. Discussing Brasillach's novels, Kaplan observes that they are seriously dated, "precious and juvenile," and, in their maudlin sentimentality and indifference to real social issues and concerns, little more than Fascist fairy tales.[83]

Similar negative conclusions can be drawn from recent efforts to reassess the work of Drieu and Rebatet. Even if one acknowledges the quality of works such as *Le feu follet*, *La comédie de Charleroi*, or *Rêveuse bourgeoisie*, it is doubtful that anyone other than a specialist would read or reread novels as bad as *Mémoires de Dirk Raspe* or *Les chiens de paille* if it weren't for the scandal of their author's Fascism and collaborationism. In other words, it is not unreasonable to argue that writers such as Drieu survive to a tangible extent *because of* rather than *despite* their politics. In the same vein, one could claim that many only read Rebatet's *Les deux étendards* because, in a hyperbolic and provocative essay published in the 1970s, George Steiner argued that not only was Rebatet a greater writer than Céline, he was more despicably pro-Nazi and collaborationist as well.[84]

But like the works of these figures, which *do* tell us a great deal about Fascist cultural modernity as well as the writers' motives for embracing collaborationism, Châteaubriant's works can add to the first discussion and provide insights into the reasons for his own complicity with Nazism. On the first score, it is worth noting that there is a significant strain of reactionary, pro-Vichy, and even pro-Nazi writing that dismisses and even abhors urban modernity and locates true values and the natural hierarchies that should govern human existence in the countryside — in the simple life of the peasant or, in Châteaubriant's case, the country squire. This is all too evident in the works of Jean Giono (see chapter 3) and is also apparent in more obscure — and surprising — places. In Paul de Man's article "Chronique littéraire," published in the Belgian collaborationist newspaper *Le Soir* on 23 December 1941, the writer speculated, in effect, on the need for a *literary* work to explore "the profound and ancient reasons that rendered the debacle [of France's 1940 military defeat] inevitable." This would be, he continued, a "handsome subject for a novelist: to show concretely, without reference to a theoretical exposé or the dryness of statistics, where the deficiency of this country lay and what breakdown caused its internal disorganization."[85]

De Man went on to offer his opinion of what precisely the problem was. Echoes of the reactionary vision and rural ethos of Châteaubriant's fiction (as well as Giono's) are quite pronounced:

> The principal flaw — as has already been noted on several occasions — was the abandonment of values that have been grouped under the rubric of "peasant" in favor of creations of the city. It is not a question here of a naive "return to the soil" but of a certain moral attitude that can be symbolized fairly precisely in the opposition between the customs of the city and the customs of the country. This entire panoply of vulgar and empty pleasures, of indifference and negligences . . . was born in the city and spread to the suburban areas. And it is only among a few peasants who have remained completely free of the nefarious effects of the corrupting city influence and among whom continue to exist the virile and strong virtues that account for the health of a country.[86]

As with de Man's identification of rural and peasant virtues with Fascism's cult of virility and force, the Manichaean oppositions he invokes and the reactionary vision of society he champions are present in Châteaubriant's novelistic universe as well.

Kay Chadwick describes the political and historical vision and attitudes that find expression in novels such as *Monsieur des Lourdines*, *La brière*, and *La réponse du seigneur* as well as in other works. Unlike reactionary predecessors such as Joseph de Maistre, Châteaubriant's politics do not reflect a nostalgia for the ancien régime and the prerevolutionary monarchy. In fact, as Chadwick explains, the writer abhorred "the modern state as created by Richelieu from the mid-1620s, then extended under Louis XIV. . . . [He] was opposed to the establishment of the Court as a fixed institution, since this promoted administrative centralization and effectively uprooted the nobility from the provinces, undermining its status by making it dependent on the king's royal favors for its existence rather than on seigneurial position." In sum, Chadwick observes, "Châteaubriant's true regret was the death of Feudal society," which he located "in the mid-sixteenth century."[87] Henceforth, the existence of what Châteaubriant described as the *cellule patriarchale* (patriarchal cell), which established the hierarchy of the rural and anachronistic utopia and was evoked longingly in his fiction, was no longer really possible.

Although Châteaubriant's "feudal" vision accounts to a significant degree for his novelistic inspiration as well as certain shared affinities with other reactionary and even *fascisant* writers, it does not explain and, in fact, runs counter to his embrace of Nazism. Despite well-known attempts by Nazi propagandists to cast Hitler in the role of Teutonic knight, including the propagation of familiar images depicting him in this guise, Nazism itself, in virtually all of its most salient features, did *not* champion a return to medieval feudalism. Historically speaking, it was profoundly *centralized*, certainly in its conception and in the majority of its institutions. Totalitarian in inspiration, Nazism's aspirations to racial and global dominance, as well as its social vision and political practices, could hardly be further removed from the localized, "microcosmic" feudalism of which Châteaubriant dreamed.

If this is the case, if Châteaubriant's politico-historical vision in its most basic and primal form diverges sharply from the reality of Nazism, how does one account, finally, for his complicity with Hitler's Reich and his archcollaborationist stance during the Occupation? The inadequacy of purely political and historical—as well as aesthetic—explanations suggests, obviously, the necessity of other approaches. It is helpful to take a final look at Châteaubriant's Christian religiosity.

In *Alphonse de Châteaubriant*, Kay Chadwick does an excellent job of discussing the nature and roots of the Châteaubriant's Catholicism, although labeling him a "Catholic" is somewhat problematic in that he was fiercely, indeed arrogantly, independent in his views and in fact broke with the Church during his youth. What

Châteaubriant seems to have drawn mostly from his faith was less a Christian ethical and moral outlook than a belief in the imminent damnation of mankind and the coming of the Apocalypse, a taste for Manichaean struggles, and an incessant longing for a Messianic figure and a "saintly" elite. All of these tendencies, as Norman Cohn's classic work *The Pursuit of the Millennium* demonstrates, coincide precisely with what he labels "millenarianism," which defines important early strands of Christian as well as Jewish thinking. For millenarian sects and movements, according to Cohn, salvation can always be pictured as

(a) collective, in the sense that it is to be enjoyed by the faithful as a collectivity;
(b) terrestrial, in the sense that it is to be realized on this earth and not in some other-worldly heaven;
(c) imminent, in the sense that it is to come both soon and suddenly;
(d) total, in the sense that it is utterly to transform life on earth, so that the new dispensation will be no mere improvement on the present but perfection itself;
(e) miraculous, in the sense that it is to be accomplished by, or with the help of supernatural agencies.[88]

Cohn adds that historically, the "world of Millenarian exaltation and the world of social unrest" do not necessarily "coincide," but they do "overlap."[89] Finally, the Messiah, originally viewed in Jewish apocalyptics as a wise and just man, increasingly came to be viewed as superhuman or indeed divine or quasi divine.

In his chapter on the tradition of apocalyptic prophecy, Cohn also describes the scenario and conditions under which the Messiah and the army of his saints shall rise up and come to power. This Cohn labels the "central phantasy of revolutionary eschatology":

> The world is dominated by an evil, tyrannous power of boundless destructiveness—a power moreover which is imagined not as simply human but as demonic. The tyranny of that power will become more and more outrageous, the sufferings of its victims more and more intolerable—until suddenly the hour will strike when the Saints of God are able to rise up and overthrow it. Then the Saints themselves, the chosen, holy people who have groaned under the oppressor's heel, shall in turn inherit dominion over the whole earth. This will be the culmination of history; the kingdom of the Saints will not only surpass in glory all previous kingdoms, it will have no successors.[90]

Considered as a whole, it is not difficult to recognize that Châteaubriant's "Christian" vision of the world and history, his adulation of Hitler and Nazism, and his understanding of the stakes at issue during the war as described in his editorials in *La Gerbe* and in his *Cahiers* coincide in virtually all their particulars with the millenarian traditions and beliefs described by Norman Cohn. In *La gerbe des forces*, it is clear, first, that mankind is being spiritually annihilated in a world dominated by the demonic power of Bolshevism and the materialistic sterility of capitalistic and democratic Europe. The discovery of the "German people"—synonymous in Châteaubriant's view with the Nazis—and above all the "revelation" of Hitler himself constitutes nothing less for the writer than the discovery of the Messiah and his army of saints. Hitler, clearly, is the semidivine leader with superhuman powers: he holds hands simultaneously with the German people and with God. As for Châteaubriant, convinced of his own role as prophet and saint in his own right, he commits himself immediately and entirely. His embrace of Nazism can be described as both a "conversionary" experience and, ultimately, a "leap of faith."

For Châteaubriant, as the *La Gerbe* editorials confirm, the coming of the war is not a *historical* or *political* confrontation but an apocalyptic struggle between Good and Evil, between the saints of God and the forces of Darkness. But the outcome—which originally promised the establishment of the Kingdom of the Saints, the hegemony of Nazism in Europe and eventually the world—turns out terribly, tragically different. Faithful to his own millenarian scenario in its entirety until the end of the war, Châteaubriant interprets the Allied victory as nothing less than the advent of the Beast, as epitomized in the dead female Allied bomber in the writer's *Cahiers*.

In the postwar period, Châteaubriant changes course and revises history, as Chadwick rightly observes, but, I would argue, not simply as a gesture of self-serving dishonesty. Throughout his career Châteaubriant clung to a misguided Christian faith shaped by his own millenarian vision and longings, and on a certain level, his embrace of Hitler and his complicity with Nazism were mandated and ratified by that faith—and not the reverse. But since the two had become synonymous from 1936 until the end of the war, in order to rescue or preserve his religious faith—such as it was—in the postwar period it was necessary, in effect, to deny Hitler and the Nazis their previously assigned roles as the Messiah and his saints. This explains why, in the passages cited earlier, the writer condemns the Nazis for failing as (Europe's) saviors, for becoming too "nationalistic" and "drunk" with victory, and, finally, for being comprised not of a (Christian) elite but of "popular elements," mere mortals after all.

Having renounced salvation in the form of a Nazi victory, Châteaubriant found himself free to renew his "spirituality" in its purer form (hence his "indifference" to his own 1948 condemnation) while maintaining that he had been right all along about decadence, the "death" of man, and the impending Apocalypse. Thus the Nazi death camps were not, ultimately, proof for him of the specific historical horror of Nazism but just one more disaster in a continuing sequence that confirmed the depravity of man in the modern world. At the same time—and perhaps equally perversely—the advent of the cold war and the necessity of Franco-German rapprochement confirmed to Châteaubriant that the form his vision of salvation had assumed had been right all along. The unification of Europe in the face of the "Bolshevik" menace was coming to pass, and the prophet, it appeared, was proving more prescient than the Messiah Châteaubriant had earlier championed—at least in his own eyes.

Having, in effect, denied history by embracing a millenarian vision of the world at the center of which he nevertheless placed the very real historical nightmare of Nazism, Châteaubriant revealed himself, ultimately, to be incapable of learning any of the *historical* lessons that World War II and its aftermath had to offer. While the vision he espoused and the values he deduced from it were very different from Montherlant's, he shared with the author of *Le solstice* a misguided and arrogant faith in his own understanding of history. This blinded him to the true nature of the cause with which he was complicit and to the full measure of the destruction that cause had achieved. But unlike Montherlant, Châteaubriant's misguided commitment to Nazism had been total, and the conflation of that commitment with a self-righteous millenarian religiosity made him even less capable of grasping the implications of his complicity with political evil and therefore of feeling, or at least revealing, any remorse whatsoever. If these are the ultimate consequences of what Chadwick labels Châteaubriant's misguided "idealism," they are disturbing indeed.

CHAPTER THREE

Jean Giono

Pacifism and the Place of the "Poet"

Much more so than is the case for either Henry de Montherlant or Alphonse de Châteaubriant, the story of Jean Giono's complicity with Vichy and Nazism begins with the experience of World War I. While the Great War certainly stimulated Montherlant's taste for force and virility and Châteaubriant's desire for Franco-German rapprochement and the creation of a "New Europe"—critical factors, respectively, in their later complicity—in Giono's case the extended experience of the fear, physical suffering, and death at the front made him a committed and indeed fanatical pacifist and helped forge his ferocious animosity to modernity in all its forms. This, in turn, shaped not only his political outlook and his vision of history but also his understanding of society and culture and, ultimately, the role and function of the artist therein. To a very significant extent, the war made him the man and the writer he became. And it led him to embrace antirepublican and antidemocratic values and to sympathize with Vichy and Nazism in ways that many in France found treasonous.

To appreciate the impact of the Great War on Giono's beliefs and perspectives, it is helpful to recall, first, the terrible material and psychological damage it inflicted on France and then to examine briefly Giono's personal experience of the conflict. In *The Hollow Years*, Eugene Weber's moving account of the political and cultural collapse of France during the 1930s, Weber stresses not only the extraordinary and indeed exceptional human destruction suffered by the French but also the fact that the trauma of these losses colored French attitudes throughout the interwar period:

> The 1930s begin in August 1914. For fifty-one months thereafter 1,000 Frenchmen were killed day after day, nearly 1 in every 5 men mobilized, 10.5 percent of the country's

active male population. That was more than any other Western belligerent would suffer: The British counted half as many dead and missing, Germans and Austro-Hungarians, who had incurred heavy losses, never got as far as 10 per cent. About 1,400,000 French lost their lives; well over 1,000,000 had been gassed, disfigured, mangled, amputated, left permanent invalids. Wheelchairs, crutches, empty sleeves dangling loosely or tucked into pockets became common sights. More than that had suffered some sort of wound: Half of the 6,500,000 who survived the war had sustained injuries. Most visible, 1,100,000, were those who had been evidently diminished and were described as *mutilés*, a term the dictionary translates as "maimed" or "mangled," and English usage prefers to clothe in an euphemism: "disabled."[1]

The damage caused by the war was evidenced not only in the sad spectacle of the *mutilés de guerre* (disabled war veterans) and in other signs of physical destruction but also, according to Paul Valéry, in France's—and the West's—loss of faith in its most fundamental values and beliefs as well as in its capacity to control its own destiny for the better. As Mary Jean Green has noted, shortly after the armistice in August 1919 Valéry proclaimed in the pages of the *Nouvelle Revue Française*, "a major 'crisis of the mind. . . . We civilizations are now aware of our mortality. . . . There is the lost illusion of a European culture and the demonstration of the impotence of knowledge to save anything whatsoever; there is science, mortally wounded in its moral ambitions, and as if dishonored in its cruel applications; there is idealism, which has won with great difficulty, but deeply wounded, responsible for its dreams; realism disillusioned, beaten, laden down with crimes and errors.'"[2]

Not surprisingly, given both the horrors wrought by the Great War and the profound cultural crisis many felt in its aftermath, the response in France and throughout much of Europe was initially less to confront the crisis than to avoid it. Buoyed by the material prosperity of the 1920s and released from the stresses of war, in political and cultural terms France turned away from its recent history. In literature, Green emphasizes, the 1920s was marked primarily by a return to and fulfillment of prewar literary traditions and tendencies. Works such as Gide's *Les faux-monnayeurs* as well as the later volumes of Proust's *À la recherche du temps perdu* simply carried out "to greater perfection the work of writers who had begun their careers before the war."[3] Some, such as the surrealists, gave themselves over to rebellious experimentation, but their various efforts and activities aimed at cultural regeneration were received "with amused tolerance by the reigning bourgeoisie." In Jean-Paul Sartre's view, the surrealists "participated in the spiritual inertia they professed to transform."[4]

According to Green, it "was not until the 1930s that the literary mainstream, along with much of its readership, turned to face the chaotic events of contemporary history."[5] It was in the 1930s, that the most important works dealing with World War I and its terrible destructiveness in material and spiritual terms first appeared in France. These included such novels as Céline's *Voyage au bout de la nuit* (1932), Drieu La Rochelle's *La comédie de Charleroi* (1934) and *Gilles* (1939), Louis Guilloux's *Le sang noir* (1935), Roger Martin du Gard's *L'Été 14* (1936), and Giono's *Le grand troupeau* (1931). The 1930s also saw the appearance of important literary works dealing with more contemporary wars, revolutions, and historical crises, including the Chinese Revolution, the Spanish Civil War, and the internal political and social crises that plagued France throughout the decade. Important works in this category were written by major figures on both the Left and Right including Malraux, Louis Aragon, Paul Nizan, Drieu, and Brasillach.

The representation of history in the major literary works of the 1930s in France was accompanied by the political polarization of the majority of the writers themselves. Numerous literary and intellectual histories dealing with the topic as well as works on specific figures from the period have underscored not only the extraordinary effervescence of political engagements by writers but the wide range of the political commitments themselves. Louis Aragon and Paul Nizan of course embraced Communism, as did, briefly, Albert Camus. Distinguished fellow travelers on the Left included André Malraux and others. On the Right, Hitler's admirers included not only the likes of Alphonse de Châteaubriant and Robert Brasillach but Céline and Drieu, among others. Drieu was also active, intermittently, in Jacques Doriot's French Fascist Parti Populaire Français. Generally eschewing party politics, the philosopher Alain (Émile-Auguste Chartier) remained a committed pacifist up through the outbreak of World War II.

Against this historical and cultural backdrop, the attitudes that led to Jean Giono's eventual complicity with Vichy and Nazism began to emerge. Giono's extensive and brutal military experience during World War I marked him profoundly for the rest of his life. Mobilized in early 1915, he remained behind the lines until summer 1916, when he saw action near Verdun. In August 1916, his regiment was decimated, largely as a result of a mistaken French bombardment.

After another period at the rear and then frontline service in a relatively calm area in the Vosges, in April 1917 Giono was transferred to Flanders, where he witnessed and participated in some of the bloodiest fighting he was to encounter during the war. He was gassed at Mount Kemmel in May 1917 during an attack and spent several weeks recovering at the rear. As the war ground to a conclusion, Giono was transferred to various postings in Champagne, Lorraine, and finally Alsace. In July and August 1918, his assignment was giving English lessons to his fellow soldiers. He was on furlough in his hometown of Manosque in Provence when the armistice was announced.

According to Giono's biographer, Pierre Citron, the future writer's attitudes toward the war while serving as a combatant, as well as the descriptions of his experiences contained in letters sent to his family, did not, surprisingly, point clearly in the direction of his militantly pacifist and antinationalist views to come. In fact, Citron notes that Giono was not consistently antimilitaristic and apparently enjoyed, for example, the camaraderie of the soldier's life. He was also on occasion given to expressions of patriotism. In a letter to his parents written in 1918, he stated, "My country has all my love."[6] Giono's letters to his parents were remarkably circumspect and even "sanitized" in their descriptions of the dangers and difficulties of his wartime existence, as opposed to the harrowing descriptions of war and life at the front that he would later pen in the cause of pacifism. Citron speculates that this was because the writer did not wish to concern his parents overmuch about his safety.

One final noteworthy aspect of Giono's wartime experience is that he rarely (if ever) encountered German soldiers in face-to-face combat. Therefore, his experience of war and combat tended to be conceived less as a human struggle than an "inhuman cataclysm,"[7] which was all the more terrifying.

Demobilized in Marseille in 1919, Giono returned to Manosque, married and became a father, and resumed his position in a local bank. He worked in the Service de Coupons underground in the bank vaults "endlessly clipping off bits of strangely colored and engraved paper and crediting them in big ledgers."[8] In 1929, he was offered a promotion to direct a branch of the bank in Antibes on the Côte d'Azur. Faced with the possibility of leaving his beloved Manosque and the surrounding countryside as well as his friends and relatives, Giono declined the offer, resigned from the bank, and devoted himself full-time to writing.

Inspired by his love of the Greek classics and their heroes as well as by the beauty and power of nature in his native Provence, Giono wrote exuberant, poetic novels celebrating the glories of peasant life and of living—and struggling—with nature. To the degree that these works generally avoided in most cases the historical realities of the interwar years, they are very much in keeping with the literary trends of the 1920s.

Giono's literary success was virtually immediate. Originally published in Marseille, his works soon appeared with the leading Parisian publishers. From Manosque, Giono produced a steady stream of fiction throughout the 1930s. His early trilogy of novels—*Colline* (1928), *Un de Baumugnes* (1929), and *Regain* (1930)—set the stage for more ambitious novels including *Le grand troupeau* (1931), *Le chant du monde* (1934), and *Que ma joie demeurre* (1935).

Not content to be merely a successful novelist, during the 1930s Giono increasingly assumed the role of cantor, extolling the virtues of peasant life and condemning the artificiality, sterility, and indeed destructiveness of urban technology and modernity. The latter he identified principally with the Third Republic, which he also held increasingly accountable for the horrors of the Great War. By now an outspoken and militant pacifist, Giono first aligned himself with the Communist Party and its "anti-Fascist" struggle by joining the *Association des écrivains et artistes révolutionnaires* in 1934. Even in this context, however, Giono's bile was primarily directed at the "Bourgeois state" as the principal perpetrator of war.

Encouraged by a growing group of admirers, friends, and sycophants, as the decade progressed Giono wrapped himself more and more in the role of sage and prophet of a superior, and indeed salvational, peasant wisdom. He became the infallible mentor of the pacifist and "primitivist" group known as the *Contadouriens*, named for the Provençal plateau where the group met and from which the new "gospel" was preached.

It was in this context that Giono published two pamphlets, *Lettre aux paysans sur la pauvreté et la paix* (1938)—addressed to his "friends," the peasants—and *Précisions* (1939). In terms of the political, social, and cultural attitudes they display, both texts are very helpful in charting the course of Giono's political evolution up to the French defeat of May–June 1940 and indeed through the Occupation.

In essence, the *Lettre aux paysans* is a paean to peasant life as well as a thoroughgoing critique and denunciation of its opposite, urban modernity. At its most fundamental, the contrast for Giono is one between authenticity and artificiality on virtually every level: material, spiritual, and even existential. On a material level, Giono establishes the superiority of the peasant over his urban counterpart—generally discussed in terms of the factory worker—by noting that the former does not work for a salary and is therefore in direct contact with the fruits of his own labor. The fruits of the peasant's labor, Giono states, "go directly from the earth to his mouth." This is why, he asserts, the peasant "is normally attached to the earth as if the latter were a part of his body."[9] To the degree that money interrupts and indeed ruptures this contact, this *bond*, it is "the greatest enemy of the peasant."[10]

By contrast, the worker is detached from what he produces as well as from the earth itself. He is "a peasant who has lost everything"[11] and the victim of "capitalist vulgarity," a scourge from which all of "the noble efforts of the present" have sought to liberate him. On this score, Giono continues, Communism initially held out hope but has failed. It has simply altered what the writer describes as "the form of capitalism" without eradicating the system and its nefarious and indeed toxic effects.[12]

As a result of the failure to destroy capitalism, "from year to year, . . . successive generations have arrived in the world with, each time, a little less of the ancient naturalness, with each time, . . . a little less force, with, each time, a little more confidence in the machine, . . . with, each time, a little less hope." Now, "[we] have arrived at the moment when this generation can no longer digest either bread or wine; it nourishes itself on industrial stimulants. It wakes up less and less."[13] And, Giono concludes, "This generation that lies at your feet is in a state of terrible despair, these phony men who no longer know how to tie a knot or generously undo the binds [that imprison], these living creatures incapable of living, that is, incapable of knowing the world and of taking pleasure in it, these terrible anesthetized sick people, they were once peasants. One doesn't need to go far into the past and back through their ancestors to find the one who abandoned the plow to go in search of what he thought was progress."[14]

Given this terrible state of affairs, Giono expresses his approval at one point for a peasant "revolt" with "all of its cruelties," although he does not specify what those cruelties might be. If, in the entire world, he continues, "the peasants of every nation united together—they all need the same laws—in one fell swoop they would install on earth the commandments of their civilization; and the ridiculous little governments—those that are now masters of everything—would finish their days as a group, parliaments, ministers, and heads of state altogether, in the padded cells of huge insane asylums."[15]

Several things are worth underscoring in these passages. First, Giono's idealization of the peasant implies a clear *hierarchy*: the peasant and his "civilization" are *superior* in every way to the city dweller and the worker and to the republican and capitalist (or Communist) culture the latter represents. Giono's outlook is neither egalitarian nor, to all appearances, democratic, and his tendency to see the city dweller as a kind of degenerate, *inferior* being smacks not only of the reactionary vision evident in the novels of Alphonse de Châteaubriant but also of the more overtly Fascistic and racist denunciations of decadence typical of the interwar period. In the *Lettre aux paysans*, Giono speaks—disturbingly—of the "purity" and "cleanliness" of the peasant as opposed to the city dweller who has been "soiled" and "burdened" with the "impurities" of "the social."[16] And in a letter to Jean Paulhan dating from the same period, Giono insists that the French peasantry "is not a *class*, it is a *race*" that in fact has more affinities with German peasants than with French workers.[17] The fact that Giono's views along these lines shared affinities with Fascism and with Nazism in particular was not lost on some observers at the time. In his 1937 book *L'Opéra politique*, Henri Pollès denounced Giono's "tarzanism or mystique of . . . the virgin forest," an attitude Giono shared with the Nazis, who were also enamored, first and foremost, with a kind of "adult scouting."[18]

It is also clear that, despite Giono's pacifism, he is not averse to speaking of an imagined and highly speculative peasant revolt with its necessary "cruelties" and social upheavals. His apparent disdain for all forms of political authority and his imagining of all the representatives of that authority being thrown into a massive insane asylum certainly constitutes at the very least a form of fantasized, *verbal* violence. And Giono indulged in fantasies such as this in other contexts as well. Already in 1931, he had spoken to André Chamson about the two men leading a peasant revolt into Paris and making "waves of blood flow."[19] Later in 1935, he had written to Jean Guéhenno on the subject of a peasant revolt to come, warning, "YOU LIVE IN IGNORANCE OF THE TERRIBLE TIMES THAT ARE COMING."[20]

All of these fantasies underscore Giono's complete lack of respect for the French Republic's democratic authorities and institutions, which for him are no better than the authorities and institutions of any other form of government, including Fascist dictatorships. On the latter score, Giono was on occasion quite blunt, noting in 1937, for example, in relation to the idea of France being invaded by Nazi Germany: "What's the worst that can happen . . . ? [The French] become Germans? For my part, I prefer being a living German to being a dead Frenchman."[21] In any case, what is clear in the *Lettre aux paysans* is that, in Giono's eyes, the "peasant good sense" and the sense of restraint that characterizes him should not prevent the peasant from undertaking extraordinary and extreme acts of *political* resistance against a governmental authority that is clearly his enemy. Although at the end of *Lettre aux paysans* Giono backs away from the idea of an actual peasant revolution and the violent overthrow of the government, he does explicitly recommend civil disobedience. And the ambivalence of Giono's prose on the subjects of revolt and cruelty, as well as his staunch militancy on behalf of the peasant "cause," leave the reader wondering what his real attitude toward political violence might be.

Despite these intimations of a justifiable—and extreme—violence, the *Lettre aux paysans* concludes with a thoroughgoing condemnation of war in all circumstances. What is so terrible about war for Giono—at least in this text—"is not its horror; it is its futility."[22] The problem is that humankind believes in the "lie of the utility of war," and for this reason they continue to wage it. Taking the example of World War I to argue against the notion that war is useful, Giono stresses that it accomplished precisely nothing. Reputedly the "war to end all wars," it failed to achieve that aim. Also supposedly worth fighting as a war to establish rights and justice, it failed in that regard as well. And, Giono continues, all subsequent wars have proven—or are proving—to be equally futile. The Spanish Civil War "is not even over yet and one can already recognize its evident futility."[23]

In *Précisions*, a pamphlet written in praise of the signing of the September 1938 Munich Accords and published a year after the *Lettre aux paysans sur la pauvreté et la paix*, Giono couples his condemnation of war with an emotional and often paranoid denunciation of France's and Europe's political leaders. According to Giono, Europe's leaders did not want peace—they wanted war. They wanted to "betray" the people, and it was only the will of the latter that constrained them ultimately to settle their differences without bloodshed. In this sense, the Munich Accords constituted nothing less than a "victory" of the people over their corrupt and murderous leaders, whose very essence is "to lie." Giono draws no distinction in this regard between France and Britain's democratic leaders and Germany's and Italy's dictators. Nor, for that matter, does he detect any impediment to future friendships between the peoples of Europe's democracies and those of Nazi Germany and Fascist Italy: "All of a sudden, we see that it is possible and that it is easy to love the Germans and to love the Italians."[24] Giono acknowledges, seemingly as an afterthought, "I know there is Czechoslovakia." But, he continues, for the Germans living in Czechoslovakia who supposedly wanted to become Germans again, "that was absolutely their right." And as for the defense of Czechoslovakian sovereignty, that was not an adequate reason for a Czech, a Slovak, or certainly a Frenchman to die.[25]

Giono was to publish one more antiwar text before the outbreak of hostilities in May–June 1940. Written in June 1939, the pamphlet *Recherche de la pureté* is at least initially more convincing than *Précisions* because the gratingly triumphalist and indeed arrogant tone of the latter text is abandoned in the opening pages of *Recherche* in favor of sober reflections on the nature of pacifism and compelling (and, according to Citron, partially fictionalized)[26] accounts of the writer's wartime experiences. Giono stresses, first of all, that contrary to what is usually assumed, to be a pacifist is to be *courageous*. Humankind's tendency in any society is to do what is easiest, not what is most courageous, and the easiest thing in contemporary society is to follow one's political leaders and one's fellow citizens in their bellicosity.

But while being bellicose is the easiest path to follow, that choice is most often based on an ignorance of what war is actually like, and so Giono turns to the horrors of warfare as he claims to have experienced them personally during World War I. He evokes the fear, the presence of death, and finally the soldiers' mutinous revolts against the political and military authorities who ordered the soldiers to their own destruction while praising their "heroism" with empty words. Here, as in other pacifist texts written during the 1930s, Giono is most forceful when describing the degradation, fear, and incomprehension of the foot soldier obliged to sacrifice himself for a cause he neither grasps nor believes in. Giono discusses the uncontrollable dysentery in the trenches and the afflicted soldiers, who had to wipe themselves with their bare hands and then wipe their hands in the mud or on the clothes of dead comrades. He also discusses the sheer terror he experienced—a terror that haunted him throughout the interwar years. In an earlier text dating from 1934, Giono had stated, "I cannot forget the war. I would like to. I might pass two to three nights without thinking of it and then suddenly I see it again, I feel it again, I undergo it again. And I feel frightened. In the war I was afraid, I tremble, I shit in my pants . . . I prefer to think about my own happiness. I do not want to sacrifice myself."[27]

In the final pages of *Recherche de la pureté*, Giono indulges once again in vitriolic denunciations of governmental authority that, in its blood lust, imposes war on peoples who do not wish it. He asserts flatly, "War is never desired by the people, it is dropped on them. There are no warlike peoples, there are only warlike governments."[28] Revisiting the opposition between natural authenticity and artificiality used earlier to distinguish between the peasant and the city dweller, Giono now employs the dichotomy to distinguish between the "simple man of the earth, the simple inhabitant of the globe" who must fight the war, and the government authorities with their "artificial obligations" who don't fight the wars they make but force others to fight them in their stead.[29] Under the pressure of an imminent conflict, Giono redraws the line between the natural and the artificial, the peaceful and productive as opposed to the sterile and destructive—in effect, between good and evil—to place the onus of the cataclysm to come squarely on the shoulders of the political authorities of the moment and, in particular, France's Third Republican leaders. Already in 1938 at the moment of the *Anschluss* (annexation), Giono had made it clear that he held his own government accountable first and foremost for militarism in general and modernity's warlike impulses: "Let me continue to struggle against militarism, and necessarily begin by fighting it in my own country."[30] There is no evidence to suggest that Giono ever recognized the real threat of war as coming from the Fascist dictatorships and Nazi Germany in particular. For him, France's leaders were at least as culpable as Hitler for the destruction to come.

It is not difficult to anticipate on the basis of Giono's militant pacifism of the 1930s his reaction to France's declaration of war in fall 1939 and to the outbreak of hostilities in May 1940. Nor is it hard to anticipate the extent to which, after France's defeat, his deep-seated animosity toward the Third Republic and the urbanized corruption of modernity he associated with it would tilt him in favor of Vichy's "return to the soil" and even the Nazi presence itself. Clearly, nothing in the discussions up to this point suggests that Giono was an admirer of republican or democratic values, and so the conservative, reactionary, and authoritarian policies promulgated by Vichy were not likely to offend his political and social sensibilities. But before turning to the Occupation years themselves, it is essential to stress that Giono's wartime complicity with Vichy and the Nazis was not linked solely to his *political* attitudes as expressed in his prewar essays. It was also bound up with his prewar aesthetics and, ultimately, with his understanding of the role and function of the writer in society. To get a sense of the former (we will return to the latter at the conclusion of this chapter), it is helpful to take a closer look at one of Giono's earliest and most celebrated fictional works, *Regain*.

A novel whose plot, characters, and landscape descriptions epitomize the writer's novelistic art of the interwar years, *Regain* tells the story of the hunter Panturle and of the small Provençal village of Aubignane where he lives. At the start of the novel, Aubignane is in the process of losing all of its inhabitants and appears destined to disappear. As the villagers move away, Panturle loses more and more contact with the human and is slowly reduced to the solitude of an animal-like existence. But Panturle's decline into savagery is interrupted when he encounters Arsule, a desperate and destitute former prostitute. Despite their differences, they fall in love, and out of their love the town of Aubignane will be reborn. The couple settles in the virtually deserted village. Panturle gives up hunting to become a tiller of the soil, and Arsule becomes pregnant. Soon another family moves into the once-dying village, cultivates the land, and forms a new community with Panturle and Arsule. At the end of the novel the inhabitants of Aubignane celebrate their "new town" or, more precisely, the recovery or renewal—*le regain*—of the old.

Nothing in Giono's novel is explicitly *political*, and it is possible to limit one's observations along these lines to the assertion that *Regain* reflects the nostalgia of a premodern—and indeed antimodern—rural life typical of much of the paintings of the period, as described by Romy Golan.[31] But to do so would be to ignore crucial aspects of *Regain* that together comprise a kind of ideological backdrop reflecting a fixed and bluntly reactionary vision of the world—a vision not far removed from the Pétainism of a decade later. First, like Giono's other novels of the period, the fictional world of *Regain* is governed by a preexisting natural rhythm that does not allow for any real change or progress. The only possible movement in the novel is essentially *backward*: Panturle returns to tilling the soil, and the village is reoccupied. No new village is created. Arsule, corrupted by the city, also returns to the purer and more innocent life of the village and the surrounding countryside. Arsule, Panturle, and their new neighbors are all "reborn," in Giono's words, but only through subordinating themselves to the ancient and timeless rhythms of nature. The fusion of their new lives and of nature itself is evoked in striking images, especially at the end of the novel when Panturle, for example, is depicted as solidly planted in the earth "like a column."[32]

In her essay "La pensée de droite aujourd'hui," Simone de Beauvoir argued that one of the "great idols" of the political Right is nature, because nature "appears as the antithesis . . . of History. As opposed to History, it offers an image of time that is cyclical, and the [resulting] symbol of the wheel undermines the idea of progress and encourages passive forms of wisdom. In the infinite recommencement of the seasons, of days, of nights is embodied the grand cosmic circle. The obvious repetition of winters and summers makes the idea of revolution ludicrous and reveals eternity."[33]

In its insistence on the sanctity of a timeless natural order and its rejection of history as well as modernity, Giono's fictional world in *Regain* — and in virtually all of his prewar novels — conforms strikingly to Beauvoir's description. Giono's validation in the novel of natural cycles that are essentially cosmic in their import suggests an allegiance to a vision of the world and of human experience that is closed and immutable and therefore impervious to the lessons of *l'actualité*. In this, Giono's vision bears a strong resemblance to Montherlant's "turnings" of the cosmic or "solar wheel" and Châteaubriant's millenarianism. For all three writers, these allegiances or beliefs entailed, ultimately, a complete misapprehension of history itself.

In regard to the Occupation and Giono's wartime attitudes as well the nature and extent of his complicity with Nazism, it is interesting to note first of all that for the writer, the real war began and ended before the commencement of hostilities in 1940. When the mobilization for war was announced in September 1939, Giono protested immediately. Along with a few friends, he placed stickers stating simply "No" on mobilization posters and other stickers on church doors affirming "Thou shalt not kill." But when the writer himself was called to service, he stunned his pacifist friends and allies by reporting for duty in Digne, where he worked briefly — in uniform — as a secretary. As Pierre Citron states, Giono's decision to report for duty was one of the most controversial acts of his life, and one that led to accusations in some quarters of cowardice and of a betrayal of the pacifist ideals.

Be that as it may, in mid-September 1939 Giono was arrested for distributing pacifist and "defeatist" tracts. Imprisoned in Marseille, he was stripped of his ribbon for the Légion d'Honneur and was initially refused the right to have visitors. Two months later, following the intervention of prominent literary friends, he was released from prison and then officially demobilized and dismissed from military service. According to Citron, Giono promised not to engage in any further antiwar activities. During the rest of the Phony War up through France's stunning defeat of

May–June 1940, Giono devoted himself to his work. In a letter to his fellow *Conta-dourien* Daniel May after the defeat, he wrote, "I am working as if nothing happened and in fact 'nothing did.'"[34] Apparently, Giono remained oblivious to the fears and suffering of his countrymen to the north, many of whom fled south in the chaotic exodus of June 1940 to escape the German conqueror. Many died of privation and exhaustion, and others were killed by the strafing and bombing of German planes.

In regard to Giono's politics during the war and the nature and extent of his complicity with Vichy and Nazism, it is important to stress at the outset that these issues were ambiguous or complicated enough for some to claim that Giono never collaborated. This, at least, is the view of Pierre Citron, for the most part a judicious, if admittedly generous-minded, observer. In his entry on Giono in *Dictionnaire des intellectuels Français*, Citron asserts unequivocally that Giono "never wrote a single word in favor of the occupiers or of Vichy" and that false assertions of Giono's collaboration were made by a narrowly sectarian faction that unjustly persecuted and harassed him at the Liberation.[35] These practitioners of a new "intellectual terrorism" also mocked and derided Giono and his work in the postwar years. The irony, according to Citron, is that Giono was in fact a *résistant*. His play *Le Voyage en calèche*, supposedly written in favor of resistance, was suppressed by the German authorities in 1944, and on occasion he also sheltered Communists, *résistants*, and Jews.[36]

But not all sources, including witness accounts and documentary sources, bear out Citron's assessment. In the second volume of his *Journal de la France* covering the period August 1940–April 1942, Alfred Fabre-Luce describes a visit to Giono in his native Manosque in Provence in October 1941. Less a visit in fact than a pilgrimage of sorts to what is for Fabre-Luce one of the high places of the spirit of Pétainism and collaboration, the stop at Manosque follows on the heels of a stay at Uriage, the famous training school for the young heads of the National Revolution, attended at different times by the likes of Hubert Beuve-Méry, founder of *Le Monde*, and the militiaman Paul Touvier.

Having arrived at his destination in Provence, Fabre-Luce first describes the beauty and purity of the Provençal sky and then climbs the hill near the top of which Giono's home looks down on the town below. Welcomed without ceremony or formality by the writer himself, Fabre-Luce launches into a description of his subject, emphasizing the blueness of his eyes, the blondness of his hair, his natural candor and simplicity, and, finally, his physical vigor and virility, suggested by the fact that he is *"plein de sève"* (full of sap).[37]

Fabre-Luce's description of Giono the man is followed by a short description of his background, covering his World War I service, his work in a bank, and the beginnings of his literary career. Up to this point, there is nothing overtly political in Fabre-Luce's portrait of Giono. Nevertheless, the description of Giono's person is clearly suggestive of the physical robustness and intellectual simplicity admired by both Vichy and the Nazis. It points as well to a curious detail that even Citron in his biography of Giono is at a loss to explain. At the outset of the Occupation, Giono dyed his hair blond and only let it return to its natural gray after the Liberation. At the time, Giono explained to friends and relatives that the sun had bleached one strand and that he dyed the rest for the sake of uniformity. Citron concedes that even Giono's family found this explanation implausible, and many were shocked by the writer's "new look."[38]

After describing Giono's physical appearance and background, Fabre-Luce's approach to and contextualization of his subject changes. He now explicitly links Giono's outlook as well as his various remarks directly to Vichy and Nazi Germany in such a fashion as to suggest that both meet with the Provençal writer's strong approval. Fabre-Luce notes that before the war, Giono the pacifist had dreamed of doing away with military conscription in favor of creating a new organization of the nation's youth. Dressed in green uniforms, these young men would be sent off to learn to live in nature. According to Fabre-Luce, "One day in June 1940, he [Giono] rediscovered his dream in the newspapers. The dream was called the *Chantiers de la Jeunesse*."[39] The *Chantiers de la Jeunesse* were in fact created by the Vichy regime and were comprised of unemployed former soldiers. They have been described as "a quasi-military mass organization for young men that embodied the ideological and functional ambitions of Marshall Pétain's National Revolution."[40]

If, according to Fabre-Luce, the Vichy regime is capable of giving concrete form to Giono's dreams, its ideology also explains the failure of at least some of Giono's efforts to help others find salvation through a "return to the soil." Fabre-Luce recalls that before the war Giono had been in the habit of taking visitors to the plateau of Contadour to gather lavender and experience the conversionary power of the beauty of nature. While the experiment succeeded in most instances, it failed dramatically when Giono's guests were Jews. Rather than appreciate the experience for itself, Fabre-Luce notes that these visitors "had invested the profits and gone to open a factory in Marseille."[41]

If the episode recounted by Fabre-Luce sounds like a parable pitting Vichy's version of all the evils of modernity—urban life, mechanization, money, and the profiteering figure of the Jew—against the rustic virtues of nature and, in effect, aligns Giono's views and experiences with that context, his conclusion evokes a second, more sinister ideological context, that of Nazism, and links Giono to that context as well. In an effort to reassure the reader after the account of Giono's failure with his Jewish visitors, Fabre-Luce claims that despite occasional setbacks, poets always end up "being right." By way of confirming the veracity of his claim, Fabre-Luce quotes Giono as stating, "What is Hitler himself, if not a poet in action?"[42] Neither man, apparently, questions the German leader's successes or sees him in anything but a positive light.

For those who have wished to tar Giono for his collaborationism during the Occupation, the writer's statement to Fabre-Luce as well as his blond hair are often cited as proof that Giono not only tolerated the Nazis but admired them and their leader.[43] Pierre Citron, however, questions the accuracy of Fabre-Luce's account. Citron adds that if Giono did in fact make the comment about Hitler that Fabre-Luce claims he made, Giono was being ironic, and the irony was lost on his interlocutor.[44]

Whatever the merits of Fabre-Luce's report or Citron's objections, the fact remains that a good deal of other evidence and anecdotal material—often second-hand in nature—sheds light on Giono's actions and attitudes during the Occupation. These sources need to be examined before any definitive conclusions concerning his political complicity can be drawn.

It is possible to presume Giono's guilt on the grounds that he was blasted repeatedly as a coward and traitor by the likes of Claude Morgan and Tristan Tzara in the pages of the clandestine Lettres Françaises, blacklisted at the Liberation by the Comité Nationale des Écrivains, and imprisoned for several months following the war. The story also goes that at the moment of liberation of Provence, the newly appointed regional commissioner, Raymond Aubrac, asked his charges why Giono had not been arrested first thing.[45] But denunciations and imprisonments do not necessarily constitute proof of guilt, nor does the fact that Giono was admired by the Nazis and Vichy for his writing and the values he supposedly espoused. Even before the war, Denis de Rougemont in his Journal d'Allemagne had remarked on Giono's popularity in Nazi Germany, noting that Giono's "anti-interventionist diatribes" and provincial primitivism led many in Germany to conclude that his views were "closer to pro-Hitlerian ideologies than the socialism he professes."[46] During the Occupation, Giono was repeatedly invited by the Nazi authorities to the European writers' conferences in Weimar, the main purpose of the conferences being to celebrate the culture of Hitler's "new European order." Giono was also one of six French authors (the others were Montherlant, Drieu, Brasillach, Jacques Benoist-Méchin, and Jacques Chardonne) whose photographs were featured in the catalogue in the German bookstore in Paris.[47] In January 1943, the German illustrated magazine Signal ran a laudatory article on Giono, complete with photographs of the author in his native Provence. A year later, in March 1944, Signal claimed erroneously that it was Giono's success in Germany that had finally demonstrated to the French what a talent they had in him.[48] In 1943, the Nazi ideologue Alfred Rosenberg's office in Germany named a Dr. Payr to be head of the *Amt Schriftum* in France and charged him with writing a report on the country's intellectual climate. The real purpose of the report, whose exalted title was *Phénix ou cendres*, was to determine which writers were considered favorable to the Nazis and which were not. Giono's name figured prominently in the first category.[49] Finally, according to Gérard Loiseaux, throughout the Occupation the Germans presented Giono not only as someone whose art and values met with their approval but, before the war, as the innocent victim of France's *bellicistes*, those Third Republican leaders and left-wing intellectuals whom the Germans, as well as Vichy, held accountable for the war.[50]

The Vichy regime and the French collaborationists in Paris also admired Giono and sought to cast him in the role of a prophet who had anticipated the National Revolution's call for a *"retour à la terre"* (return to the soil) as well as its condemnation of a mechanized, urban modernity. In the *Journal de la France*, Fabre-Luce asserts that Giono's pagan appreciation of nature harmonized with the austerity of Uriage's more disciplined primitivism to create a hymn to France's "new reality." Fabre-Luce adds that Marcel Pagnol's film version of Giono's novel *Regain* could serve as a propaganda film for Vichy and its message.[51]

In Paris especially, Giono was revered as a prophet of the new reality. His works enjoyed immense success, and his message inspired a number of enthusiasts espousing the cultural politics of Vichy as well as more militant forms of engagement with the German occupant. Giono's play *Le bout de la route*, written before the war, was first performed at the Noctambules Theatre in June 1941 and was performed almost a thousand times by May 1944.[52] Financial support in the form of payments for rehearsals, guarantees to actors, and expenses for publicity were paid by *Jeune France*, a support group for the theater funded by Vichy to promote the cultural goals of the regime. In his discussion of the success of the play, Fabre-Luce states, "These are things that Paris waits for but would not dare to write. The proud capital now seeks its gods outside of itself. It is grateful to Giono for not being willing to uproot himself, for not even having consented to come to the first performance of his play. It is with a sort of piety that the capital receives on Mount Sainte-Geneviève the message from Manosque."[53]

Giono's wartime literary successes were not only in the theater. When his book *Triomphe de la vie* appeared in early 1942, Giono went to Paris, where he was feted by French collaborationists and German cultural authorities alike. The publisher of *Triomphe de la vie*, Bernard Grasset, threw a large party on 18 March to celebrate the book's author. Giono also met with collaborationist luminaries including Alphonse de Châteaubriant of *La Gerbe* and Jean Luchaire, editor of *Les Nouveaux Temps*. From Châteaubriant, Giono received a contract worth twenty thousand francs for the rights to serialize his novel *Les cavaliers de l'orage* in *La Gerbe*.[54] This and other lucrative transactions would prompt Claude Morgan to write bitterly in the pages of the underground *Les Lettres Françaises* in June 1943, "After the return to the soil, the return to the bank."[55]

Giono and his work were also celebrated throughout the Occupation in the pages of collaborationist publications, especially *La Gerbe* and *Comoedia*. Both periodicals announced his arrival in the capital in March 1942 with great fanfare. On 19 March, *La Gerbe* published a lengthy "conversation" between Châteaubriant and Giono, both portrayed as "shepherds" of the people in Pétain's France. The 19 March 1942 interview was not the only one with Giono published in *La Gerbe*. The first issue of the paper appeared on 11 July 1940 and included an interview with Giono titled *"Gens de lettres et de coeur."* In the interview, Giono describes his imprisonment by French authorities in 1939 and asserts that he was jailed for refusing to write pacifist tracts that were to be dropped exclusively over German lines. Giono insisted on distributing the tracts among French soldiers as well.[56]

Laudatory articles devoted to Giono and his work written by such *La Gerbe* staff writers as Gonzague Truc and Christian Michelfelder (who also wrote a book in praise of Giono before the war)[57] also appeared regularly in the paper. Even in high cultural reviews such as the *Nouvelle Revue Française*, Giono and his work were appreciated. Not only did Giono publish in Drieu La Rochelle's *Nouvelle Revue Française*, but in 1942 Giono's name was floated for a new editorial board for a review that would be more pleasing to the Germans than the one in place at the time.[58] According to Montherlant, also one of those proposed for the new board, "One wants people who will reassure the occupying powers."[59] The project ultimately came to nothing.

Given Giono's visibility and the celebration of his works and the values they espoused in the officially sanctioned media, it is not surprising that he inspired enthusiasts and militant supporters of the regime and the politics of collaboration. In his book on the theater under Vichy, Serge Added notes that *Jeune France*, the Vichy organization that helped fund the staging of *Le bout de la route*, had been inspired from its inception by "the Contadour movement calling for a return to the soil."[60] The official acting troupe of the Ministry of National Education also found inspiration in Giono's work, taking as its name Regain, from the title of his 1930 novel.[61]

Other forms of inspiration were less innocuous but found their roots as well in Giono's antimodern primitivism. Among Giono's younger admirers, Marc Augier had been a leader of youth movements before the war and became a writer for *La Gerbe* in summer 1940. At the same time, he published a militant tract titled *Solstice en Laponie* in Giono's pacifist publishing venture, the so-called Editions du Contadour. He also joined the Légions de Volontaires Français and fought alongside the Germans on the Eastern Front. *La Gerbe* published heroic and idealized accounts of the fighting dispatched by Augier from the battle lines. Another young admirer of Giono, Philippe Merlin, ended up joining and fighting in the Waffen-SS.[62]

It is not difficult to conclude on the basis of the evidence just cited that Giono was deeply implicated in the politics of collaboration and that his philosophy of a "return to the soil" coincided precisely with Vichy ideology and, to a lesser degree, with National Socialism itself. But how does such an interpretation square with Citron's claim that Giono was not a collaborator, that he was in essence apolitical, and that in the final analysis he believed that de Gaulle "was right"?[63]

Concerning Vichy's embrace of Giono's call for a "return to the soil," Citron's argument that Giono had been espousing these views for years before the war and could not be held responsible for Vichy's ideological choices appears sound enough, although, as noted in the discussion of *Regain*, the writer's novelistic vision in the 1930s was inherently reactionary in a number of important ways that dovetailed nicely with the aims and vision of Pétain's National Revolution. (The extent to which Giono deliberately linked his views to Vichy's will be considered later in the chapter in a discussion of his 1942 book *Triomphe de la vie*). As for Giono being apolitical or even Gaullist, little if any evidence supports these claims, and much of the existing evidence points in the opposite direction. Giono did, after all, accept being interviewed in *La Gerbe* and profited financially from his relations with the paper in agreeing to the serialization of *Les cavaliers de l'orage*, even if the novel itself, begun before the war, contains no clear political message. Citron argues that at least when Giono was first interviewed in *La Gerbe*, he was not aware of the paper's ideological slant or the fact that it was funded by the Nazis, although it is hard to imagine anyone either insipid or naive enough to remain ignorant on this score, given the circumstances at the moment of *La Gerbe*'s creation or the track record of the paper's founder.[64] Under any circumstances, Giono could certainly have been under no illusions concerning *La Gerbe*'s pro-Vichy and pro-Nazi views when he agreed to be interviewed by Châteaubriant in its pages in March 1942.

Citron attributes Giono's contacts with Nazi Germany's cultural emissaries while he was in Paris in 1942 to broad-mindedness. Unlike many of his compatriots during the Occupation, Giono, in Citron's opinion, could distinguish between Nazis and "ordinary" Germans. It is the latter with whom Giono supposedly met during his visit.[65] While many would object to the distinction Citron draws and to which Giono supposedly adhered, the fact remains that, as Philippe Burrin notes, Giono took the initiative himself to meet with Nazi cultural representatives Karl Epting and Gerhard Heller. During these meetings, according to Heller, Giono showed himself to be "extremely well disposed toward collaboration."[66]

It is important to note at this stage, however, that contextualizing Giono's choices and actions in historical terms and accepting Heller's account of his attitude toward collaboration are not proof positive that Citron's views are completely unfounded and that Giono was in fact pro-Vichy or pro-Nazi. Ultimately, the best sources for understanding Giono's politics during the Occupation are his own statements and writings of the period. These sources include the interviews in *La Gerbe*, occasional letters to the German authorities, the 1942 book *Triomphe de la vie*, and, most significantly, Giono's *Journal de l'Occupation*, covering the period 1943–1944 but not published until 1995.

Although the timing and venue of the interviews in *La Gerbe* are in many respects damning in and of themselves, Giono's remarks either tend toward reiteration of earlier positions or are too vague or elliptical to constitute outright praise of Vichy or the Nazis. Other writers who wrote essays for *La Gerbe* or who were interviewed in its pages were often more direct in their political pronouncements. Nevertheless, Giono's comments do tend to ridicule Third Republican authority, as in the 1940 interview dealing with Giono's imprisonment, or to praise Vichy indirectly, as in the March 1942 interview. In the latter interview, Giono applauds the fact that France "has rediscovered its true and pure face"—that of a France faithful to its peasant and artisanal roots.[67] Although Vichy is not explicitly named, Giono's meaning seems clear enough.

In communications dated September 1942 to Nazi authorities in Marseille concerning their invitation to Giono to attend a writers' conference in Weimar, Giono is much more explicit. He laments that his mother's health prevents him from making a journey that he had anticipated with great pleasure, "all the more so because [the trip] would have allowed me to continue with even greater faith this project of a Franco-German rapprochement that I have pursued since 1931." Giono adds: "I am truly disappointed [*désespéré*] but I hope it will be possible for me to make the next trip, to attend the next meeting of the Association of European Writers, of which I am so proud to have been chosen to be a part."[68]

It is possible to argue that in making statements such as these Giono was simply looking for a plausible pretext to avoid attending a conference of which he secretly disapproved, regardless of what he stated to the Germans. If this were the case, his comments, obsequious as they are, would constitute proof of bad faith and perhaps even cowardice, but not of collaboration or complicity. Unfortunately, the views expressed in the *Journal de l'Occupation*—which were not written for public consumption—confirm a tolerant and even occasionally favorable attitude toward the Germans and, more disturbingly, present evidence of a persistent hostility toward the Resistance and a deep-seated anti-Semitism. Acknowledging the presence of occasional "disagreeable" comments concerning "the character of the Jew" in Giono's journal, Citron chalks this up to "a certain, understandable exasperation."[69] He ignores all references to the Germans and to the Resistance. However, it is only by taking all of these attitudes into account that a clear picture of Giono's political outlook during the crucial years 1943–1944 emerges.

In the opening passages of the *Journal de l'Occupation*, the perspective on events Giono claims to adopt is not explicitly partisan in nature but consists of a haughty disdain for the "religions" of "our modern, mechanized world." Modern man embraces these new faiths and even participates in the "wars of religion" they provoke simply to "give the impression that in spite of everything he is a thinking creature."[70] That all of these creeds are ultimately the same is suggested by the image Giono uses to distinguish past idealisms from present ones. When knights-errant pursued the Holy Grail in premodern times, they followed a "single path" leading to one and only one grail. Even Don Quixote, in his madness, "walked in a straight line." But today's seekers, by contrast, scatter to the four winds: "Today one could say that the grail has shattered and that its shards are pursued in all directions." Giono, for his part, chooses not to participate in these pursuits but prefers instead to treat them all with the same disdain: "As for me, I think that the most important thing is not to be a dupe. . . . I want to reserve the right to laugh [at others] and comfort myself with a *precisely* applied disdain."[71]

Whatever one may think of Giono's "*precisely* applied disdain"—which as late as April 1944 he claims made him a "stranger" to the Germans, the English, the Americans, and the Russians alike—it is hardly apolitical in nature. It does, after all, constitute a *political* judgment affirming that all these conflicting ideologies or "religions" are *equivalent*. On this score, Giono's views have clearly not changed since the prewar years. Resistance is the same as collaboration, and Nazi Germany is in reality no different from the democracies that oppose it: "I make no distinction between the Germans and the Anglo-Americans, they resemble each other." Even their crimes are identical: "The Germans machine-gunned those fleeing during the [1940] exodus; the Anglo-Americans bomb Forcalquier for pleasure."[72]

Giono's vitriolic antimodernism, then, appears to level the political playing field to the point of denying any real difference between the conflicting ideologies and their adherents. But even in the opening passages of the *Journal de l'Occupation* and indeed throughout the text, the writer's supposed detachment gives way to political animosities directed first and foremost against the Resistance. Giono's pessimistic, indeed nihilistic, assessment of modernity that opens the journal is triggered in this context, he claims, by disappointment on learning that a former comrade from Contadour has betrayed his pacifist principles to distribute arms for the Resistance. For Giono, the comrade in question has failed to "to escape in the direction of *la hauteur*."[73] Giono does not explain what that *hauteur* (higher moral ground) might be.

As the Liberation approached and the activities of the Resistance become bolder and more widespread, Giono's animosity toward its members and their actions only increased. In January 1944, he learned that the son of a former fellow pacifist had joined the Resistance in Grenoble, had been arrested by the Germans, and would in all likelihood be shot. As described in the journal, the fate of the young *résistant*, Alain, fails to arouse sympathy in Giono. In fact, it provokes the opposite reaction. Alain is characterized as "the biggest imbecile that I've ever encountered," and his "patriotism" is simply the label this "hoodlum . . . has found for his misdeeds."[74] All of this is merely a "comedy," and the Germans are certainly not to blame for arresting or killing Alain, since, Giono claims, *he*, Alain, took up arms against *them* in the first place. The fact that Germany invaded and Occupied France in 1940 and invaded the Free Zone in violation of the terms of the armistice in November 1942 does not figure in Giono's calculus of guilt and responsibility.

In the entry dated 20 January 1944, Giono discusses another episode involving a conflict between the Resistance and the Germans—this time, the Gestapo. What Giono labels *"combats de guerre civile"* (battles in a civil war) consist of efforts by the local Resistance to liberate the town of Banon. Here again, Giono's wrath is directed against the *résistants*. For Giono, these are not patriots but simply rabble settling old scores: "They care as much for their country as they do for their first sock."[75] The motives of the Germans are not called into question.

On 8 May, Giono describes what he labels the *"attentat de Voiron"* (attack of Voiron).[76] Of all of the passages in the journal dealing with the Resistance, this is perhaps the most disturbing in its revelation of Giono's attitudes:

> An entire family killed by revolver shots, from the eighty-year-old grandmother to a three-year-old child shot in its cradle with *three* bullets in the back of the head and one in the gut. The assassins (what other word can one use?) are students and teachers at the town professional school! A group of Communist youth. These youths laid the groundwork for the crime by first making friends with the family. They thereby learned the password to get into the house. They then spent several amicable evenings at the home. One night they arrive, chat in a friendly fashion with their hosts, and then

massacre everyone including the child. They are arrested. They admit everything. They say they were carrying out orders. They are shot. . . . All the professors in the school are accomplices. The entire school knows and says nothing.[77]

Having painted a portrait of unparalleled horror, Giono does not even feel compelled to denounce explicitly the motives of the *résistants* who carried out the attack. The pretext of a feigned friendship on the part of the "assassins," their apparent unquestioned willingness to obey orders to murder, and the unspeakable brutality of the killing of the child are sufficiently damning.

Conceding the terrible nature of the events described, the problem is that there is much more to what happened at Voiron than Giono allows in his journal, and the details of his account are not entirely accurate. By modifying some of the facts and eliminating the *context* of the killings, Giono casts the entire episode in starkly Manichaean terms: the victims are wholly innocent, and the perpetrators are purely and inhumanly malevolent. But the realities of the situation were in fact much more complex. The murdered family members all belonged to the Jourdan family. The father, a former member of Action Française, was head of the local Milice and is described by Jacques Delperrié de Bayac in his history of the Milice as "a man without scruples, a stool pigeon, a thief," indeed the individual responsible for the majority of the crimes committed by the Milice in the region.[78] The students who murdered the Jourdan family did not feign friendship for them but rather joined the Milice under false pretenses to gain access to the Jourdan house, which was itself guarded constantly by other Miliciens. Having gained entry into the Jourdan house, the *résistants* killed the guards and then shot the family members. Giono's account is accurate in stating that when the *résistants* were captured, they confessed to the killings and were shot. What he fails to mention is that they were shot in the back of the head in front of twenty of their classmates and professors, who, after witnessing the executions, were deported to Germany, where most of them died.[79] Delperrié states that the Voiron episode was recounted widely at the time by those who wished to discredit the Resistance. Giono's version of events clearly serves the same end. It also whitewashes the Miliciens, whom, in other contexts, Giono praises for their courage.[80]

If Giono's version of the Voiron episode and other passages in the *Journal de l'Occupation* confirm a strong aversion to the Resistance—composed, he believes, of violent hooligans bent on social disruption and mayhem—his animosity toward the Jews is of a very different sort. In fairness to Giono, the journal reveals that during the Occupation he did on occasion help individual Jews. Also, in reading Karl Epting's anthology of German poetry, Giono lamented the absence of works by

Jewish authors "if the works are beautiful."[81] But such actions and sentiments did not prevent him from voicing his belief that the Jews are a race *apart* and that their fate during the war was fundamentally a matter of indifference to him. On 12 November 1943, Giono writes that "Jews are exactly Jews. Jews of the ghetto. One only has to see their communities in Manosque and Fourcalquier clearly separated, voluntarily separated from the rest of the population."[82] And in an entry dated 2 January 1944, Giono describes a conversation with a Jewish acquaintance: "He asks me what I think of the Jewish problem. He wants me to take a stand. I tell him that I don't give a damn, that I care as much about the Jews as I do about my first diaper: that there are better things to do on earth than concern oneself with the Jews. What narcissism! For him they are the only subject of discussion, the only thing that counts. As for me, I'll concern myself with other things."[83]

Given the situation for Jews in France at the time—with which Giono was certainly familiar—his attitude is shocking. His comments concerning the Jews, at least in this instance, are more than simply "disagreeable," as Citron describes them. Ironically, in his journal Giono displays a great deal more "sensitivity" toward the Germans in chastising his neighbors for their lack of "nobility and dignity" in taunting Wehrmacht prisoners as they are driven through Manosque in trucks following the Liberation.[84] Earlier, in May 1944, Giono had in fact been happy to sign copies of his books for German soldiers who came to visit, although he had come to realize that such actions were by then dangerous and politically suspect.[85]

As the *Journal de l'Occupation* clearly demonstrates, Giono's prewar pacifism and especially his visceral and obsessive hatred of modernity, indissociably linked in his mind with Third Republican France, not only blinded him ultimately to the realities of history unfolding around him but contributed to his complicity with Vichy and Nazi Germany, even in their most horrific aspects. In late 1943, when the journal opens—and when the full extent of Nazism's brutal global ambitions as well as its *technological* bellicosity are fully evident—Giono is willing to insist that *nothing* distinguishes Nazism from its enemies. All the antagonists in the war are merely misguided knights-errant of different religions in pursuit of shards of the grail, and all are equally worthy of his disdain. The same dismissive attitude was already apparent in the writer's comment during the 1930s concerning the "futility" of the Spanish Civil War. In historical and ideological terms, Giono had apparently learned nothing.

But Giono's willful blindness where history was concerned did not prevent him from *sympathizing* and indeed *empathizing* with Nazism's and Vichy's most brutal representatives, as is evidenced in his anger over the deaths of "innocent" Miliciens, his rage against their Resistance killers, and his concern for the dignity of German troops. Nor did his disdain for the "religions" confronting each other prevent him from sporadically embracing and voicing the ugliest feature of Vichy's and the Nazi's respective "religions," their anti-Semitism. Giono's anti-Semitism had not been evident and had certainly not been voiced before the war in the way that it is in the *Journal de l'Occupation.*

But, in the final analysis, should one attribute Giono's complicitous stance with regard to the regimes of Pétain and Hitler primarily or exclusively to his outlook on history or to his political attitudes and prejudices? As the earlier discussion of the novel *Regain* should suggest, Giono's historical vision and ideology are ultimately inseparable from and in fact derive in part from the writer's *aesthetic* vision. As other texts written during the Occupation confirm, they are also indissociably linked to the role and function Giono ascribes to the "poet"—to himself—in society. I want to conclude, then, with a consideration of the "aesthetic" dimension of Giono's political complicity.

In a particularly striking (and insensitive) passage in the *Journal de l'Occupation,* Giono expresses a feeling of unparalleled joy while living through France's experience of national humiliation. On 24 September 1943, he writes that "I have never been this happy. Books have never been so succulent. Never has love been so peaceful, so colorful, so fanciful. Never have the days been so admirably harmonious. Never have I worked this patiently. Never have I appreciated so fully my riches."[86] As this comment suggests, Giono's newfound sense of self-fulfillment during the Occupation is essentially an *aesthetic* experience to the extent that his well-being is tied to an appreciation of the beauty of life and the ability to *create.* As he puts it, he has never worked so "patiently" or so thoroughly embraced his "riches." The apocalypse of the nation's defeat and the destruction of Third Republican modernity are apparently followed by a personal "renewal" that is *also,* it would seem, a renewal of the kind of world that grounds Giono as an artist and that he feels destined to celebrate. The advent of Vichy—of Vichy's "return to the soil"—is thus an affirmation in the *real world* of the truth of Giono's artistic vision and the rhythm it espouses. Vichy affirms the sanctity of the myth of the simplicity and beauty of provincial life, that is, the world celebrated in Giono's novels and essays, but it also affirms the cycle of loss or destruction followed by renewal that animates the writer's vision in *Regain* and other prewar novels.

It is precisely this vision and the cycle of renewal that are articulated with precision and clarity in Giono's 1942 book *Triomphe de la vie.* A hellish vision of the modern city, Marseille, with its cafés and "their halls full of Neros, Caligulas, Caesars, and triple-chinned Vitellius,"[87] opens the essay and is followed by a denunciation of the modern world with its faith in progress, reason, technology, and "intelligence." Marseille is a city peopled by automatons living in "petrified forests." Worst of all, it is a city whose inhabitants have given up the idea of what Giono labels *"créer par coeur"* (creating through the heart).[88]

The infernal, and indeed apocalyptic, vision of Marseille—of modernity itself—soon gives way to an idyllic vision of a peasant village whose inhabitants are governed by an alternating rhythm of work and celebration. It is this world, Giono affirms, that only too recently has been mocked and disdained by a modernity drunk with the notion of progress, a powerful form of inebriation that led ultimately to its downfall in 1940.[89] But it is also this world, this *monde de l'artisanat* (artisanal world), on which one is now constructing, "simply and naturally, what one can truly call a great nation."[90]

And where is the "poet"? Exiled from the "petrified forest" of modernity, he resides, along with the baker and the saddler, in Giono's rustic village paradise, where he opens his *magasin à merveilles* (store of marvels). There, he satisfies the entire population's most profound need, because it is he, we now learn, who "creates through the heart."[91]

If Giono's antimodern utopianism and his self-defined role of poet and "creator through the heart" are inseparable and in fact mutually dependent on one another, they must depend for their achievement on Vichy itself. In one of the most telling passages from the 19 March 1942 interview in *La Gerbe*, Giono is asked by his interlocutor if he could have written *Triomphe de la vie* before the war. Giono responds, "No, I could not have conceived it then. We could not have imagined yesterday that the destiny of France would be to move toward a peasant, patriarchal civilization. But since then, we have lived through a great experience, we have learned about ourselves in a few short months of these events more than what we learned during years of errors. Our characteristics, our essential virtues, are now clear to us."[92]

And if Giono reveals himself in the *Journal de l'Occupation* to be viscerally hostile to the Resistance and to Jews—but shockingly tolerant of Germans and the Milice—it is perhaps because the former represent not so much the vestiges of a corrupt past but the threat of a new apocalypse that will eliminate the idyllic world created, in Giono's view, by France's defeat and the advent of Vichy. And if that world is eradicated, it will of necessity silence the poet who "creates through the heart"—Giono himself. If, moreover, Giono can espouse collaborationist views in the *Journal de l'Occupation*, all the while claiming to be nonpartisan, it is because he sees his engagement not as narrowly political but as a defense of his *vision* of community and of the *possibility* of artistic creation itself. It is therefore not surprising that after the German defeat and especially the disappearance of Vichy, Giono's artistic vision and his self-perception as "poet" underwent a radical trans-formation in the postwar years.[93]

In the case of Jean Giono's complicity with the authoritarian and racist politics of Vichy and the Nazis, then, it is not possible to separate the political from the aes-thetic, and not simply because the one may serve as a convenient or simplistic metaphor for the other. Indeed, the inseparability of reactionary politics and aes-thetics in Giono's artistic production up through the Occupation underscores his limitations as an artist, a writer, and a thinker. Unwilling or unable to analyze and perhaps reconcile through art the incompatibilities and conflicts he perceived be-tween modernity and his vision of the virtues of peasant and rural existence, Giono absolutized both in a hyperbolic and moralizing language that ultimately lost touch with the objects it set out to describe. While for some this may not make Giono less of an artist, it does make him a less than reliable and objective witness of his time.

CHAPTER FOUR

Alain Finkielkraut

Croatian Nationalism and European Memory

Before turning to the 1990s, it is important to recall very briefly those events and de-velopments—political, historical, and cultural—of the late 1980s that prepared the intellectual terrain and defined the parameters of political engagement for the decade to come. Foremost among these for our purposes here was a growing na-tional preoccupation with—and malaise over—the memory of World War II, the Vichy regime, and French complicity in the Holocaust. This memory provided a distorting lens that skewed perceptions of many political crises and historical de-bates and offered a pretext for justifying often misguided engagements.

Equally important, of course, to shaping political perspectives, sympathies, and commitments in the 1990s was the collapse of Communism in 1989. The postwar pro-Soviet or pro-Communist leanings of the majority of France's writers and intel-lectuals had been eroding steadily for decades under the impact of events, begin-ning with the Soviet suppression of the Hungarian revolt of 1956 and including the fragmentations and disillusionments of May 1968, the publication in French of Aleksandr Solzhenitsyn's *Gulag Archipelago* in 1974, as well as other events. But it was 1989 that sounded the death knell for such leanings and redrew the political (and geographical) map that would redefine future commitments. The cold war was over; Communism, it appeared, had failed; and Europe was about to undergo dra-matic and unsettling changes.

In France, the political seismic shift of 1989 was accompanied by the commem-oration of the two-hundredth anniversary of the French Revolution, an event that in itself spelled remarkable changes in the nation's political and historical outlook. The failure of the Soviet experiment, itself in principle the product of the revolutionary legacy stretching from 1789 up through the Bolshevik Revolution of 1917, confirmed for many that, in the words of François Furet, "the Revolution is over." Internal political developments in France in the 1980s served to confirm this perspective. The election of François Mitterrand in 1981 initially promised massive social and especially economic changes in French society, but by the late 1980s this "revolutionary" outlook had changed very significantly. Among other developments, the Socialist president had shared power with a Gaullist prime minister during the first period of "cohabitation" in French history after 1988. Furet took this as a sign that French democracy had finally matured, stating that "the universal acceptance of the political institutions and constitutional settlement of stability of the Fifth Republic" confirmed that "fiercely partisan political disputes of the past had finally subsided. The 'spectacular peculiarity' of France's political identity, its perpetually unstable state forms (constantly under challenge from the Jacobin Left and the Catholic Right) had been transformed into the routines of constitutional representative democracy."[1]

But if French political life in the late 1980s had, broadly speaking, achieved a new consensus or *juste milieu* (happy medium), if intellectuals had lapsed into an occasionally lamented "silence" with the electoral victories of the Socialist Left, and if it was possible to debate the "end of history" following the Soviet demise, this state of affairs did not last long. Despite Furet's claims for a new French political consensus, the disturbing presence and continuing success of Jean-Marie Le Pen's extreme right-wing and xenophobic National Front revealed fissures in the political and ideological landscape that became most spectacularly visible more than a decade later with Le Pen's first-round victory in the presidential elections in spring 2002. From the outset, Le Pen's anti-immigrant xenophobia was linked to more "traditional" forms of racism that included a defense of a blue-eyed and blond "Frenchness"; obscene, anti-Semitic jokes about the names and "dual nationality" of some Jewish leaders; and, finally, the claim in September 1987 that the gas chambers were "a minor detail in the history of World War II." No wonder, then, that many in France saw Le Pen and his movement as a return of Fascism and indeed concrete evidence that the Nazi and Vichy pasts were not completely past.[2]

If the 1991 war in Kuwait and Iraq riveted attention outside France and Europe at the very outset of the decade, developments in the former Eastern Bloc, and especially troubling signs that the violent breakup of the former Yugoslavia was imminent, began to draw scrutiny closer to home. From the beginning, analyses by intellectuals of the general situation in Eastern Europe after the demise of Communism pointed toward a return to other, familiar forms of political extremism from the Right: nationalism, ethnic hatreds, and Fascism itself. Summarizing Jean Baudrillard's

likening of the situation to a kind of glacial melt that allowed for a generalized thaw-
ing of virulent reactionary political strains, Bernard-Henri Lévy wrote:

> Communism had frozen everything. It froze what had pre-existed its hegemony. It had
> petrified that which it had conquered. We're speaking here of the famous sheet of cold-
> ness—which, rather than kill the germs that make societies live, or die, had conserved
> them, exactly as they were, with all their virulence. Well now, the ice floe is melting.
> And as in all debacles, and as in all snow melts, everything covered by the icy blanket
> comes back to the surface; nationalisms, xenophobias, debris of anti-Semitisms, racisms,
> populisms, accents from yesterday and the day before yesterday, residues of fascisms—
> a sunken Atlantis, completely intact, with its cortege of monsters, unfinished deliriums,
> and ghosts.[3]

Having colorfully described Baudrillard's "thaw," Lévy offered up a different but
equally imaginative metaphor to describe the political and ideological conditions in
the post-Communist East:

> Imagine . . . that Europe is a laboratory.
>   In this laboratory there are some test tubes.
>   In these test tubes, there are mixtures through which currents of extraordinarily
> high intensity pass.
>   Imagine that some molecules break up.
>   Some recombine to form new molecules.
>   Now imagine political atoms subject to unheard of pressures that free them and
> combine them into new molecules.
>   These political atoms are familiar. Each one has a familiar place in our repertoires,
> in our politico-chemical taxonomies. Except that the violence of the shock, the power
> of the big bang, the arbitrariness of the encounters, both collisions and attractions, has-
> ten the new combinations that are themselves unfamiliar.[4]

But lest one conclude from Lévy's laboratory analogy that his predicted political outcome for Eastern Europe would be very different from Baudrillard's, he hastened to
add that although the area was not simply witnessing a reemergence of old, familiar
demons, it was undergoing a process of "catalysis . . . perfectly comparable to the one
in the past that engendered the German nightmare."[5]

Jacques Julliard in his *Ce fascisme qui vient* . . . avoided fanciful meteorological
or scientific metaphors but also foresaw a similar outcome, as the title of his book indicates. But for Julliard, the problem was not simply a recrudescence of xenophobia
and racism in the East, it was also a resurgence of extreme nationalisms and the ex-
acerbation of economic woes in the West. All of this recalled for Julliard the Germany

of 1933 at the moment of Hitler's ascendancy and, later, the Western democracies' impotence in the face of the annihilation of the Spanish Republic.

The widespread and growing fear of a return of Fascism and even the advent of a new form of Nazism in Europe were firmly and indeed inextricably linked to the violent breakup of Yugoslavia and, in particular, to Serb aggression against its neighbors. To gauge the nature and extent of this linkage and to provide an appropriate context for Alain Finkielkraut's complicity with Croatian nationalism, we must briefly examine the history of the mobilization of French intellectuals and to a certain degree public opinion, first on behalf of Slovenian and especially Croatian independence, and then on behalf of Bosnia.

Fighting in Yugoslavia began in earnest in the summer of 1991, but the political and social developments leading directly to the outbreak of hostilities had been underway for several years. By virtually all accounts, the most crucial contributing factor was the rise of Slobodan Milosevic in Serbia. Named head of the Serbian Communist Party in 1986, Milosevic had first attracted considerable attention in spring 1987. Sent by Yugoslav President Ivan Stambolic to quell ethnic unrest between Serbs and Albanians in the province of Kosovo, Milosevic did the opposite. He took advantage of the situation and exacerbated ethnic tensions by vociferously supporting the Serbs. Having exploited this initial opportunity to make himself the champion of a renascent Serb nationalism and provide himself with a powerful political base in the country as a whole, in May 1989 Milosevic succeeded in becoming president of Serbia. Over the next several months, his efforts were focused on extending his own and Serb hegemony in the rest of Yugoslavia.

A second major contributing factor to political tensions and later hostilities was the May 1990 electoral victory in Croatia of the nationalist Franjo Tudjman and his Hrvatska Demokratska Zajednica (HDZ) Party (both will be discussed in greater detail later in the chapter). Tudjman's fiery pro-Croatian rhetoric, his efforts to increase his own power, and his party's and supporters' relegation of Croatian Serbs to the status of minorities enraged the Serb population. The eventual revolt of that population against Tudjman's authority in the area around the town of Knin in the Krajina region set in motion a series of events that eventually led to war.

Following Tudjman's victory, tensions between Serbs and Croats mounted in the region, as did ethnic and regional tensions in the country as a whole. In January 1991, Tudjman and the Slovenian leader Milan Kučan authored a joint declaration stating that Yugoslavia could only survive as a "voluntary league of sovereign republics," thus further confirming the power of centrifugal forces within the country.[6] As talk of secession increased throughout the spring not only in Croatia and

Slovenia but also in the republics of Bosnia and Macedonia, Serb leadership in Serbia and elsewhere indicated that there was no question of these republics "taking their Serb minorities with them."[7]

In March 1991, the Serb revolt expanded with the takeover of the police station in the town of Pakrac. Ethnic tensions and confrontations between Serb paramilitaries and Croatian police increased throughout the spring, with heavy anti-Croatian propaganda being broadcast on Belgrade television. In May 1991, matters reached a crisis point when Serb efforts prevented the Croatian representative Stipe Mesić from assuming his post in the rotating presidency of Yugoslavia. Although a solution to this particular crisis was found, bloodshed increased dramatically throughout the summer as Serb paramilitaries took over Croatian towns, especially in Slavonia, and killed dozens of ethnic Croats. In June, Slovenia officially declared its independence and was invaded by the Yugoslavian army, which was strongly pro-Serb. A brief period of confused fighting ensued, and Slovenian independence was finally recognized following negotiations between Kučan and Milosevic.

But in Croatia, fighting only increased as international peace efforts failed and the Yugoslav federation continued to slide toward dissolution. In the fall, Serb forces intensified attacks on the Croatian cities of Vukovar and Dubrovnik. The former was bombarded mercilessly. The latter, a symbol of Croatian resistance, finally fell in November 1991, and its fall was, according to Marcus Tanner, "an agonizing psychological blow to most Croats."[8] But by Christmas, things improved considerably from the Croatian perspective. The nation's independence was recognized by Germany and other EU nations. In January 1992, a cease-fire negotiated by UN representative Cyrus Vance brought an end to the fighting in Croatia. In the process, however, the Vance agreement ceded one-fourth of Croatian land to the Serbs.

Bosnia declared its independence in February 1992, and the war moved next door, so to speak. The horrors of that conflict are widely known, as are the names of such places as Sarajevo and Srebrenica. The war in Bosnia lasted three years, until the Dayton Accords brought an end to the conflict. Before Dayton, however, in the spring and summer of 1995, Croatian forces launched attacks against weakened Serb forces to recover former Croatian territory, especially in the Krajina region.

Given the fact that by 1995 the intensity of the reactions of French intellectuals, writers, and artists to the war in the Balkans prompted comparisons with earlier watershed moments of political engagement in French history, including the Dreyfus Affair and the Spanish Civil War, it is perhaps surprising that the early response to the violence in the Balkans was generally low-key. By way of explaining this state of affairs, Frédéric Martel notes that initial signs of trouble in Yugoslavia in the late

1980s and at the outset of the 1990s went largely unnoticed because the Parisian intelligentsia was still preoccupied with the Gulf War.[9] But in the summer of 1991, with the declaration of Slovenian independence and the intensification of hostilities and increased bloodshed in Croatia, the intellectuals began to speak out. In one of the earliest interventions concerning the conflict, Alain Finkielkraut, along with Milan Kundera and others, defended Slovenian independence in accordance with the principle of a people's right to self-determination. In October, a petition appearing in *Le Monde* and signed by the distinguished historians François Furet, Marc Ferro, and Jacques Le Goff, as well as by Milan Kundera and Alain Finkielkraut, advocated French recognition of the legitimacy of Slovenian and Croatian claims to independence.

With the siege of Vukovar by the Yugoslavian national army (JNA) and the fall of the city in November 1991, the rhetoric became more charged. In editorial pages and elsewhere, writers and intellectuals began comparing the events in Yugoslavia to the worst memories of recent European history. In the Parisian daily *Libération*, the writer Annie Lebrun titled her 13 November 1991 editorial on the destruction of Vukovar "Today Guernica Is Called Vukovar." The implicit comparison of Nazi destructiveness with Serb aggression would become a refrain that French intellectuals voiced increasingly as the war continued.

Added to the list of those who spoke out in opposition to Serb aggression in Croatia in the following months were figures long familiar in the United States, such as the playwright Eugene Ionesco. Others included the *nouveau philosophe* André Glucksmann and Pascal Bruckner, the latter Finkielkraut's former coauthor and a successful public intellectual, moralist, and novelist in his own right. Following the fall of Vukovar, Glucksmann's commentary on the conflict titled "Un Pearl Harbor Moral," which appeared in *Le Monde* on 11 December 1911, extended the range of historical comparisons with the Second World War by comparing Serb aggression to that of the Japanese.

But not all those who spoke out in the first year of the conflict defended Slovenian and Croatian claims to self-determination and blamed the Serbs as the sole perpetrators. Fearful of a renascent nationalism in the region, Bernard-Henri Levy, Jorge Semprun (novelist and Nazi camp survivor), Elie Wiesel, and the novelist Mario Vargas Llosa published a petition in *Le Monde* in November 1991 in which they stated that they did not wish to choose one "nationalism" over another in the war. They perceived the war as being essentially a "civil war," pitting "past against past, religion against religion, the dead against the dead," and noting that "the entire country risks sinking into an endless vendetta." They also called on the "Yugoslav" people to settle their differences in the name of unity.[10] As Martel explains, the pe-

titioners were motivated in part by what they perceived to be strong cultural and political links between Franjo Tudjman's newly elected nationalist regime in Zagreb
and Croatia's Ustaša—and Nazi-affiliated—past.[11]

By the end of 1991, then, French intellectuals were divided into two camps over
the war: those who saw the Serbs as the aggressors and the Croats as the victims,
and those who believed that both nationalities or ethnic groups were equally responsible for the conflict. For the latter group—which, in general terms, still held
to the idea of Yugoslav unity and feared Croatian nationalism—the events of
December–January 1991–1992 brought good news and bad. On 29 November 1991,
French president François Mitterrand reminded his interlocutor in an interview
published in the German newspaper *Frankfurter Allgemeine Zeitung* that Croatia
had been "part of the Nazi bloc" during World War II. Mitterrand also stated his
belief that Serbia was making war not to conquer Croatia but to protect Serb minorities there. This was music to the ears of those who supported Serbia outright as
well as those who wished to reduce Serbia's culpability by tarnishing any favorable
reputation Croatia might enjoy. In this fashion, any meaningful difference between
the roles of the two countries in the war could be discounted. This, in turn, justified renewed calls for Yugoslav unity.

For those insisting on equal culpability among the warring factions and calling
for a new Yugoslav national unity, Germany's decision in December 1991 and the
European Community's decision shortly thereafter to recognize Slovenian and
Croatian independence were, by contrast, heavy blows. The historian and former
Communist Annie Kriegel, who would move more and more toward the Serb camp
as the war progressed, expressed strong regrets over these positions, arguing that Serb
ambitions focused more on the maintenance of a "Lesser Yugoslavia" than on a
"Greater Serbia." The process of fragmentation in Europe into smaller and smaller
nations, undesirable in itself, would only accelerate as a result of these decisions.
Finally, in Kriegel's view, the sole legitimacy and substance that these smaller
"nations" in the former Yugoslavia enjoyed was attributable to their status as "victims" of an exaggerated Serb "aggression, imperialism, fascism, communism . . . barbarism." The etiquette chosen in condemning the Serbs was inconsequential, as
long as it underscored their fundamental evil and brutality.[12]

Elie Wiesel lamented the recognition of Croatia, arguing forcefully in an article
in the political review *Lignes de Fond* that since World War II, Croatian national aspirations had been linked to the "hatred of the other" associated with the Ustaša
regime. That regime, he continued, had been an "unconditional ally" of the Nazis,
and the atrocities committed in its name occasionally surpassed those of the Germans themselves. Unlike Kriegel, during the course of 1992 Wiesel would slowly

redirect his hostility toward the Serbs; in early 1993 he announced that he had in effect been duped by their propaganda.

The renowned sociologist Edgar Morin followed a similar trajectory, entertaining—at least initially—serious reservations about Croatian independence and expressing his belief that a renewal of Ustašan Fascism was a genuine threat. As to the origins of the conflict, Morin argued that the "arrogant politics" of Milosevic and Tudjman were equally responsible. These views, articulated in Le Monde in early 1992 in two successive articles jointly titled "The Yugoslav Agony," also implicitly challenged the position that the small nations such as Slovenia and Croatia had the right to self-determination. At what point, asked Morin, did one stop? What of the smaller "nations" within those nations, which, according to the same principle, likewise had a legitimate claim to self-determination? By March 1993, however, Morin's position had changed. He now saw Serbia, previously yoked in its "arrogant politics" to Croatia, as representing a new and greater threat to the degree that it embodied a new ideology, "Total Nationalism."[13]

With the outbreak of war in Bosnia in the spring of 1992, the engagement of France's intellectual elite vis-à-vis the conflict expanded in scope, while the issues at stake underwent significant changes. As Martel notes, many of those who opposed Croatian and Slovenian independence as a dangerous expression of ethnic nationalism did not encounter the same difficulty in the case of a supposedly more tolerant and multiethnic Bosnia. For many, Bosnia came to represent an idealized, peacefully diverse, and cosmopolitan state that fully exemplified Europe's supposedly "communal" values. Although the realities of the situation were more complex and certainly less harmonious, Bosnia's fate came to symbolize for a large number of intellectuals the fate—and future—of Europe itself. The nation's sovereignty and integrity therefore had to be defended at all costs. Disagreements remained over conceptions of nationhood and citizenship, dating from the war in Croatia. But inaction on the part of the international community and especially of France itself as regards the war in Bosnia provoked among virtually all the intellectuals a strongly indignant response that served to unite them in spite of their differences.

The revelation in the summer of 1992 of the existence of Serb concentration camps and of the full horror of ethnic cleansing intensified this indignation. Although the debates over Maastricht temporarily drew attention away from the conflict in Bosnia, by the end of 1992 the war once again took center stage. On 21 November, a demonstration beginning at the Place du Pantheon and winding its way to the Place Montparnasse brought together a large group of well-known writers, historians, philosophers, and other public figures, who marched under the banners "1991:

Vukovar. *1992:* Sarajevo. *1993:* . . . ?" and "This time, we will not be able to say that we did not know." A petition signed in association with the demonstration included the names of philosophers and historians, including Paul Ricoeur, Pierre Vidal-Naquet, and Jean-Pierre Azéma, as well as Cardinal Decoutray, a leader of the French Catholic Church; the politicians Jacques Toubon and Alain Carignon; and the movie directors Patrice Chéreau and Roman Polanski. Alain Finkielkraut, Pascal Bruckner, and Edgar Morin—all already associated with French activism regarding the conflict—also signed the petition. The demonstration and the signing of the petition proved to be one of the most visible activities of the group known as the Sarajevo-Vukovar Committee.

The demonstration at the Pantheon constituted in many ways a watershed event that accelerated public indignation over the war in Bosnia and encouraged a number of intellectuals to assume ever more prominent roles. Foremost among these was Bernard-Henri Lévy, whose resources and influence as arguably France's most powerful public intellectual resulted in a number of highly visible (if occasionally somewhat ridiculous) efforts on behalf of the embattled Bosnians. On 21 December 1992, with a group of colleagues, Lévy organized a public meeting at the Mutualité Hall, a building already memorable for earlier meetings by the Parisian intellectual elite in the service of various political causes. At that meeting, Lévy announced his intention to purchase arms for the defenders of Sarajevo. Shortly thereafter, he was instrumental in bringing Bosnian president Alija Izetbegovic to Paris to request support for his besieged nation, a visit that accomplished little.[14]

Lévy had also been instrumental in convincing François Mitterrand to go to Sarajevo in June 1992, a trip that resulted in the temporary reopening of the airport so that humanitarian supplies could get in. Like one of his heroes, André Malraux, who during the Spanish Civil War had made a memorable film adaptation of his prorepublican novel *L'Espoir*, Lévy in 1993 began filming his documentary *Bosna!*, which was released to widespread public acclaim in April 1994. Finally, in May 1994, a number of intellectuals led by Lévy proposed the creation of a pro-Bosnian list for the European parliamentary elections. This maneuver did much to divide the French Socialist Party, and to a certain degree the organizers themselves. Lévy's last-minute decision not to vote in the election disconcerted his colleagues and brought accusations of insincerity and publicity seeking.

France's intellectuals continued to speak out vehemently against Serb aggression and to call for international intervention in the conflict right up to the time of the final cease-fire and the signing of the Dayton Accords. It is fair to say that the agitation of the intellectuals—and the creation of the Bosnian list for the European elections—did force a number of politicians to deal with the issue and, in some cases, to take a strong stand in favor of Bosnia; this was certainly true in the case of the Socialist leader and one-time prime minister Michel Rocard. As events reached their climax in the summer of 1995, the new French president, Jacques Chirac, took more forceful steps than had his predecessor to bring about an end to the conflict, although, if Bernard-Henri Lévy is to be believed, this was ultimately not attributable to pressure from the intellectuals. Whatever the case, for Lévy at least, the cessation of hostilities and the signing of the Dayton peace agreement did not ultimately mark a victory for those who had agitated so long for international intervention on behalf of the Bosnians and against Serb aggression. Instead, in partitioning Bosnia along ethnic lines, the Dayton Accords spelled the tragic defeat of what Lévy continued to view as a Bosnian cosmopolitan and multiethnic utopia. As Lévy concluded, somewhat melodramatically, in the 28 December 1995 entry of his Bosnian diary, "Defeat of Bosnia? No. The debacle of Europe."[15]

Of all of French intellectuals who took stands in relation to the conflict in the Balkans in the first half of the 1990s, certainly among the most longstanding and controversial commitments was that of Alain Finkielkraut, who was an early proponent of Slovenian and especially Croatian independence. In regard to Croatia, he states that he committed himself "without reservation" in the face of a "double scandal": the "invasion" of that country by Serbia and the "indifference" of the world. Later, Finkielkraut became a supporter of Bosnian independence when the conflict moved to Bosnia-Herzegovina, although he stressed in 1999 that he never shared the view of Bernard-Henri Lévy and others that Bosnia represented a cosmopolitan utopia. For him, there were always ethnic tensions beneath the surface in that country, which others chose to ignore. And what many described—and championed—as "cosmopolitan" was, in Finkielkraut's view, nothing more than "nomadism, interbreeding, versatility, 'creolization.'"[16] Throughout both conflicts, Finkielkraut was also, of course, a fierce critic of Serb brutalities and atrocities.

As early as 1991—long before many of his colleagues followed suit—Finkielkraut was writing editorials in Le Monde and Libération and giving interviews in the press in an effort to make his compatriots come to terms with the growing disaster to the east. In 1992, these early commentaries on the Balkan conflict were gathered together and published as a book under the title Comment peut-on être Croate? (How can one be Croatian?). Following publication of that book, Finkielkraut continued to write opinion pieces for the Parisian dailies (mostly Le Monde) and to publish essays and interviews in intellectual reviews assessing the implications of the military, political, and diplomatic developments in the region. One of the latter essays, originally published in Finkielkraut's own journal, Le Messager Europeen, was expanded and published in pamphlet form in 1994 under the title *Le crime d'être né: L'Europe, les nations, la guerre* (The crime of being born: Europe, nations, war).

Since the conclusion of the war, Finkielkraut has continued to stress the importance of the conflict in the Balkans in the early 1990s—as well as its "sequel" in the 1998 NATO bombardment in Kosovo—and to reiterate the reasons for his involvement and for his controversial pro-Croatian stance in particular. He has also discussed his views on the region and the conflict in *L'Ingratitude* (1999) and *L'Imparfait du présent* (2002). Finkielkraut discussed the Kosovo bombardment—and especially Régis Debray's controversial opposition to the NATO intervention (see chapter 5)—in *Une voix vient de l'autre rive* (2000).

What reasons does Finkielkraut offer in these works to justify his engagement, and how does this engagement entail complicity with antidemocratic and even racist politics? To respond to these questions, we must first examine the more general or "abstract" premises justifying his support for Croatia, premises that, to a certain extent, draw on positions Finkielkraut had articulated earlier. It will also be necessary to look more closely at some of the details of the conflict as well as the politics and policies of the Tudjman regime in Croatia.

In the foreword to *Comment peut-on être Croate?*, Finkielkraut alludes to a number of general themes and issues that recur regularly in his reflections on the Balkan conflict discussed in the book and in subsequent works. The first of these is what he perceives to be the failure and indeed the moral bankruptcy of humanitarian efforts in the region and of the humanitarian project itself. For Finkielkraut, humanitarian efforts mask a real and terrible indifference to the actual cost of the fighting in terms of human lives, since these efforts are carried out *in place of* more serious and beneficial attempts to stop the massacre and find a political solution to the conflict. In focusing exclusively on the *physical* sufferings of all human beings involved, the humanitarian perspective not only reduces human life to "life in the strictly biological sense of the term," it betrays a disdain for every other aspect of human experience and suffering.[17]

In political terms, this misguided humanitarianism refuses to distinguish between perpetrators and victims, and, as a result, Serbs, Croats, and later Bosnians are all put in the same category and judged to be the same. Not only does this perspective exonerate the Serb aggressors in advance, it reinforces one of the more widely held prejudices concerning the Balkan region—that all Balkan peoples are essentially bloodthirsty brutes, members of primitive "tribes" who gladly kill one another on the slightest pretext. This, in turn, justifies the inaction of Europeans and others in the West, who throw up their hands helplessly in the face of this "ethnically driven furor," lament the situation "on a full stomach," and denounce it "with well-chosen insults directed at the rabid hordes on all sides."[18]

A second reason underlying Finkielkraut's commitment can be described as a strong and indeed visceral reaction against the mediazation of the world and the ways in which this process alienates humans from the present as well as the past, thereby stripping human experience of meaning and profundity. The media, he argues, floods us daily with horrific images of one conflict, famine, or catastrophe and then, just as quickly, drops the first disaster in order to move on to a new one. Overwhelmed by this endless stream of images, the television viewer is at once anesthetized by them and detached from them, despite their apparent proximity. Living *everywhere* simultaneously through these images, the television viewer—that is to say, modern humankind or "planetary man"—in reality lives *nowhere* at all. We simply beam into one situation or crisis through the television screen and then beam back out just as easily. The reality of the events leaves no trace on us, nor are we truly affected by what we witness—for example, the very tangible sufferings of the people of Sarajevo. As Finkielkraut caustically remarks concerning the latter, they are not merely "the telespectators of their own sufferings."[19] They actually bleed and die.

In a number of important ways, Finkielkraut's critique of the media (television in particular) and his efforts to make his readers aware of their detachment and, implicitly at least, of the very *real* suffering and dying of the victims of Serb aggression, derive and are indeed inseparable from earlier critiques of the commodification of culture and what might be described as the "disappearance" of history. In his highly polemical 1987 book *La défaite de la pensée* (The defeat of the mind), Finkielkraut denounces in the same breath the emergence and domination of identity politics, the reduction of culture to its lowest common denominators, and the media for replacing bourgeois culture with adolescent culture. He argues that a fundamental shift has occurred from a time when democracy made culture available to everyone to the present moment, when democracy "implies that everyone has a right to the culture of his or her own choice (or to identify as cultural any urge of the moment)."[20] The result of the convergence of these trends is that the "mind" is receding to make room for the encounter of "the fanatic and the zombie."[21]

In *La mémoire vaine* (Remembering in vain), published in 1989, Finkielkraut examines the impact of this mediatized, infantilized world on our capacity to understand and *absorb* history and its lessons. In his discussion of the Barbie trial and the ability of the average (French) person to grasp its meaning, Finkielkraut writes, "In the age of entertainment, 'news' has usurped the place of historicity; moments no longer follow one another according to a reasoned and recountable order; they succeed one another like meals in an unending cycle. With the world transformed into a multiform and permanent object of consumption, its destiny is to be continually gobbled up by its consumers." Finkielkraut sums up, quoting Régis Debray, "Now, everything is now."[22]

The fact that the world can now enter our households through the television does not mean that a person has greater access to or appreciation of the world in its complexity, but rather that "the home can impose itself on the world." As a result, even the most terrible of events or, conversely, the most admirable of accomplishments are "domesticated," so to speak, and reduced in scale to such an extent that they are incapable of inspiring awe or horror. As Finkielkraut asserts, nothing on television is large enough to "make us stop eating our apple or talking back to the screen."[23] If this is the case, then, in regard to the war in Yugoslavia, Europeans as well as others are, in Finkielkraut's view, incapable of understanding the gravity, the "historicity," and the tragedy—the *reality*—of the conflict because they view it on television. And in protesting the "postmodern condition," Finkielkraut is also, it would seem, attempting to sensitize Europeans to the full dimensions of the conflict and thereby to *mobilize* them.

Another crucial component of and reason for Finkielkraut's engagement is—as he indicated at the moment of the breakup of the former Yugoslavia and on numerous occasions since—his belief not only in the right of small nations in Europe to independence and self-determination but also in the historical and cultural importance of those nations. Finkielkraut bristles at the suggestion of Annie Kriegel that Croatia and Slovenia have no real identity or legitimacy outside their claims to being the victims of Serb aggression. He argues rather that Croatia in particular perfectly fits Otto Bauer's definition of a nation in that it constitutes a "body of men united by a community of destiny and a community of character."[24] Finkielkraut also insists on the falseness of the view of what he describes as the antitotalitarian Left, which is that the fewer nations there are, the more democracy there is. In fact, history suggests the reverse. As the epigraphs to both *Comment peut-on être Croate?* and *Le crime d'être né* point out, the disappearance of small countries in Europe in the recent past was linked not to democracy but to the triumph of authoritarian ideologies and totalitarian regimes. The epigraph appearing at the outset of part one of *Comment peut-on être Croate?*—titled, appropriately, "Le retour de l'idéologie"— is a quote from Friedrich Engels: "I am authoritarian enough to consider the very existence, right in the middle of Europe, of such small, primitive peoples to be anachronistic."[25] Similarly, the epigraph to *Le crime d'être né*, taken from Pierre Drieu La Rochelle's wartime journal and dated May 1940, reads: "No more Holland. The number of small, obsolete countries is shrinking in Europe."[26]

Given these historical circumstances, Finkielkraut finds it ironic that for many of his contemporaries, the mere existence of these small, ethnically based countries

is viewed as a threat to a unified, cohesive, and peaceful continent because they supposedly represent a rebirth of new and lethal forms of nationalism. As an example
of this attitude, Finkielkraut points to the 1992 "Europe or the Tribes" conference
(held in Paris and dealing with the Yugoslav conflict). As the conference title suggests, for the organizers at least, the choice is perceived as being one between a unified "European" civilization and a hodgepodge of small, barbaric nation-tribes. Having been ascribed the status of primitive, indeed prehistoric, peoples by the title of
the colloquium itself, the inhabitants of the newly independent East European nations are, as Finkielkraut asserts, all the more easily lumped together as "all those
Southern Slavs!" To comprehend the absurdity and offensiveness of such a perspective, Finkielkraut asks what the reaction of a Western European would be to an
Eastern European who, when asked about the history of Franco-German conflicts,
dismisses the entire issue with "They're all just Franks!"[27]

The final and most crucial component of Finkielkraut's commitment to the
Croatian cause for our purposes here concerns his reading of the conflict in historical terms, and specifically with reference to the horrors of World War II. How is it,
Finkielkraut wonders, that in a Europe haunted by the memory of Nazism and
claiming to remain vigilant to avoid its recurrence, a person can fail to recognize a
renewal of Nazism's worst excesses in Serb-sponsored acts of aggression, brutality,
and genocide? In *Comment peut-on être Croate?*, Finkielkraut stresses that a part of
the answer concerns the effectiveness of Serb propaganda. In insisting on their own
victimization, the Serbs have succeeded in reversing the tables and casting themselves in the role of the Jews. As a "guardian" of Jewish memory, Finkielkraut considers it his obligation to combat this distortion.[28]

Another part of the response concerns the power of the memory of the Nazi
genocide and what might be described as "the will to vigilance" themselves. According to Finkielkraut, the desire of Europeans and their leaders to remain "irre-
proachable" and not to repeat the past is so strong that they refuse to see, or are simply incapable of recognizing, a recurrence when it occurs. Reinforcing this notion
is the view—or, more accurately, the prejudice—that the Balkans are ultimately
peripheral and their conflicts regional and "tribal" in nature. For "vigilant" Europeans, these conflicts could not possibly measure up to the Nazi nightmare. As a
result, in Finkielkraut's view the real nature and dimensions of the Serb threat are
underestimated and misunderstood.

In France, this problem is complicated by and filtered through the memory of
Vichy. So powerful is that memory and so overwhelming the urge to deal belatedly
with the nation's criminal past that, according to Finkielkraut, the French would
rather spend their energies bringing the aging and inconsequential former Milicien

Paul Touvier to trial for crimes committed fifty years ago than stopping similar crimes in the present in the Balkans. Such self-indulgence on a national level in what Finkielkraut dismisses derisively as "navel contemplation" is inexcusable.[29] That this tendency would continue into the 1990s with the trial of Maurice Papon would, for Finkielkraut, be nothing short of scandalous. He would become one of the most vociferous critics of the lengthy and often controversial proceedings in Bordeaux against the former Vichy official. As the trial got underway in October 1997, Finkielkraut published an editorial in *Le Monde* titled, simply, "Papon, Too Late."

A final part of the response to the question of European blindness in relation to Serbian aims and actions concerns Croatia's own past. Given the Croatian Ustaša regime's racism, anti-Semitism, and above all collaboration with Nazi Germany and Fascist Italy during World War II, and, more importantly, the links between the contemporary Croatian nationalism and that dubious past, many argued that Croatia, and not Serbia, should be condemned in the present conflict. This perspective is roundly criticized and in fact forcefully rejected by Finkielkraut, both in *Comment peut-on être Croate?* and in subsequent works.

The question of Croatia's past and the links of that past with the fledgling nation's bid for independence and recognition in the early 1990s lead us, finally, to the crux of Alain Finkielkraut's complicity with antidemocratic, xenophobic, and even racist politics. As they are presented in *Comment peut-on être Croate?* and subsequent works, all of Finkielkraut's general arguments in support of Croatia and Croatian independence are fundamentally sound, well argued, and certainly in keeping with liberal and democratic principles. Apparently the worst that can be said of his engagement is that his militancy and stridency were on occasion excessive, leading some of his critics to refer to him derisively as "Finkielcroate." But there exists what might be described as a darker, more ambiguous side to Finkielkraut's pro-Croatian stance that borders on apology for xenophobia and historical revisionism, although this is certainly not the writer's intent. To approach these issues judiciously and assess Finkielkraut's position fairly and completely, it is necessary to look first at Croatia's World War II past, the cultural politics of Franjo Tudjman's HDZ Party, and finally the events that precipitated the war in Croatia.

Croatia's Ustaša past during World War II was often decontextualized and distorted by those who sought to tar not only Franjo Tudjman and his HDZ Party but, more broadly, Croatian aspirations to independence in the early 1990s. For example, the number of Serbian victims and Jewish victims of the Ustaša regime were exaggerated by Serb propaganda, and the fact that the Ustaša was essentially a puppet regime put in power by Hitler and Mussolini, and *not freely chosen by Croatians*, was ignored. In fact, the Ustaša movement, founded in 1929 by Ante Pavelić, had

spent many of the prewar years in exile in Fascist Italy. Initially welcomed by Mussolini (they were allowed to set up training camps on Italian soil), the Ustaša fell into
disgrace following the assassination of King Alexander I of Yugoslavia in Marseille
in 1934. Mussolini interned the Ustaša on the island of Lipari. Mussolini's foreign
minister Count Galeazzo Ciano dismissed them as a "band of cutthroats."[30]

But Hitler's declaration of war on Yugoslavia in April 1941—which the Croatians
blamed on the Serbs—paved the way for the imposition of the Ustaša regime on
Croatia. Pavelic was brought back from exile and placed in power. He immediately
set about creating a state that was, according to Marcus Tanner, "a carbon copy of
Nazi Germany."[31] Among the new regime's first acts was to forbid the use of the
Cyrillic alphabet, a symbol of Eastern, Serbian, and non-Aryan culture. Other acts
included outlawing marriages between Croats and Jews and forbidding Jews to trade
with non-Jews. In October 1941, anti-Semitic legislation decreed the complete con-
fiscation of Jewish goods. Jews were also forced to wear the yellow star, and non-
Catholics were forced to convert.

Six months after assuming power, the Ustaša regime began deporting undesirables, including Serbs, Jews, and gypsies. Prison camps for political undesirables
were established, but there was worse: the wholesale killing of Serbs and others got
underway quickly. Marcus Tanner reports that "at least 20,000 Serbs were killed
in . . . pogroms in the summer months of 1941."[32] The small populations of Jews in
Croatia and Bosnia—just under forty thousand—were, as Tanner puts it, "easily
dealt with."[33] Eighty percent of the Jewish population in both countries would eventually perish.[34]

By the end of the war, the number of Serbs, Jews, and other political undesirables
killed by the Ustaša was enormous. Communist authorities told the UN after the
war that some 1.6 million people had perished in Ustaša camps and that six hundred
thousand of these deaths occurred in Jasenovac, the most notorious of these camps.
These figures are quite exaggerated, but even conservative estimates suggest some-
where in the neighborhood of one hundred thousand killed in Ustaša camps.

Given the horrors and criminality of the Ustaša, it is not difficult to understand
lingering Serb animosity toward the regime as well as fear and hatred of any political movement that might maintain its legacy. All of this was deftly exploited by Slobodan Milosevic, who never failed to insist that Croatian aspirations to independence in the early 1990s were unequivocally Ustaša-inspired and represented the
same mortal threat to Serbs that they had in the 1940s. And this raises the issue of the
connections among Franjo Tudjman, his HDZ Party, and the legacy of the Ustaša.

To get a sense of the complexity of this issue, it is helpful to look briefly at the
itinerary of the author of Croatian independence, Franjo Tudjman. Even a cursory

glance at some of the obituaries published following the Croatian president's death in 1999 gives a sense of the degree to which the man and the movement he embodied are still shrouded in disagreement and controversy. Praised in some quarters as "the father of his country" and a national hero who successfully navigated his country through war to achieve sovereignty and international recognition, in other quarters he is dismissed as a "racist," an anti-Semite, and worse.

In fact, Tudjman began the postwar period as a Communist, although, as Tanner observes, Yugoslavia's postwar Communism under Tito did not succeed in erasing continuing subterranean tensions and animosities among Serbs, Croats, and Muslims. By the late 1960s, Tudjman was a dissenter. In 1971 he participated actively in the Croatian Spring—Yugoslavia's answer to the Prague Spring—for which he was briefly jailed. But most importantly, Tudjman was evolving into a staunch nationalist, and it is in this context that the thorny issue of his relationship to the Ustaša past emerges. When the HDZ Party was formed in 1990, Tudjman did not hesitate to seek financial support from the Croatian emigré community in Canada and elsewhere, despite strong Ustaša links to that community. Earlier, Tudjman had written books on Croatia's past that were most disturbing in how they dealt with the Ustaša regime. While Tudjman acknowledged that it was a "quisling organization and a fascist crime," it was also "an expression of the Croatian nations's historic desire for an independent homeland." This "peculiar phraseology," as Tanner describes it, seems to suggest that "the Ustche was a malevolent manifestation of a benign impulse."[35]

But there was more. Already in the 1960s, Tudjman had scandalized many historians by insisting that the total number of Ustaša concentration camp victims was only sixty thousand, well below all other reliable estimates. And in his autobiography, he had ventured into the very dangerous waters of historical revisionism, the Holocaust, and Middle Eastern politics. Among other things, he labeled Israelis "Judeo-Nazis" for their treatment of Palestinians, argued that the Jewish God Jehovah originated the notion of genocide and offered a justification for it, and claimed that the Holocaust and Israel's treatment of the Palestinian's were identical in the sense that "when a people feels threatened in its very survival, it will do everything possible and use all available means to conquer and even destroy" their enemy. As for Croatia's own genocidal past, Tudjman apparently insisted that the Jasenovac was a "labor camp" and not a death camp and that Jews murdered gypsies there.[36]

As a candidate for president of Croatia in 1990, Tudjman "campaigned squarely on the national question."[37] In that role, he was prone to making very disturbing assertions. On 17 March 1990, he stated baldly, "Thank God my wife is not a Serb or a Jew." Other remarks on the campaign trail suggested that he had expansionist aims in Bosnia.[38]

According to Misha Glenny, Tudjman and his HDZ Party were "overtly" racist,[39] and if for some this view is overstated, Tudjman and his party's initial actions on assuming power after their electoral victory certainly suggest a strong xenophobia reminiscent of the Ustaša. Once elected president, Tudjman immediately denounced what he considered to be the excessive presence of Serbs in Croatia's police force, media, and officialdom.[40] Especially where the media was concerned, the HDZ Party acted quickly to assume full control. The republic's television station, according to Tudjman's lieutenant there, was to be turned into a "cathedral of the Croatian spirit."[41] Tudjman took the initiative to rename streets and squares in Zagreb to emphasize past Croat glories and heroes (the Square of the Victims of Fascism was renamed the Square of Croatian Great Ones). He also chose to reintroduced the traditional Croatian checkerboard flag—the same flag used by the Ustaša. Finally, in another echo of Ustaša politics, Cyrillic was once again banned and Latin adopted as the only official script.

In addition to these gestures intended to celebrate Croatian nationalism and culture, the new constitution drafted by Tudjman and the HDZ Party declared that Croatia was no longer "'the national state of the Croatian nation and the state of the Serbia Nation in Croatia' but the homeland of the Croatian nation alone." This, in effect, reduced Serbs and Hungarians, among other ethnic groups, to the status of minorities.[42] It was also a key factor in setting off the Serb revolt at Knin. The new constitution invested "enormous executive authority" in the presidency, making Tudjman, in effect, a virtual dictator. Finally, in consolidating its power, the HDZ, according to Glenny, carried out purges and practiced intimidation. And if these moves were not troubling enough, Glenny argues that Tudjman on several occasions revealed his disdain for Bosnian Muslims. In this regard, the Croatians were hardly sure allies for the Bosnians against the Serbs once the fighting started in Bosnia. It is now widely acknowledged that even before the war in Bosnia, Tudjman and Milosevic met secretly to discuss partitioning Bosnia in March 1991. During the war in Bosnia, Croatia sold oil and other supplies to Bosnian Serbs.[43]

If Alain Finkielkraut had been ignorant of Croatia's troubling ideology and politics, it would be possible to characterize his engagement as a case of misguided idealism that could be justified in terms of Croatia's right to independence and, of course, Serb aggression, brutality, and destructiveness inside Croatia and elsewhere. It is also fair to point out that at the outset of hostilities, Croatia was woefully undermanned and ill-equipped and therefore easily victimized by Serb militias and the JNA. Finally, Tudjman and the HDZ toned down their nationalist and xenophobic rhetoric once the fighting began, not only because that rhetoric played into the hands of Serb propaganda, but because a more measured tone was likelier to stir the sympathies of a largely indifferent international community.

Nevertheless, in its prewar nationalistic rhetoric and xenophobia, Croatia exemplified precisely the strain of particularist, ethnic, and narrowly nationalist ideology that Finkielkraut had earlier identified and denounced in *La défaite de la pensée* — precisely the ideology that many *tier mondiste* (third world) liberation movements had unfortunately taken up in their efforts to liberate themselves from their European colonial masters. However, when deployed within Europe by Croatia, Finkielkraut chose to see this ideology in a different light.

It is important to stress as well that Finkielkraut was also aware of the uglier side of Croatia's new nationalism as embodied in the views of Tudjman and his HDZ Party, and on several scores he was willing to attenuate and even justify these views. In *Comment peut-on être Croate?*, Finkielkraut argues—implausibly—that the reason Tudjman had sought to reduce the number of the supposed victims of the Jasenovac camp was not that he was trying to "excuse the massacres for which the Pavelic regime is guilty." Rather, Tudjman was trying to "put an end to the chain of violence and quash the *logic of victimization* that drives the Serbs to justify their present hegemony with their past suffering."[44] Here Finkielkraut casts Tudjman in the unlikely role of peacemaker while neatly shifting the onus of what René Girard terms "the victim-turned-victimizer" onto the Serbs.[45] On the subject of changing the name of the Square of the Victims of Fascism to the Square of the Croatian Great Ones, Finkielkraut argues that the change was less to celebrate Croatian nationalism than to express Croatians' "profound distaste of language of anti-fascist coinage" from the Communist era.[46] Finally, on the subject of Tudjman's comparison of the Israeli treatment of Palestinians to the Nazi treatment of Jews, Finkielkraut states rather lamely that the Jewish community in Zagreb protested these "slips" (*dérapages*) at the moment when Tudjman's book was published, and, besides, these statements had no visible effect in securing Tudjman votes during the elections of 1990 and 1992. Finkielkraut concludes by pointing out that the party that did openly embrace the Ustaša past during these elections only received 5 percent of the vote.[47]

In these comments in *Comment peut-on être Croate?*, it seems clear that, to use a memorable phrase from the Touvier affair, Finkielkraut "proceeds in order to exonerate." In Finkielkraut's view, Tudjman—and through him, the aspirations of Croatian nationalism—are incapable of any but admirable motives and the most tolerant of outlooks. No matter how troubling the expression of these aspirations, there is always a laudable reason for it, or, at least, an excuse. Conversely, where the Serbs are concerned, Finkielkraut reveals himself capable of the most zealous "vigilance" of the type he attributes to Europe's memory militants, a vigilance that blinds them, in his view, to the real historical implications of *l'actualité*. In carrying his support of Croatian independence to these extremes, Finkielkraut makes himself complicit with its darker and decidedly undemocratic and xenophobic side.

Given these circumstances, it is perhaps not surprising that in the years following the conclusion of the war, Finkielkraut has had occasion to offer a dubiously one-sided defense of Croatia that would seem to belie the principles upon which he based his arguments for Croatia's right to exist in the first place. In two brief essays in *L'Imparfait du présent*, Finkielkraut stridently criticizes the International Criminal Tribunal at The Hague, and Carla del Ponte in particular, for seeking to arrest and prosecute Croatian military figures for human rights abuses in Croatia's reconquest of the Krajina region in 1995. In attempting to prosecute Croats and Serbs alike in the name of "Humanity," the tribunal erases the "fundamental distinction between the defense of the homeland and a war of annexation."[48] As a result, in Finkielkraut's view, justice is denied. The "school mistress" Carla del Ponte is seeking to reduce history to a "night where all cats are gray." And, similar to the way in which the war in the Balkans started, with all the antagonists dismissed as so many tribes, it concludes with an indiscriminate and "generalized incrimination."[49] Here, Finkielkraut obscures not only the fact that there *were* Croatian crimes and human rights abuses committed against the Serbs in the Krajina, but, equally important, that Croatia's right to exist and form part of the international community would seem to imply that crimes and excesses committed by *its* citizens should be subject to international law as well.

Finally, if Alain Finkielkraut's pro-Croatian engagement seems deeply flawed in the ways described here, the question arises as to which feature of that commitment skewed the judgment and perspective of an intellectual widely—and rightly—admired for his perspicacity. The answer, I would argue, lies in Finkielkraut's "insertion" of the Balkan conflict of the 1990s into the historical context of World War II and his insistence that the Serbs are, in effect, the Nazis of this scenario. As he has argued very recently in his pamphlet on contemporary anti-Semitism, *Au nom de l'autre*, the horror of Nazism was such that subsequently its victims, the Jews, came to exemplify the Other—the innocent and defenseless "brother," of sorts—whom humanity must henceforth defend at all costs. In the postwar world that Other has also become the victim of European colonialism and, most recently, the Palestinian. For Finkielkraut, the danger is that once a group assumes—or is ascribed—the role of the Other, its own perpetual innocence is assured, and its own violence, its own crimes, are justified in advance. As a result, true historical understanding loses its hold.

In ascribing in absolute terms the role of the Nazis to the Serbs, Finkielkraut inevitably casts the Croats in the role of the Other and proceeds to justify their excesses and abuses and explain away those actions and views that are decidedly not in keeping with the innocence of history's truest victims, its most authentic Others—if such peoples actually do exist. If this is the case, Alain Finkielkraut in his complicity with Croatian nationalism turns out to be less a victim of his own intellectual idealism than, ironically, of the skewed and indeed false vision of history he has so often sought to combat.

CHAPTER FIVE

Régis Debray

The Debray Affair

The philosopher and medialogist Régis Debray's complicity with antidemocratic politics and, according to some of his critics, his articulation of a post-Holocaust revisionism and negationism during the NATO bombardments of Kosovo in the spring of 1999 serve as a kind of mirror image to Alain Finkielkraut's earlier complicity with Croatian nationalism at the outset of the 1990s. Whereas Finkielkraut cast the Croatians in the role of victims and the Serbs in the role of genocidal persecutors, for Debray the Serbs under Slobodan Milosevic were wrongly accused of attempting to ethnically cleanse the Kosovar Albanian population and were in fact themselves the innocent victims of a brutal American-led aggression. Like Finkielkraut, Debray also justified his interpretation of the conflict and his determination of who were the victims and perpetrators with references to recent history as well as to World War II and France's *guerre sans nom* (war without a name) in Algeria in particular. But, Debray reversed the terms of the comparison proposed by Finkielkraut and others, casting the Serbs in the role of anti-Fascist *résistants* and Milosevic—the Balkan Hitler, according to many—at least obliquely in the role of a heroic Charles de Gaulle. Ultimately, just as Finkielkraut's earlier support for Croatian independence entailed a blinkered and dangerous complicity with a dubious Croatian nationalism, Debray's protest of the victimization of the Serb population by NATO bombings led to willful misperceptions of Milosevic, the nature of his power, and Serbia's nationalist ambitions. This made Debray complicitous with not only a dangerous and antidemocratic nationalism but a disturbing historical revisionism.

As was the case with Finkielkraut's support of Croatia, to appreciate the full implications and impact of Régis Debray's engagement on behalf of the Serb cause it is helpful to situate that engagement in relation to the positions taken by other intellectuals with regard to the NATO bombings as well as Serbia's, France's, and especially America's role in the conflict. Given the number and range of responses of these intellectuals to the wars elsewhere in the former Yugoslavia in the early to mid-1990s (see chapter 4), it is not surprising that NATO's bombing of Serbia and Serbian military targets in Kosovo beginning in March 1999 following the collapse of the Rambouillet talks provoked a strong and sustained reaction among the Parisian intelligentsia.[1] As was the case during the fighting in Croatia and Bosnia, when NATO began its air strikes in Kosovo, committees were formed, petitions were signed, demonstrations were organized, and, most visibly, strident and numerous editorials, op-ed pieces, and interviews were published by and with intellectuals of all stripes and hues in the pages of the French press. Following precedents set earlier by groups such as the Comité Vukovar-Sarajevo—a committee founded in 1992 that petitioned Europe to intervene militarily to stop the bloodshed in the Balkans—in early April 1999 the Comité Kosovo published a petition calling on NATO to send in ground troops "as quickly as possible in order to stop this crime, the proportions of which have not been seen in Europe since the Second World War."[2] Many of those who signed the Comité Kosovo's petition had also been signatories on the earlier petition, and the same people—most notably Pascal Bruckner and Olivier Mongin—were essentially the principal organizers of the two committees. On 10 April 1999, a rally on behalf of the Kosovar Albanians occurred in downtown Paris and was attended by the likes of André Glucksmann, whose photo at the rally was prominently displayed in an article titled "The Intellectuals Jump on the War" that was published in the 13 April 1999 edition of Libération. Glucksmann's support of the Kosovar Albanian cause and NATO's attacks on Serbia was not limited to an occasional attendance at a rally. Throughout the conflict, he, like Bernard Henri-Lévy and many other intellectuals including Jacques Julliard, Jean Daniel, Pascal Bruckner, and Alain Finkielkraut, wrote numerous articles in favor of the bombings. On several occasions during the conflict, some intellectuals called for the introduction of ground troops into the region as well.

The reasons these intellectuals offered to justify their positions were, as a whole, quite similar, deriving not only from an awareness of the recent history of the region but a commitment to human rights. In a 26 March editorial in Libération, Bernard-Henri Lévy mockingly recalled François Mitterrand's earlier stand against intervention in the region. Lévy then argued that the NATO offensive against Milosevic should have happened eight years earlier.[3] Jacques Julliard denounced Serb ethnic cleansing and asserted that even if it was impossible to make the rights of the individual respected throughout the world, the least that Europe could do was to stop the barbarism on its own soil.[4] On the same *Libération* editorial page where Lévy's comments appeared, Alain Finkielkraut labeled the bombings "inevitable." Kosovo, he continued, was in reality only the most recent episode in a war that had started a decade earlier. It was therefore an appropriate final battleground of the conflict. Finkielkraut also chastised those who opposed the bombings for allowing their anti-Americanism to blind them to what was obviously a "duty to humanity."[5]

As Finkielkraut's statement suggests, while the earlier conflicts in Croatia and Bosnia had produced a nearly unanimous denunciation of Serb expansionism and brutality by French intellectuals, the 1999 bombing generated no such consensus. Many intellectuals, in fact, unequivocally condemned the NATO war effort. Even before Régis Debray's famous *intervention* in the pages of *Le Monde* in mid-May 1999, to be discussed in detail shortly, others on the Right and Left had denounced the bombings and expressed their displeasure and even their disgust with French complicity in what they perceived to be the actions of an illegitimate and arrogant NATO-American imperialism. In an op-ed piece published in early April in *L'Événement du Jeudi*, Serge Faubert argued that in reality the United States cared very little about the Kosovar Albanians; the true purpose of the bombings lay elsewhere: "Clinton intends to remind Europe, economic giant but political pygmy, that America remains the world's only real military power. [The bombings are] a show of force that should make Paris, London, Rome and Bonn think. Henceforth, Washington will intervene in the heart of Europe in the same offhand way that it previously intervened during its expeditions in Granada or Panama. The 'World Company' has extended its backyard to cover the entire world."[6]

In the Communist *L'Humanité* a few weeks later, the philosopher Jean-Louis Sagot-Duvauroux echoed similar sentiments. Being the only "World Empire," the United States had to remind not only Europe but the entire planet whose responsibility it was to maintain order anywhere in the world: "A political war. A state war. A war undertaken to freeze, organize and stabilize relations of force. A war of self-defense led by the Imperial State in order to maintain its status as the general organizer of planetary civilization. A spanking."[7] In a brief editorial published in *Le Figaro* in late March, the right-wing novelist Jean Dutourd voiced similar views but directed his animosity primarily at the weakness of France's leaders in allowing themselves to be pressured by the Americans into fighting against France's former allies. According to Dutourd, this would not have been possible under Mitterrand and would have been simply inconceivable under de Gaulle.[8]

If the majority of these positions taken against the bombings grew out of the perceived threat of American imperialism and European and French subservience, that is, out of a traditional French anti-Americanism, others derived from a variety of different motivations and perspectives—some practical or factual, others more specifically moral in nature. Near the outset of the bombings, a petition appearing in *Le Monde* and signed by Pierre Bourdieu, the historian Pierre Vidal-Naquet, the Marxist philosopher Daniel Bensaïd, and others expressed opposition to what it described as a "false dilemma: to support the NATO intervention or to support the reactionary politics of Serb power in Kosovo." This supposedly either/or choice was completely misguided since, the petitioners argued, the bombings might limit the operations of the Serb army, but they would increase the power of Milosevic in rallying the nation around him. Worse, the bombings would also unleash the worst elements of the revenge-minded and murderous Serb paramilitaries against the Kosovar Albanians.[9]

Others argued that the actual situation in Kosovo was being misrepresented to justify the bombings, while still others took the position that the conduct of the war itself was cowardly and morally unhealthy to the point of being obscene. On the first score, in a late-April editorial in the pages of *Le Figaro*, Patrick Besson argued that it wasn't just the Serbs who were doing the killing, and he blasted Bernard-Henri Lévy for supposedly making precisely this claim. Besson also asserted that such simplistic and mechanical thinking was unworthy of intellectual debate and more suited to children's books.[10] But Besson's own credibility, and certainly his impartiality, were undermined by the fact that he was known to have written poems in Alexandrine verse in praise of Radovan Karadjic, the Bosnian Serb leader indicted for crimes against humanity.

In an essay published in *L'Humanité* toward the end of the conflict, François Salvaing raised a more troubling moral issue, certainly even for those who supported the bombing, that centered on the problem of fighting a war in which one's own side suffers no casualties, no material damage, no privations—in fact, not even the slightest inconvenience. Under these circumstances, following the progress of the conflict is like following a tennis match at Roland Garros—"seated in one's comfortable chair." And one is even allowed to indulge in the moral smugness not permitted the French in 1940: "Morally . . . we have reason to feel a lot more proud than we did in 1940. This time, we have resisted Hitler from the outset, right off the bat we are in the Allies' camp and we don't hesitate to condemn the deportations of whole populations. M. Papon had no luck, being Secretary-General of the Gironde prefecture a full half century too soon."[11]

It is against this backdrop that some eight weeks after NATO began the bombings, Régis Debray published an open letter in *Le Monde* to President Jacques Chirac titled "Lettre d'un voyageur au président de la République" (A voyager's letter to the president of the republic). In his letter—more often than not patronizing in tone—Debray states that his purpose in writing is to share with Chirac the knowledge he had gleaned from a week-long visit to Serbia and to the war-torn areas of Kosovo. Debray also states that, unfortunately, Chirac and France itself have gone seriously "off course" in their policy toward the conflict. Dismissing the views expressed by other intellectuals as so many "peremptory and grandiloquent approximations," Debray stresses that he will speak only of the facts and as one "man of the soil" to the other.[12]

Debray's account begins with an explanation of how and why he decided to go to Kosovo. On assignment in Macedonia for the magazine *Marianne*, Debray was interviewing Albanians fleeing Kosovo. The experience convinced him that while some of the tales of horror he heard were true, others were concocted less with the intent of exposing the truth of the events than with an eye to arousing the sympathy of world opinion. Debray's language suggests a conspiratorial dimension to these testimonies, since most were recounted by "sympathizers or militants of the KLA [Kosovo Liberation Front]" who eagerly watched for "newly arrived foreigners" to recruit to their cause. He also suggests that the magnitude of the persecutions was grossly exaggerated in the accounts he heard, but he does concede that there must be an "undeniable kernel of truth" (*un fond indéniable de réalité*) in them.[13]

Thus dissatisfied with these supposedly partial and partisan perspectives, Debray states that he decided to visit the other side, that is, Serb-controlled Kosovo. There he discovered, among other things, the "extreme and inexact nature of some of these accounts [of the refugees]." However, the way in which Debray gained access to Kosovo and was able to verify, or dismiss, what he had been told in Macedonia is itself revealing. Disdaining what he describes as "Intourist style" tours and "journalistic bus trips," Debray explains that he requested of *Serb authorities* that they provide him with "my own translator, my own vehicle, and the right to speak to anyone I pleased. The request was granted."[14]

In his discussion of the war, Debray's analysis is couched in terms of a critique of a public statement made by Chirac concerning the nature of the conflict, the motives and actions of the Serbs, and the justification of and objectives for the NATO bombings. As quoted by Debray, Chirac had affirmed that the bombing was aimed not at the Serb people but at the "dictator" Slobodan Milosevic, who, refusing all negotiations, had "programmed the cold-blooded genocide of the Kosovars." Any collateral damage from the bombardments to civilian populations and targets was regrettable, according to Chirac, but not reason enough to suspend NATO operations against the continuing ethnic cleansing of Albanians by Serbs in Kosovo.[15]

Dismissing Chirac's claims as "trickery" (*duperies*), Debray goes on the offensive and undertakes a point-by-point dismantling of the president's contentions. First, in responding to Chirac's statement that the war was not a war against the Serb people, Debray counters by asserting that the bombing campaign had already destroyed three hundred schools and cultural centers, including the Belgrade children's theater, and had left half the Serb population unemployed. Expanding on these claims, Debray states that the "carnage" caused by the bombardments included those bombed in refugee camps and in trains as well as, from his own experience, "little girls" and "grandparents" in isolated cottages. For good measure, Debray also refers to "four hundred thousand Serbs" deported earlier by Croatians from the Krajina region. The plight of these Serbs, he continues, was not even registered by the cameras and microphones of the international media. (Debray fails to mention, however, that it was the Serbs, encouraged by Milosevic, who first drove *Croatians* from their homes in the Krajina at the start of the Balkan conflict.) By way of accounting for such examples of the world's indifference to Serb suffering, Debray quotes a Serbian girl who observes, following the accidental deaths of Chinese embassy workers during the NATO bombings of Belgrade, "When one kills four Chinese, citizens of a great country, the world is indignant; but when four hundred Serbs are killed, that doesn't count. Curious, no?"[16]

A week after the open letter to Chirac was published, Debray responded to the initial outcry over the letter in an article appearing in *Le Nouvel Observateur*. He denied a partisan attitude in support of the Serb people, stating bluntly, "I am neither pro- nor anti-Serb." But the philosopher's fundamental sympathy for the suffering of the Serbs—their apparent *innocent* victimization—is all too evident in the open letter to Chirac, as is his admiration for Serb resolve, courage, and sangfroid. Debray pointedly stresses that Serbia's "sacred union" has not been dented by the bombings—an obvious reference to the *union sacrée* of the French people facing aggression during World War I. He also mentions a Serb army sergeant picked up while hitchhiking who notes that in defending bombed Kosovar towns without electricity, the Serb troops had to drink their Cokes "lukewarm." The soldier casually states, "It's a pain, but we made do." He makes no mention of the danger he and his fellows faced. Later in the letter, Debray emphasizes the collective courage of the Serb army as it waits impatiently and firmly for foreign troops to invade on the ground. He states that these troops are "getting on like a charm" despite allied bombings and goes on to cite another soldier who is eager for the fight and disdainful of NATO's war from the sky. "In a real war," the soldier is quoted as saying, "there are deaths on both sides." And, in an affirmation that must have offended the French military as well as the French people, Debray implies that if the French army were to enter Kosovo, it might well be beaten. Don't send "our Saint-Cyrians," he warns, because they will be facing an army of Serb "volunteers" for whom the struggle will be "sacred."[17]

Debray then turns to Chirac's characterization of Slobodan Milosevic himself. Conceding that the Serb leader is "autocratic and manipulative," Debray nevertheless rejects Chirac's contention that Milosevic is a dictator. Debray argues that Milosevic keeps no political prisoners, respects the Serb Constitution, and does not rule through a single-party apparatus. He has also won election three times, which means that by definition he cannot be a dictator: "dictators get themselves elected once, not twice." Milosevic does not attempt to control the Serb population through the imposition of a "totalitarian charisma" and freely allows himself to be criticized in the cafés of Belgrade.[18]

As to comparisons of Milosevic to Hitler and Kosovo to Munich supposedly implicit in Chirac's statement and voiced explicitly by others, for Debray such claims are the height of folly. The comparisons reverse the relationship of power between the weak and the strong and attribute motives to Milosevic and the Serbs that are not their own. What, Debray wonders, does an isolated and poor country of ten million whose leader seeks only to reestablish sovereignty within its borders have in common with an expansionist, powerful, and populous Nazi Germany and its megalomaniacal leader? Besides, Debray reminds his readers, in making comparisons between the current situation and World War II, it is important to remember that there were "Albanian, Muslim and Croatian SS divisions, but never Serb ones." Moreover, the Serb people are "philosemitic," not anti-Semitic.[19]

The comparison with Nazi Germany also raises the issue of genocide, and, here again, Debray seeks to discredit Chirac's and NATO's claims. Stating that the "genocide of Kosovars" constitutes a "terrible chapter," Debray then proceeds to counter the implications of this assertion by denying, justifying, or minimizing Serb actions against the Kosovar population. Debray had seen no genocide or any ethnic cleansing, and he even quotes some sources as affirming that the hordes of Albanian refugees were fleeing American bombs rather than Serbs or simply taking advantage of the situation to join "cousins" who had already immigrated to wealthier European countries such as Switzerland and Germany. Debray does identify two "reliable" journalists he encountered, a Serb and a Canadian, who had observed the burning of homes as well as pillaging and rapes committed by Serb forces. But, the journalists affirmed, these crimes occurred *only* following a "deluge of bombs" and *only* during the first three days of the NATO attacks. After that time, there were no more "crimes against humanity."[20]

Having both acknowledged and minimized Serb crimes—which, Debray's language suggests, occurred in response to the "deluge" of NATO's bombs—he then proceeds to undercut the notion that there are deep-seated and indeed murderous animosities existing between the two ethnic groups. He had seen Serb soldiers guarding Kosovar bakeries—an apparent sign of solidarity—although Debray does not address the question as to why the soldiers would need to defend the bakeries in the first place. He states as well that he had also observed Serb and Kosovar Albanian victims of the bombings lying side by side in hospitals in Kosovo. All of this, of course, tends to undermine the very bases upon which genocide and ethnic cleansing would take place, and Debray is quick to take advantage of this to label the conflict as "a local civil war" exacerbated by the bombings.[21]

Needless to say, Debray is not unaware of—nor does he attempt to ignore completely—the history of the conflict between Serbs and Kosovar Albanians stretching back for a decade and beyond. But in referring to that history, Debray slants it in favor of the Serbs to underscore *their* victimization. He asserts that in 1998 three hundred Serb police and soldiers had been killed. Also, the KLA had kidnapped more than three hundred Serb hostages, of which no more than one hundred had returned alive. And when the NATO bombings started, he notes, KLA "snipers" went to work against the Serbs.[22] Debray uses the English word "snipers" because, as the Communist novelist Didier Daeninckx later observed, this word had earlier been used to describe Serb snipers shooting down on civilians from the heights surrounding Sarajevo. For Daeninckx, it is clear that Debray wants to suggest at least a fundamental *equivalence* between the two sets of gunmen and, at the same time, to stir a similar international outrage against the KLA fighters as had earlier been directed against the Serb snipers around Sarajevo.[23]

Under the circumstances Debray describes, when the bombing started the Serbs had no choice but to deal with NATO's "fifth column." They had therefore logically ordered the Kosovar Albanians out of the region. (This assertion, of course, seems to be in logical contradiction to the hearsay Debray cites that the Kosovar Albanians left essentially under their own volition or in an effort to flee NATO bombs.) These evacuations, which Debray describes provocatively as being "in Israeli style" (*à l'israélienne*), were similar to those carried out, apparently justifiably for Debray, by the French in Algeria in displacing one million civilians and putting them behind barbed wire.[24]

At the end of his letter to Chirac, Debray reinforces the analogy between the Serb situation in Kosovo and France's Algerian crisis by adding another twist. He states that the potential defeat of the Serb army and especially of its irregulars in Kosovo might eventually transform the latter into a Serb OAS (Organisation Armée Sécrète), and Milosevic would then find himself in the same kind of dangerous situation that had threatened de Gaulle's life years before. The comparison, of course, ignores Milosevic's role in stoking ethnic hatred and, at least indirectly, in supporting the Serb army as well as Serb irregulars in their exactions. Whatever the complexities of de Gaulle's role vis-à-vis Algeria and the French army, he certainly was not culpable of similar activities.

Not content to compare Milosevic and de Gaulle solely within the context of the Algerian war and its aftermath, Debray goes on to propose another important similarity between the two: their vehement opposition to NATO. Citing de Gaulle's assertion that NATO is the "organization imposed on the Atlantic Alliance and is nothing more than the military and political subordination of Western Europe by the United States of America," Debray chastises Chirac for forgetting this basic principle of Gaullism. He reminds Chirac, finally, that the price of this amnesia is high. In Belgrade, Debray had asked one of Milosevic's opponents why the Serb president had been happy to meet with an American envoy during the bombing campaign but not a French envoy. Debray's interlocutor replied that it was "better to speak to the master than to his servants."[25]

Régis Debray's open letter to Chirac brings into sharp focus and summarizes many of the criticisms of the NATO bombings (cited at the beginning of this chapter) and especially the political and ideological attitudes underlying them. Echoing the likes of Faubert and Dutourd, Debray voices a blatant anti-Americanism and suspicion of American imperial ambitions in Europe that is shared by many on the extreme Left as well as on the extreme Right. (On the latter score, members of Jean-Marie Le Pen's National Front warned that if America was ready to intervene in the internal affairs of a sovereign state such as Serbia to impose its will, it would certainly not hesitate to do the same thing in other European countries, including France.) As Debray states in his open letter to Chirac, not only does the United States impose its will militarily, subjugating and humiliating friend and foe alike, but where it cannot succeed with force it simply pays for the political conditions it wishes to impose. Along with his evident anti-Americanism, Debray also expresses his distaste for French subservience to U.S. hegemony, a sentiment also echoed by many other critics of the bombings. And while Debray's pro-Serb stance—despite his protestations of impartiality—was not noticeably shared by the majority of French intellectuals, in its expression in the open letter it is reminiscent of the attitude of another well-known European intellectual and writer, Peter Handke, who made himself a pariah by vocally supporting Serbia and going to Belgrade during the bombings to denounce the campaign as an "invasion of Mars." As opposed to Debray, however, Handke's overt support of the Serbs had been a matter of record since the earlier fighting in Bosnia and especially since the 1996 publication of his *Un voyage hivernale vers le Danube, la Save, la Moravia, et la Drina.*[26]

But to credit Debray merely with having written a kind of distillation of the motivations and attitudes of those who opposed the NATO bombings would be to

greatly minimize his role and impact. The letter to Chirac created, in fact, a veritable firestorm of controversy and served as a touchstone not only for those intellectuals who shared Debray's views but for those who opposed them. It also raised
timely issues concerning the media and especially its role in relation to the policies
of the French government. Most importantly for our purposes here, it underscored
again the dangers involved in deploying misguided historical analogies in an effort
both to understand current crises and to justify taking a partisan stance. These analogies and their pitfalls are important in analyzing Debray's complicity with Serb
nationalism and determining its political and historical implications.

To get an idea of the magnitude of the controversy provoked by Debray's open
letter to Chirac, it is worth stressing that virtually every leading intellectual from all
points on the political spectrum waded into the fray with editorials, interviews, and
open letters published in the press. But this was not all. The day after the publication of Debray's letter, *Libération* published an entire dossier titled "The Debray
Case" in which Debray's claims were dissected and for the most part apparently de-
bunked. In the days and weeks that followed, national magazines published numerous interviews, editorials, and background pieces. While magazines favorable to
Debray such as *Marianne*, which had originally hired him to do a piece on Kosovo,
denounced his attackers and claimed to expose their real motivations in its "The
Underside of a Failed Media Lynching,"[27] other magazines were hostile to Debray.
For example, *L'Événement du Jeudi* ran a feature on the affair titled, tellingly, "The
Treason of the Intellectuals."[28] In June 1999, Edwy Plenel, managing editor of *Le
Monde* (and the individual who encouraged Debray to write the open letter to
Chirac), published *L'Épreuve*, a book condemning not only Debray's position concerning Kosovo but the political philosophy of National Republicanism that, at least
ostensibly, subtended it. All the while Debray was publishing numerous responses,
clarifications, and refutations in *Le Monde diplomatique*, *L'Humanité*, *Libération*,
and elsewhere. In spring 2000, Debray, still smarting from these attacks, published
a book of his own about the controversy and about Kosovo. *L'Emprise* sought to have
the last word with his critics and denounced the press once again, this time as an
"industry" fabricating modern conscience.[29]

According to Pierre Péan and Philippe Cohen, to a significant degree the intensity and indeed violence of the media's response to Debray's open letter to Chirac
was the result of a behind-the-scenes campaign to discredit Debray orchestrated by
none other than Edwy Plenel. Péan and Cohen argue that before the letter was published, Plenel gave it to Bernard-Henri Lévy and Debray's friend Alain Joxe, among
others, so that they could attack it immediately. Lévy's harsh response appeared in

Le Monde the next day, as did Joxe's. The latter titled his polemic "International Cretinism."[30]

But if Péan and Cohen's scenario suggests that the media circus generated by Debray's letter was manipulated and in fact artificial—perhaps nothing more than score settling or an opportunity for Paris's media-hungry intellectuals to mount their soapboxes—there were other reasons for the intensity of the media response as well. In an editorial included in *Libération*'s dossier on the letter published the day after it appeared, Jacques Amalric stated that Debray's letter required a response not because it was newsworthy but because it constituted nothing less than an all-out assault on the integrity of the media itself: "we were not simply dealing with a provocative piece of writing by a 'writer and philosopher' [Debray described himself in these terms in signing the letter] . . . but rather with the charge of a light-horseman that itself announced a much vaster offensive intended to persuade the maximum of French that most of the media lied to them and sought to brainwash them in regurgitating without verification or conscience one-track thinking [*la pensée unique*] of those in charge."[31]

Not surprisingly, given Amalric's remarks, the authors of the *Libération* dossier chose to attack Debray's letter at what would be, at least for a journalist, its weakest point—the reliability of the so-called facts he presented. In an interview included in the *Libération* dossier, Debray was forced to concede that his reported number of schools destroyed (three hundred) was hearsay, although, apparently, that number was later verified); that he had greatly underestimated the number of Kosovar refugees; and that he was perhaps in error in accusing NATO officials of lying. But having conceded these shortcomings in *Libération* a few days after the publication of his letter, in the June issue of *Le Monde diplomatique* Debray went on the offensive once again, this time upping the ante by denouncing the "media bombardiers" for following up on the rocket attacks with murderous editorials: "the army of Good strikes the evil-doers twice—first Tomahawk missiles, then with editorials." More focused in his attacks on the press than he had been in his original letter, however, Debray singled out for criticism primarily those newspapers such as *Libération* and *Le Monde* that had treated his original claims most harshly. At the same time, Debray lamented the fact that those newspapers that defended him, such as *Le Figaro* and *L'Humanité*, "are not read." His conclusion: "The dominated read the dominators, not the reverse."[32]

If the media, or at least a good portion of it—already under fire in the 1990s for a variety of reasons by a number of *intellos*—felt obliged to defend itself by challenging Debray on the level of the facts, others who disagreed with Debray sought instead to expose and denounce the political, ideological, and even psychological

motives underlying his statements about the war. Echoing the spirit of the article in
L'Événement du Jeudi titled "The Treason of the Intellectuals," Bernard-Henri
Lévy, in an article in *Le Monde*, denounced Debray's naivete in swallowing whole
Serb propaganda and, subsequently, in uncritically regurgitating it. And in a statement clearly intended to cast Debray in the worst possible light—and that provoked
its own fair share of outraged retorts—Lévy compared him to the ultimate intellectual traitor and wartime collaborator with Nazism, Drieu La Rochelle: "Debray is
not Drieu. And Belgrade is not Berlin. But, in the final analysis . . . in a very real
sense that is where we find ourselves. What we understand through books we are
now apparently given to experience in our lives. Hatred of democracy and Europe?
Hatred of oneself? A passion to blind oneself, to disappoint. The suicide, live, of an
intellectual. Too bad. Goodbye, Régis.[33]

If Lévy's ad hominem attack on Debray proved the most shocking to many—Max
Gallo denounced Lévy's disdain for responsible thinking in comparing Debray to
Drieu[34]—it was certainly not the only such attack. Benoît Rayski saw Debray's letter
as proof of his monstrous egotism, asking "what could be more delectable for the ego
of Régis Debray than to live like a Prometheus who rears up in the face of the Jupiter
of the White House or like a modern Antigone, rebellious against American state interests that supposedly subjugate the world?"[35] Eschewing mythological references
in favor of more contemporary ones, Gilles Tordjman argued that the "tragic" part
of Debray's situation was that he had survived his Warholian quarter of an hour of
fame by thirty years. All that remained of the formerly heroic guerrilla was "a kind of
bitter courtesan showing off in the face of a history made without him."[36]

In an editorial in *L'Express*, André Glucksmann abandoned the psychological for
the ideological in explaining Debray's motives. For Glucksmann, Debray's refusal to
see Serb destructiveness and hatred of Albanians recalled a writer's assertion on the
front page of *L'Humanité* in 1956 that he had seen smiles on the faces of the people
of Budapest following the Red Army's brutal conquest of that city. Like the writer for
L'Humanité, and despite the collapse of Communism in 1989, Debray could not escape the ideological bind dictating that all Communists and former Communists, including the likes of Milosevic and his Serb army and police, were ultimately sympathetic and well intentioned, while all those who have truck with NATO and with its
éminence grise, American imperialism, were either dupes or traitors.[37] Offering a
similar perspective, Rony Brauman argued that Debray radically rejected "everything
that comes from America while showing reverence for anything that resists it."[38]

If the criticisms of Debray's open letter to Chirac offer a number of plausible—
and not so plausible—explanations for his pro-Serb engagement, none make a sys-

tematic effort either to situate that commitment in relation to the historical vision suggested in the letter or to explain Debray's stance in relation to his own past or his broader political views. All of these factors played a vital role in determining Debray's attitude toward the conflict and, ultimately, shaped his complicity with Serb nationalism.

As many of the commentaries on the bombing of Kosovo confirm, just as in the earlier wars in Croatia and Bosnia, the memory of World War II, Nazism, and Vichy often served as a prism through which French intellectuals interpreted the conflict as well as a frequent basis for choosing sides. As his open letter to Chirac clearly indicates, Debray was no exception to this rule. For Debray, Serbia's historical resistance to Nazism coupled with the collaborationism of Albanians and others in the region (Debray refers in passing to the latter's "SS divisions") clearly inclined him to cultivate a heroic image of the Serbs and disinclined him to view their motives or their actions as in any way similar to those of the Nazis. Debray thus exhibits a frankly shocking impulse to downplay Serb animosities, crimes, and ethnic cleansing and even to question the motives of the Kosovar Albanians fleeing their homeland.

In *Une voix qui vient de l'autre rive*, published a year after the conclusion of the NATO bombings of Kosovo, Alain Finkielkraut offers an astute assessment of Debray's misguided engagement and traces its source directly to Debray's skewed historical framing of the conflict. According to Finkielkraut, at the root of the problem is a kind of historical "telescoping" on Debray's part that links the "present instant" directly to the "Nazi apocalypse" and assigns the Serbs the heroic role of the resister. But this "telescoping," Finkielkraut continues, also succeeds in erasing everything in between including, notably, recent Serb abuses and crimes in the region. In reading Debray's letter, one could believe that "practically nothing happened in Yugoslav space between 8 May 1945 and 24 March 1999: not the suspension of Kosovar autonomy and the subjugation of the region to an oppressive and discriminatory Serb regime; not the removal of all Albanians from public employment; not the banning of the Albanian language from television; not the 'Serbization' of teaching; not the decision of Slovenia and then of the other republics to secede when faced with the threat of 'Kossovisation.'"[39]

And one could add to this list other Serb crimes and abuses. As Rony Brauman stressed in his response to Debray's letter, among the terrible events effaced by Debray's historical telescoping is the destruction by Serbs of the Croatian town of Vukovar in 1991 and, later, the Bosnian Serb General Radko Mladjic's horrific ethnic cleansing of the Bosnian Muslim enclave of Srebrenica in July 1995. Both of these events were, of course, indelibly linked to Slobodan Milosevic's dreams of a "Greater Serbia."

Also a result of Debray's historical telescoping, according to Finkielkraut, is the fact that for the philosopher and medialogist "everything begins . . . with NATO. [Debray] went to Kosovo to verify this certitude which was invisible to the naked eye: the will of the United States to make war to put into effect its strategy of globalization and to prove their world supremacy. And the rest, the rapes, the pillaging, the torching of houses, the destruction of identity papers, the planned expulsion on the Bosnian model of three hundred thousand Albanians before 24 March [1999] and a million afterward—is nothing but an exaggeration and a humanitarian smoke-screen."[40]

In his analysis of Debray's open letter to Chirac, Finkielkraut is himself culpable of distorting some of Debray's assertions and ignoring others. For example, Debray does acknowledge Serb crimes, including rape and pillaging, although he downplays them. But the overall thrust of Finkielkraut's argument is correct in its claim that Debray's insistence on framing the conflict, at least in one section of the letter, in relation to World War II and Nazism does lead to a dangerous revisionism and even a form of negationism where Serb crimes are concerned. This—justifiably— drew the ire of Debray's critics. Ironically, it is Alain Finkielkraut—himself the victim of egregious blind spots as a result of his own misguided historical references to World War II—who diagnoses the nature of Debray's myopic and distorted vision and one of the major reasons for it.

Before turning to the other historical context invoked by Debray, the Algerian war, and the figure who, inevitably, links the two historical contexts together, Charles de Gaulle, it is important to stress that Debray's willingness to dredge up the World War II past and to situate the Yugoslav antagonists in relation to it also resulted in his own "caricaturization" within that context. Bernard-Henri Lévy's depiction of Debray as a latter-day Drieu may have struck many as offensive and even defamatory, but it is not without interest—or justification. As Lévy himself was probably aware, in the autobiographical *Les masques*, published more than a decade before the conflict in Kosovo, Debray acknowledged that the intellectual figure from the interwar years, the "sacred monster" with whom he felt the greatest kinship and even fraternity, was not André Malraux, as one might assume, but Drieu La Rochelle:

> Let's leave aside the fascination with force (which has nothing to do with efficaciousness) and the chaos of a spirit even more confused than the age within which it lives [a spirit characterized by] a philosophical superficiality better given to creativity than to the intellectual baggage of an *agrégé* in philosophy). The rest of Drieu, his nocturnal side, is more fraternal to me [than Malraux]; the "empty suitcase" side [of his

nature], the hatred of the self, his inability to escape himself, his taste for isolation and his regret for missed communions which require an incessant coming and going between the public forum and the convent, the curiosity about death and the inability to live.[41]

If Debray readily identifies in *Les masques* with the side of Drieu that is disabused and even nihilistic and also, apparently, with his incessant longing for a form of "communion" or transcendence, there are other intriguing links between the two men that also shed light—at least obliquely—on Debray's position vis-à-vis Kosovo. First, like Drieu, who achieved fame as a champion of martial virtues associated with trench warfare during World War I, Debray, since his early days as a Latin American revolutionary and confidant of Che Guevara, has also championed these virtues in the revolutionary's struggle against oppression. There are, of course, echoes of this in Debray's celebration of the courageous resistance of Serb forces when faced with the overwhelming and unassailable might of the NATO bombers.

Also like Drieu, Debray's taste for "isolation" has led him to embrace deliberately iconoclastic attitudes toward specific political issues and to voice disdain, on occasion, for the views, as well as the posturing, of his fellow intellectuals. This has resulted in frequent diatribes against the superficiality and media-mindedness of Paris's intellectual elite, most recently in *I.F. suite et fin*, published two years after the NATO bombings. Just as Drieu enjoyed shocking his more politically correct fellows with his political views in the 1930s and 1940s, so Debray's occasional denunciations of such "sacred cows" of the Left as May 1968—and certainly his position vis-à-vis Kosovo—have afforded him the possibility to shock many of his fellow intellectuals while expressing disdain for their superficial and media-driven sophistication. Echoes of this same disdain are evident in his claim to be speaking to Chirac in the open letter not as an intellectual but as one "man of the soil" to another.

In his comments in *Les masques* on shared affinities with Drieu, Debray makes no mention of Drieu's political attitudes and trajectory or his own, but there are interesting, if highly debatable, similarities here as well. Like Debray, who began his career as a leftist revolutionary or revolutionary sympathizer in Latin America, Drieu began his career at least on the "cultural Left" as a friend of the surrealists. He only moved to the Right politically well into the interwar years, becoming a supporter of Jacques Doriot's Fascist Parti Populaire Français in the 1930s and an admirer of Hitler during the same decade, an admiration that continued during the Occupation. According to Jacques Lecarme, at the end of World War II, with the defeat of Nazism imminent, Drieu lost faith in Nazi Germany and largely abandoned politics to devote his last years before his suicide to the study of Eastern religions.[42]

Bernard-Henri Lévy's likening of Debray to Drieu in his response to Debray's open letter to Chirac is, it appears, clearly intended to suggest a similar itinerary on Debray's part. And, according to Pierre Péan and Philippe Cohen, Edwy Plenel sought to make this claim explicit in his book *L'Épreuve*: "Debray . . . went from Castro to Mitterrand, and from Mitterrand to [Jean-Pierre] Chevènement, to end up with Milosevic. Plenel doesn't say it but the reader can guess it; Debray's itinerary is that of the scoundrel. In summary, the book declines the thought [of Bernard-Henri Lévy] which compared Debray to Drieu. Case closed, next case!"[43]

For Péan and Cohen, the comparison of Debray to Drieu is nothing short of scandalous, if not outright defamatory, and they are right to the extent that Debray's trajectory, while apparently moving from Left to Right as did Drieu's, in no way means that he ended up Fascist or pro-Nazi. But the comparison is pertinent to the degree that it reflects Debray's move away from support for the (leftist) revolutionary aspirations of oppressed populations to a position of sympathy for a politics of national sovereignty and hegemony. What is clear in Debray's letter is that he has no sympathy for the efforts of the majority Kosovar Albanians—and not just the militants of the KLA—to get out from under the yoke of Serb dominance and oppression. And if this stance reflects a loss of a certain political idealism in the same way that Drieu's embrace of Nazism and collaborationism reflected a deep pessimism about France's and Europe's future, it is also worth noting that as was the case with Drieu, Debray's deep political pessimism seems to have led to a newly rekindled interest in religion, the idea of God, and the latter's role in the history of humankind. If there is not necessarily an evolution of sorts implicit in Debray's current interest in religion, then at least it would appear to echo what Debray identified as his and Drieu's taste for shuttling between the "convent" and the "public forum."

In the final analysis, of course, the comparison of Debray to Drieu, provocative and evocative as it is, is more anecdotal than it is illuminating when it comes to explaining Debray's troubling support for Milosevic and his complicity with Serb nationalism and hegemony. To ascribe the latter to a Drieu-like self-hatred, a fascination with death, and an urge to betray—as does, ultimately, Bernard-Henri Lévy— certainly provides a simple and simplistic psychological explanation of Debray's stance, but it does not do justice to the more profound motivations underlying Debray's commitment, to his vision of history, or to his deeply held political convictions.

To return, then, to Debray's vision of history, the second, broader historical context invoked to explain the stakes in Kosovo is the Algerian war and, to a lesser degree, the cold war. For Debray, the two are joined in the figure of Charles de Gaulle, who dominated both in French politics as well as in French memory. The figure of de Gaulle is, of course, more overshadowing still, since he is also the French nation's greatest hero in the struggle against Nazism. But while Debray's readers, at least in the 1990s, would in all likelihood associate the General de Gaulle more closely with the defeat of the Nazis and the Liberation than with any other historical context, Debray appears to skirt any possible linkage between Milosevic and the "Man of 18 June," that is, the World War II hero. His focus is instead on comparisons between the two men, their attitude toward NATO, and the similarities between their respective roles in the Algerian crisis and in Kosovo. But are these comparisons justified?

Stated bluntly, other than their shared hostility to NATO, which was itself the result of very different historical circumstances and motivations, absolutely nothing justifies any form of comparison between de Gaulle and Milosevic. Milosevic was certainly no war hero or popular leader at the outset of his career, but rather an opportunistic Communist Party bureaucrat who exploited ethnic tensions and animosities to create a place for himself on the Yugoslav national political stage. As for the comparison of Algeria to Kosovo, little if anything justifies the analogy, and certainly nothing legitimizes comparing de Gaulle's role in Algeria to Milosevic's in Kosovo. De Gaulle, after all, *ended* the war in Algeria on his own initiative and was certainly not responsible for its outbreak. By contrast, in the late 1980s Milosevic deliberately stirred up tensions between Serbs and Albanians in Kosovo, and, as Finkielkraut points out, implemented pro-Serb and antiegalitarian policies in the region, which only stoked the fires of ethnic hatred.[44]

Given these obvious *dissimilarities* between arguably France's greatest statesman of the twentieth century and a now-deposed Serb leader currently on trial at The Hague for crimes against humanity, one is at a loss to understand Debray's logic in strictly *historical* terms. And the linkage becomes even more difficult to comprehend when one takes into consideration Debray's genuine, broadly based admiration for the founder of the Fifth Republic and president who helped secure his release from a Bolivian prison in 1970. Debray's 1991 book À demain de Gaulle!, for example, describes de Gaulle as nothing less than the "futurist of the nation" (the subtitle of the English translation). In the foreword to the English edition, Debray praises de Gaulle's prescience, stating, "All of de Gaulle's predictions—the transience of World communism, the reunification of Germany, the resurrection of the old Russia, the collapse of the Empires, and so on, have come true since his death."[45]

But de Gaulle's prescience is by no means his sole or even his most distinctive virtue in Debray's eyes. According to Keith Reader, Debray's admiration focuses on his perception of de Gaulle as a defender of the "institutions of the republic and the state" and as the embodiment of a "verbal culture . . . jeopardized by the omnipresence of the visual."[46] At least equally important, argues Donald Reid, is that de Gaulle exemplifies for Debray a faith in France's "special mission in the world," a faith primarily evident in de Gaulle's "far-reaching foreign policies." That mission and that vision have subsequently been terribly eroded in the bland, superficial, and consensual "mediocracy" France has become.[47]

At the time of the Bicentennial of the French Revolution in 1989, Debray also cast de Gaulle—at least implicitly—in the role of champion of France's Jacobin, revolutionary tradition in the face of Philippe Pétain's efforts to repudiate that tradition in proclaiming his own National Revolution. Debray wistfully acknowledges that in his youth he misunderstood the fact that de Gaulle was in reality the true rebel and revolutionary he sought to emulate all along: "To find the rebel, I turned my back on him; to reach 1940 London I fled from 1960 Paris." To drive the point home, Debray also affirms, "I became a Gaullist—the term is incorrect but appropriate—around May 1968."[48]

Given all these attributes, it is perhaps fair to say that, in the final analysis, de Gaulle exemplifies for Debray nothing less than the ideal of the French Republic, as Debray conceives of it, with its revolutionary tradition and heritage; its long, continuous and continuing history of struggle; its "special mission" in the world; and its embodiment of the sacred idea of the French nation—"a certain idea of France," as de Gaulle would say. In any number of texts published during the past two decades, Debray has in fact articulated a vision of the republic in keeping with these characteristics. In *Que vive la République*, for example, he affirms that "The Republic is not just one political regime among others. It is an ideal and a struggle (*un combat*). It requires not only laws but faith, not only social services but distinct institutions . . . , not only users and consumers but citizens united not around mere objectives but transcendent ends, like liberty and equality."[49] He continues along these lines in *La République expliquée à ma fille*: "The Republic has always been a 'between-the-wars.' [It has had to struggle against] enemies on the outside as well those within. It has had to mobilize, regiment, battle, arm, decorate, galvanize. With the drum and with the bugle. Barricades and trenches. This trooplike quality has put males in the first rank. Of necessity. But this wasn't the fault of the Republic, but rather of its enemies."[50] But if de Gaulle has come to exemplify in Debray's eyes the quintessential features of the French Republic as both a reality and an ideal, as these passages describe, in recent years and in other texts Debray has articulated a more troublingly *nationalistic* conception of France and the republic that leads, finally, back to Kosovo and helps explain Debray's pro-Serb stance.

In April 1999, at the height of the war in Kosovo, Debray published a monograph titled *Le code et la glaive: Après l'Europe, la nation?* Based on a lecture delivered at the Sorbonne in November 1998, *Le code et la glaive* sketches out a position that, as Debray describes it, seeks at once to be anti-European without being reactionary, "national" without being "nationalistic," "universal" without succumbing to the pseudouniversalism of the "global village" dominated by American imperialism and its "might makes right" attitude, and respectful of the "rights of man" without denying the "rights of a people."[51]

As admirable and indeed all-embracing and equitable as are these ambitions in the abstract, in his own more detailed discussion of his position Debray makes it clear that, after all, there must be priorities and hierarchies. So, for example, while Debray aspires to be both "national" and "republican," he confesses that for him the *"nation precedes the Republic"* just as, in Sartrean terms, *"existence precedes essence."* In "simple terms," he asserts, "I am French before being a republican, and a republican before being a socialist."[52] In other words, an *essentialist* notion of national identity takes precedence over the republic and its political institutions, even including, it would appear, democracy itself.

It is not difficult to see how the simple formula articulated in *Le code et la glaive* accentuates—to a disturbing degree—the "national" and frankly "nationalistic" over the "Republican" in Debray's "National-Republicanism." More importantly, this "hierarchy," understood less as a reasoned political perspective than as a kind of visceral, instinctual stance according to which all politics and political conflicts are ultimately judged, also goes a long way toward explaining Debray's disconcerting engagement vis-à-vis the NATO bombing of Kosovo. If in Debray's view the nation in effect constitutes the first priority and supercedes both the (republican) form of government and the (humanitarian) ideology that is Socialism, his visceral reaction in favor of the Serbs, whose "nation," at least from his perspective, clearly included Kosovo, is understandable. Having relegated republicanism and humanitarian Socialism to a secondary status, Debray would naturally not be overly concerned with the niceties of democratic politics in Serbia and the bases of Milosevic's power or visibly preoccupied with the fate of the refugees fleeing Kosovo. Finally, having equated a "bad" universalism with American hegemony and dismissed Europe as essentially an empty shell incapable of inspiring the passions that the idea of nation inspires,[53] Debray could hardly do anything but condemn NATO's war effort. If NATO served American interests, as so many French intellectuals were quick to point out, in principle at least it served those of Europe as well.

If Debray's position on Kosovo does indeed reflect the basic tenets of his National Republicanism, then it is frankly difficult to see how this supposedly new political philosophy leads to a perspective significantly different from the cold war perspectives revived, according to Edwy Plenel, by the Kosovo conflict. Debray's knee-jerk anti-Americanism, his denunciation of NATO, his instinctual sympathy for Milosevic—after all, a former Communist—all lend credence to Plenel's analysis.

But there is also another twist. In *Ce Fascisme qui vient* . . . , Jacques Julliard warned of a renascent Fascism in Eastern Europe, many of whose political strongmen, former Communists such as Milosevic, were embracing the worst and most primitive strains of ethnic nationalism and exploiting them in the bloodiest of power plays. The result was what Julliard labeled a new *Brun Rouge* (Brown Red) ideology, marrying old-style Fascism and even Nazism with the remnants of Communism in a new and lethal mixture. When the war in Kosovo began, André Glucksmann, among others, was quick to identify this ideology as the source of Serb hegemony and political practice.[54] Given Debray's own turn to National Republicanism combined with his pro-Communist past, it is not difficult to read into his position vis-à-vis Kosovo at least a tacit acceptance of *Brun Rouge* ideology, and it is perhaps this apparent acceptance, more than the specifics of his comments about the war itself, that led figures such as Lévy to denounce Debray. Indeed, a month before Debray's letter appeared in *Le Monde*, Julliard also denounced in an editorial what he described as France's "nationalists of the left" and their embrace of the Serb position. Julliard's vitriolic critique of the views of these "nationalists of the left" sounded more like an attack on Debray's National Republicanism than anything else. "They are sons of the French Revolution that they admire, and of the Republic, that they venerate. But go figure: recently they have repudiated the universalism and the abstract notion of the rights of man. A strange posture: They only rediscover a taste for the universal when one intervenes to stop one tyrant and they are scandalized that one doesn't stop all the others at the same time. In short, these are humanists who don't care for the humanitarian, anti-Americans who are not resigned to the notion of Europe, generalists taking refuge in the particular."[55]

Julliard's critique of France's new "nationalists of the left" is both telling and persuasive. But it fails, ultimately, to capture the sad ironies of Régis Debray's National Republicanism and where that led him. Debray's passionate and indeed idealistic commitment to a heroic vision of the French Republic is sincere and in many ways admirable. But his "Republicanism" is also fatally tainted with a strain of nationalism that not only encouraged traditional French and cold war prejudices but led Debray ultimately to identify with the Serb position and to become complicitous, in his own pronouncements, with Serb crimes.

CHAPTER SIX

Stéphane Courtois

Historical Revisionism and the
Black Book of Communism Controversy

The heated debates surrounding the multiauthor *Livre noir du communisme* (Black book of communism), whose volume editor was the historian Stéphane Courtois, occurred a year and a half before the NATO bombardment of Kosovo and Régis Debray's controversial engagement vis-à-vis the conflict. Those debates dealt less with current events and their inflection through the memory of World War II than with a comparison of that memory with the memory of another terrible historical trauma, the history of Communism and its crimes.

I have chosen to treat the *Black Book* controversy last for two reasons. First, there is obviously a historical, geographical, and political continuity between Alain Finkielkraut's pro-Croatian commitment and Régis Debray's later stand condemning Nato's attack on Kosovo and Serbia. Those two subjects therefore needed to be treated sequentially. Second, as the discussion of Debray's reasons for, in effect, supporting Serbia suggest, during the 1990s the memory of World War II, of Vichy and Nazism, began to lose its hold as the *sole* and *absolute* historical paradigm of evil to which events of the present were inevitably compared. As Debray's open letter to Chirac confirmed, Algeria also began to serve as a historical yardstick. And as the *Black Book* controversy reveals, so too did the history and memory of Communism, dormant for the most part since 1989. This controversy is the backdrop for determining Courtois's commitment to the memory of Communism's crimes and, through it, his complicity with a reactionary historical revisionism.

As the title of Jacques Julliard's diary *L'année des fantômes* suggests, 1997 was the "Year of the Ghosts,"[1] marked by several major "eruptions of memory." The first such eruption, which concerned the Vichy past, was of course the trial of Maurice

Papon in Bordeaux on charges of crimes against humanity for his role in the deportation of several trainloads of Jews from the Bordeaux area during the Occupation. The trial, which began in October 1997, continued interminably for six months. We will return to the Papon trial shortly.

The second major eruption of memory occurring in France in the fall of 1997 dealt with a very different past, but one to which the French public, perhaps surprisingly, proved at least as sensitive. In November 1997, the Éditions Robert Laffont published *Le livre noir du communisme*, or *Black Book of Communism*, a massive, 850-page multiauthored work detailing the crimes of Communism worldwide.[2] Originally scheduled to appear on the eightieth anniversary of the October Revolution, the project had been delayed by a number of factors. The first of these was typical, given a project of this size and scope: several of the authors were unable to finish their individual chapters on time. The second factor concerned the untimely and tragic death of one of the project's moving forces, François Furet, who succumbed to a head injury received while playing tennis. The *Black Book* had in fact been conceived in large part by Charles Ronsac, the editor of Furet's own very successful history of the idea of Communism, *The Passing of Illusion* (which we will return to shortly). Furet had agreed to write the preface to the *Black Book*, and the introduction to the volume was to be a collaborative effort of all the contributors.

With Furet's death and the deadline approaching, the contributors to the *Black Book* requested a six-month delay from the publisher. The request was refused. As a result, the volume editor, Stéphane Courtois, volunteered to write a general introduction, which he completed in early September. When Courtois's introduction was shown to the other contributors, however, two of the latter, Nicholas Werth, author of the section dealing with the Soviet Union, and Jean-Louis Margolin, author of the chapter on China, were outraged by its contents and refused to sign off on what Courtois had written. When the publisher decided to move forward with production with Courtois's introduction intact, Werth and Margolin consulted a lawyer to see if they could withdraw their respective contributions from the book. They were advised that they could not. Given the circumstances under which the *Black Book* finally appeared, it is not surprising that part of the controversy surrounding the book's publication was generated by the contributors themselves.[3]

Upon publication, the *Black Book of Communism* provoked a veritable uproar. In the editorial pages of daily newspapers, in magazine articles and intellectual reviews, on television, and even on the floor of the National Assembly, the book's publication inspired vehement statements of support or denunciation, vitriolic exchanges, and, in the heat of the moment, a fair number of exaggerations and indeed whopping distortions of history. An example of the latter occurred when Socialist Prime Minister Lionel Jospin was attacked on the floor of the National Assembly by right-wing deputies for including a Communist Party still unrepentant over its "criminal past" in his governing coalition. Some of the deputies even brandished what appeared to be copies of the *Black Book*. Jospin responded to these attacks by stating that he was proud of his Communist allies because the French Communist Party (*Parti communiste français* [PCF]) had always supported the struggles of the Left in France, and its Soviet sponsors had been with the Allies in the struggle against Nazism. For good measure, Jospin also asserted that the PCF had never encroached on anyone's liberties.[4] Interviewed in *Le Figaro* about Jospin's claims, Jean-François Revel scoffingly noted that Jospin overlooked the fact that the PCF had refused to join the *Cartel des Gauches* in the 1920s. Revel also pointed out that Jospin had selectively reported on the Soviet Union's wartime record, making no mention of the Hitler-Stalin pact of August 1939. As for the claim that the PCF had never abridged anyone's civil liberties, Revel underscored the obvious: the PCF had never been in power. Given its Stalinist tendencies, respect for individual freedoms would in all likelihood not have been one of the hallmarks of its rule had it achieved power.[5]

While Jospin chose to defend his political allies by offering a very selective and indeed expurgated version of Communism's past, the PCF leader, the avuncular Robert Hue, opted for a somewhat more judicious strategy. Lamenting the excesses of Stalinism as well as the PCF's own Stalinist past, Hue asserted that the PCF was now looking at that past "with courage" and that the French people as a whole still had confidence in a party that had been a mainstay of the Popular Front (*Front populaire*) in the 1930s and later of the Resistance, as well as a leader in anticolonial struggles. Hue concluded that it was "ludicrous and grotesque" to ignore all of these accomplishments while reducing the memory of Communism to a "macabre" tally sheet of its crimes.[6]

In making reference to a list of Communism's crimes, Hue was referring, of course, not to the number of victims of the PCF but rather to the supposed total number of victims of Communist regimes worldwide from 1917 to the present. And while each chapter of the *Black Book* offered harrowing accounts of suffering and death as well as estimates as to the number of victims of starvation, execution, etc., the tally sheet of Communism's victims—or, more accurately, the body count—was in fact provided in its most succinct and shocking form in Stéphane Courtois's introduction titled, simply, "The Crimes of Communism." Here, Courtois arrived at the astonishing figure of 100 million dead. He asserted baldly that the Soviet Union was responsible for 20 million dead, China 65 million, North Korea 2 million, and

Cambodia 2 million. Other Communist regimes accounted for the remaining 10 million.[7]

The sheer enormity of the number of Communism's victims cited by Courtois was certainly one reason for the succès de scandale of the *Black Book*. But for many of Courtois's critics, including some of his coauthors, it wasn't so much the size of the figure that scandalized, it was the fact that Courtois had grossly exaggerated it. In an interview in the magazine *L'Histoire*, for example, Nicholas Werth pointed out that in his own section of the book dealing with Soviet crimes, he had come up with the figure of 15 million, not the 20 million cited by Courtois.[8] Presumably, there were other exaggerations as well.

But if Courtois's exaggerated figures of Communism's crimes outraged many, at least equally shocking—and more disturbing and compromising in the long run— were the uses to which he put these figures in historical terms. In effect, Courtois's body count became the starting point, first, for a comparison of Communist and Nazi crimes and then, more broadly, of Communism and Nazism themselves. The nature of these comparisons, and Courtois's zealotry and single-minded efforts to condemn Communism unequivocally, led ultimately to his complicity with a dangerous historical revisionism with very real *political* implications in the present.

The first stage of Courtois's comparison, then, was simply statistical. Having established, to his own satisfaction at least, the figure of 100 million dead as the result of Communist regimes, Courtois then compared that figure to the number of those killed by the Nazis, which he estimated at 15 million dead. On the basis of this comparison, Nazism appeared significantly less murderous.

But Courtois did not stop there. If the numbers appeared favorable to the Nazis, a moral comparison—where Nazism was generally considered much the worse of the two—pointed, in Courtois's view, to a moral *equivalency*. In his introduction Courtois argued that death by starvation, deportation, or exhaustion during the process of "decossakization" or "dekulakization" in the early years of the Soviet Union was in reality no different from the murder of Jews by similar means at the hands of the Nazis. Reprising an analogy originally proposed by the Soviet writer Vassili Grossman, Courtois stated that "the death of a Ukranian Kulak child deliberately starved by the policies of Stalinism 'is equal to' the death of a Jewish child in the Warsaw ghetto deliberately starved by the Nazis."[9] And he concluded, in the same vein, that class genocide equals racial genocide. Or, to put it more cagily, "the genocide of a 'class' may well be tantamount to the genocide of a 'race.'"[10]

Having insisted on the essential moral equivalency of the two crimes (he did concede the "uniqueness" of Auschwitz and the "industrial" killing of the Shoah in one sentence, and then moved on), Courtois then proceeded to attempt to establish a *legal equivalency* by, in effect, indicting those responsible for the crimes of Communism in accordance with the legal categories used at Nuremberg. These categories include crimes against peace, crimes of war, and, most controversially, crimes against humanity.

As for crimes against peace, Courtois asserted that Stalin committed crimes of this nature in secretly negotiating with the Nazis in August 1939 to divide Poland and to allow the Soviet Union to annex the Baltic States in August 1939.[11] The Soviet Union was also guilty of crimes against peace in launching its war against Finland. In addition, Stalin and the Soviets committed crimes of war in murdering thousands of Polish officers in the Katyn forest and later in quietly killing German prisoners of war in the Gulag.

But it was to the category of crimes against humanity and genocide that Courtois devoted most of his attention, and here as well Communist regimes and the Soviet Union in particular were found guilty on numerous counts. In discussing the Nuremberg statutes in this context, Courtois noted that these statutes were of course applicable only to the Axis powers, Nazi Germany in particular. To address Communist crimes against humanity and genocide, Courtois made a rapid transition to French law. Here he found real grist for his mill. He cited in full the statutes governing both genocide and crimes against humanity in the 1992 French criminal code. In French law, both crimes are in essence defined as the complete or partial destruction of religious, ethnic, or national groups, or any other group arbitrarily designated, as part of a concerted plan that is politically motivated and deploys means including deportation, enslavement, and executions. These definitions are obviously broad enough to include any number of crimes committed by the Soviet Union as well as other Communist regimes.

On the face of it, Courtois's transition to French law was not unreasonable, in that statutes governing crimes against humanity and genocide are in fact incorporated into current French law, and the Nuremberg statutes were indeed only intended to be applied to the Axis powers. (As we have already seen, however, Courtois's scruples on this score did not prevent him from applying Nuremberg statutes concerning war crimes and crimes against peace to Soviet abuses). But given the moment that the *Black Book* appeared, when the Papon trial was fully underway in Bordeaux and stirring historical and legal controversies as well as painful memories, Courtois's move could not have been more provocative. In insisting on Communism's supposed crimes against humanity, Courtois was in effect further blurring the historical focus on Vichy and Nazi crimes and implying that a justice system that dealt only with the crimes of the latter was selective at the very least. In this light, Papon's trial appeared almost arbitrary, and it is no surprise, therefore, that Papon's lawyer, Jean-Marc Varaut, attempted to introduce the *Black Book* into evidence. The judge refused Varaut's request, but the point had been made nonetheless.

Courtois's initial numerical and moral comparisons of the Communist and Nazi crimes in his introduction to the *Black Book* were denounced and refuted by a number of critics from a variety of perspectives, historical as well as moral. In his interview in *L'Histoire*, Nicholas Werth reacted not only to Courtois's Communist body count but also to the figure Courtois had come up with for the number of Nazi dead. Werth asserted that while the figure for Communism's crimes was exaggerated, the body count attributed to Nazism was substantially underestimated. Werth insisted that any accurate count of Nazism's victims should also include the 50 million who died during World War II, because Nazi Germany was responsible for the conflagration. In an article in *Le Monde* coauthored with Jean-Louis Margolin, Werth also pointed out that Courtois's insistence on the equivalency of the victims obscured profound moral differences in the aims and ideals of the regimes in whose name these crimes were committed. Werth and Margolin stressed the fact that despite its crimes, Communism's dream was the liberation of the majority of mankind, whereas Nazism's racist ideology sought to "force most human beings into the shadows."[12] Making the same point in more concretely historical terms in his review of the English translation of the *Black Book*, Anson Rabinbach conceded that Courtois's claim that a Kulak child starved by Stalinism was worth no less than a Jewish child starved by Nazism was "irrefutable." Nevertheless, the statement said "nothing about the differences between a state-induced famine designed to subdue an independent peasantry and a state-directed genocide designed to eliminate the possibility of Jewish children now and forever."[13]

To his credit, Courtois was not without a pointed and indeed plausible rejoinder to the implications of this line of criticism. In the pages of *Le Monde* in late December 1997, he asserted bluntly: "One has the right to ask in what way it is more excusable to kill in the name of a hope for a better tomorrow than to murder for a racist doctrine. In what sense can self-delusion and hypocrisy be considered extenuating circumstances for mass crimes?"[14] Jacques Julliard, for one, agreed with Courtois in this instance. In his column in the weekly *Le Nouvel Observateur*, Julliard pointed out that if one insists on the inherent goodness of Communism because of the nobility of its ideal, in effect one reduces its crimes to so many "accidents"—a ludicrous perspective, to say the least, but one that served the interests and eased the consciences of nostalgic former Marxists still unable to swallow the bitter pill of reality.[15]

In *Stalinism and Nazism: History and Memory Compared*, published two years after the *Black Book*, Henry Rousso went at the problem differently, arguing first that on "the level of morality, there is absolutely no reason to hierarchically rank the victims of Nazism, Stalinism, or any other political system practicing terror."[16] While insisting that equal respect for *all* innocent victims of political evil in the name of memory is certainly legitimate, from the standpoint of historical analysis this says nothing about the "equivalency of the crimes of the executioners" or the political system or ideology in whose name the latter are acting.[17]

If Courtois's ultimate aim in comparing numerically, morally, and legally Communism's victims to Nazi victims was essentially to "tear down the mental Berlin Wall" that he claimed existed and to recognize Communism's victims and honor their memory, then this goal is not only morally legitimate, as Rousso's comment implies, it is in fact laudable. However, as Rousso and other critics have pointed out, from a historical perspective Courtois's aim is misleading. As Rousso asserts, in the postwar period there has been no lack of recognition or discussion of Communism's victims.[18] They have been described in the powerful testimonies and writings of Margerete Buber-Neumann and Vassili Grossman, not to mention Aleksandr Solzhenitsyn's monumental *Gulag Archipelago*, a bestseller in France in the mid-1970s.[19] In fact, as Anson Rabinbach points out, during the cold war period not only were Stalinist crimes discussed, "they were brought to the attention of the Western public long before there was any significant discussion of the Holocaust."[20]

Still, within the French context itself, Courtois's aim is not without merit. In the postwar period, of course, any number of French intellectuals, Communists, and fellow travelers have sought to justify, diminish, or even deny Communism's crimes not only out of sympathy for the Soviet Union but also, as Sartre would have it, not to discourage or disillusion France's own pro-Soviet workers. And from the late 1980s through the late 1990s and the moment the *Black Book* appeared, the memory of the Nazi Final Solution and especially Vichy complicity in that enterprise very much dominated national memory and certainly the national media. With these considerations in mind, Courtois's "memory militancy" on behalf of the victims of Communism is obviously not altogether misplaced.

The larger problem, not only from the standpoint of memory but of history, is that Courtois's crude comparisons of Communism and Nazism through their respective numbers of victims, their crimes against humanity, etc., were not put exclusively to the service of remembering Communism's victims. In fact, from the outset some of Courtois's harshest critics accused him of much baser aims and motives. Among those who condemned Courtois for his strategies, language, and ultimate aims was the distinguished Holocaust historian Annette Wieviorka. Wieviorka argued in *Le Monde* shortly after the *Black Book* appeared that in presenting exaggerated body counts, dwelling on the full range and horror of Communism's crimes, and, in effect, putting these crimes on at least an equal footing with Nazism's crimes, Courtois was attempting to *substitute* the memory of Communism's crimes for the memory of Nazi crimes. *The Black Book of Communism* was intended, Wieviorka believed, not to serve as a companion volume to Vassili Grossman's and Ilya Ehrenburg's *Black Book of Nazism*, which chronicled Nazi atrocities on the Eastern Front, but to displace it. Courtois's strategy, Wieviorka asserted, was also to distort the memory of the two crimes, and even history itself, by arguing that the memory of the Shoah, widely disseminated by the "international Jewish community" since the immediate postwar period, had completely overshadowed the crimes of Communism. Wievioka wondered to which international Jewish community was Courtois referring, given that the memory of the Shoah had only become predominant in the 1980s, not in the immediate postwar years. Courtois's argumentation and distortions of the facts were clearly not ideologically innocent. Finally, Wieviorka pointed out that Courtois's language was offensive as well, smacking as it did of the worst excesses of the *langue de bois*—the propagandistic rhetoric—of the Communist system he was denouncing. Courtois's introduction included liberal sprinklings of words such as "extermination" and "deportation" in discussing Soviet practices. The terms, Wieviorka maintained, had been directly lifted from Raul Hilberg's lexicon in *The Destruction of the European Jews* to hammer home the analytical identity of the Nazi Holocaust and Soviet crimes.[21]

In his response to his critics, Courtois dismissed Wieviorka's central charge that he was attempting to downplay and even efface Nazism's crimes and the Shoah in particular. "The victims of Communism do not erase the victims of Nazism," he wrote.[22] But as Courtois himself must have been fully aware, this pithy rejoinder hardly addressed the broader implications of Wieviorka's attack. In effect, she had accused Courtois not only of dangerous historical revisionism but of "negationism" itself. His credibility as a historian and, by extension, his personal politics were called into question, and in an extremely serious way.

Was there any legitimacy to Wieviorka's charges, and if so, what are their implications for our purposes here? In answering these questions, it is necessary to examine the broader debate over the comparison of Fascism and Communism, and especially Nazism and Communism, as it was renewed and debated in France in the 1990s. The starting point for the debate is not 1997 and the publication of the *Black Book* but 1995 and the publication of François Furet's *The Passing of an Illusion*.

The Passing of an Illusion is primarily a history and an indictment of Communism in the twentieth century. But in a chapter titled simply "Communism and Fascism," Furet discusses at length Communism, Nazism, and Italian Fascism and finds that all three shared two crucial characteristics. The first was a deep and abid-

ing hatred of the bourgeoisie, and the second—which resulted from a common experience of the horror and futility of trench warfare during World War I—was a
ready willingness to resort to violence and to appeal to elemental passions for the
purpose of achieving political ends.

In the course of these comparisons, Furet also discusses the viability of the totalitarian model. To its credit, he observes, it allows for valuable structural comparisons between Communism and Nazism in particular. But the danger is that it ignores specific historical circumstances that are crucial to understanding the origins
and crimes of both Soviet Communism and Nazism.

On the other hand, if we put aside the totalitarian model to focus almost exclusively on historical realities and their possible interconnections, we risk falling victim to false historical causalities such as the one proposed notoriously by the Berlin
historian Ernst Nolte that played a crucial role in launching the Historians' Debate
in Germany in the 1980s. Summed up succinctly by Ian Kershaw in a lecture given
at the German Institute in Paris in 1995, that causality affirms that "the Gulag was
the original, Auschwitz was the copy."[23] We shall return to the details as well as the
implications of Nolte's argument shortly.

Although it did not provoke a public controversy comparable to the one resulting from the publication of the *Black Book*, Furet's *Passing of an Illusion* certainly
generated extensive commentary and debate, especially on the subject of the comparison of Communism and Nazism. Historians including Renzo de Felice, Eric
Hobsbawm, and Ian Kershaw (whose lecture at the German Institute was in large
part a response to Furet) agreed or disagreed with Furet in the pages of *Le Débat* and
Commentaire, among other venues. Of these responses, the most fascinating and
troubling—and certainly the most illuminating where Stéphane Courtois and the
Black Book are concerned—was articulated by Ernst Nolte in a series of letters ex-
changed with Furet that were first published in the pages of an Italian journal, then
in *Commentaire*, and finally in a book titled *Fascism and Communism*.[24]

In their letters, Nolte and Furet cover not only the history and origins of the Nazi
and Soviet regimes and the viability of the concept of totalitarianism but more del-
icate matters such as the uniqueness and origins of the Shoah and the question of
historical revisionism. Early on, Nolte reveals a ready willingness to revisit his argument made during the Historians' Debate concerning the origins of Auschwitz and
even to give it a newer and more general, but equally insidious, twist. For "anyone,"
Nolte writes, who sought in a "resolute and consequent" manner to oppose Bolshevism and its "abolition of classes," would an analogous "radicality" not have been
essential? And what "radicality," what objective, could possibly be more logical,
under the circumstances, than to target the Jews?[25]

Nolte does not stop there. Even if one dismisses what is for Nolte the obvious causal link between the Gulag and Auschwitz, or even Soviet class war and Nazi "eliminationist anti-Semitism," to use Daniel Goldhagen's phrase,[26] there would still be what Nolte describes as a "rational core" to Nazi anti-Semitism. Jews were, after all, well represented in Germany's educated and wealthier classes and were therefore presumably well placed to serve as scapegoats for other groups. There was a preponderance of Jews in Socialist and Communist leadership roles, and since, for Nolte, Nazism would not have existed except in opposition to Marxism, the hatred of these Jews was "rational," if not normal.[27]

In the latter stages of his correspondence with Furet, Nolte raises two final issues that are worth stressing here. The first concerns the question of "historical revision" and specifically the denial of the Holocaust, and the second concerns the crimes of the Wehrmacht. In discussing the former, Nolte is perhaps at his most insidious. First, he argues that the facts and figures of the Holocaust are constantly being revised and that much of this revision is carried out by scholars with impeccable credentials. According to Nolte, Raul Hilberg, for example, argued in the mid-1980s that 2.5 million Jewish victims could not possibly have been killed at Auschwitz and that the number had to be revised downward to approximately 1 million. This figure, Nolte states, was subsequently generally accepted.[28]

If historical revisions of this magnitude can be proposed by legitimate scholars and accepted unproblematically, Nolte continues, what sense does it make to completely dismiss from the realm of possibility *any revision*, no matter how small, proposed by those who question the existence of the Holocaust? Why not consider the Holocaust deniers a kind of radical historiographical fringe, whose research does nevertheless reveal elements of the truth on occasion? This seems much wiser than to unjustly prosecute them under the law, as is the case in both Germany and France.[29]

In turning to the crimes of the Wehrmacht, Nolte is concerned primarily with the famous exhibit that circulated in Germany and caused a good deal of controversy. What really concerns Nolte is less his distaste for the exhibit and its inspiration—which he does denounce—than the fact that the seemingly endless emphasis on German crimes during World War II overshadows and in fact completely obscures Soviet and Red Army crimes that are treated as "nonexistent."[30]

In his exchange of letters with François Furet, Nolte draws, of course, on ideas and interpretations developed over many years and published in a series of books and articles that have become increasing controversial, if not scandalous. Nolte's insistence on Auschwitz and the Holocaust as a copy of and preemptive response to Soviet crimes in the East was a major, if not *the* major, precipitating event of the Historians' Debate in 1980s' West Germany. But Nolte had already achieved renown well before that, especially with the publication of *The Three Faces of Fascism*. Hailed at the time as an original and indeed groundbreaking comparative study of Charles Maurras's *Action Française*, Mussolinian Fascism, and Hitlerian National Socialism, in light of Nolte's subsequent works—and views—*The Three Faces of Fascism* has fallen on harder critical times. In an essay on Nolte in *Le Débat*, Denis Trierweiler has argued recently that the real aim of the work was to "de-Germanize National-Socialism in analyzing it as a European phenomenon."[31] In the same vein, the French historian Edourd Husson has described the work as "a passionate and failed attempt to definitively establish the fact that the principal sources of Nazism are not to be found in German history."[32] Nolte more or less concurs, stating in a recent interview that "it was not through the intermediaries of Bismarck and Bethmann Hollweg that I sought to open myself up to an understanding of Hitler and National Socialism, but rather through the intermediaries of Mussolini—and of Charles Maurras." Nolte continues by noting that what characterized all three of the latter was less hatred than "fear."[33]

If it is possible now to see *The Three Faces of Fascism* as perhaps an intellectually elaborate attempt to free Germany of its essential responsibility for Nazism, that assessment has emerged largely as the result of what might be described as the radicalization of Nolte's trajectory as a historian. The crucial move was the argument that it was Hitler's fear of a Soviet genocide that unleashed the Holocaust, but this move was anticipated by other claims that many historians find objectionable, to say the least.

In the foreword to the French edition of *The European Civil War*—the work that more than any other exposed the broad outlines of Nolte's revisionist view—Nolte reaffirms a definition of Fascism that defines it almost entirely as a reaction and opposition to Marxism, thus stripping it of other salient features, including an ideological "autonomy." More importantly, it tends to cast Fascist violence as a *defensive response*, thus reducing its culpability. "Fascism is an anti-Marxism that aims to destroy its enemy by developing an ideology radically opposed to the former's, even though it is close to it, and in applying methods almost identical to Marxism methods, but not without having transformed them in a characteristic manner, but this always within the unshakeable framework of self-affirmation and national autonomy." As Nolte also acknowledges, "This definition implies that Fascism's principal adversary, Marxism, must also be characterized as an exterminating ideology and that its practical application, Bolshevism, must be recognized as an exterminating reality as well."[34]

In *The European Civil War* and in interviews about the book, Nolte elaborates on many of his views expressed during the Historians' Debate as well as many of the dubious and troubling positions articulated in his exchanges with Furet. He affirms, for example, that his approach is one of "historico-genesis," which dismisses the widely accepted view that Fascism and Communism are "parallels." Nolte argues instead that Communism is an "original phenomenon" while Fascism—and especially Nazism—is a "derivative phenomenon" and that their confrontation shaped and determined the "European civil war" that began in 1917. As one might expect, this sets the stage for or, better yet, contextualizes the attendant and crucial claim that Nazism's criminality was a copy of and response to Bolshevism's criminality and that it grew out of a radical fear of Bolshevism whose destructiveness Germany was in a privileged position to appreciate. Nazism—a "radical fascism" in Nolte's view—was ultimately nothing more than an "imitative opposition."[35]

Also in *The European Civil War* and in other texts discussing its theses, Nolte takes up the notion of the "rational core" of Hitlerian anti-Semitism discussed in the exchange with Furet, which he describes as an "'extremization' of a rational perception, an excess." He stresses that the sharpest criticisms of the notion of the rational core come from what he describes as "Jewish thought" (*la pensée juive*), which in Nolte's view wrongly sees in the "rational core" a "justification" for Nazi crimes.[36]

Nolte's positions and interpretations articulated in *The European Civil War* have, of course, come under heavy fire on historical grounds. Charles Maier notes that Nolte seriously misapplies the notion of "civil war" in the first place. And in reducing Fascism to a "simple reaction to Bolshevism," Nolte denies not only Fascism's own (innate) capacity for prejudice and violence but the fact that Fascist hatred was directed not so much at Marxism as toward "government founded on discussions, elections, and free speech."[37] Edouard Husson offers a similar assessment of Nolte's myopic historical approach, asserting that in "the entirety of his notion of a European civil war, Nolte underestimates the reality of international conflicts as well as the endogenous character of a phenomenon like German nationalism."[38] Husson also points out the fundamental irrationality of Nolte's claims as to Hitler's overriding fear of Bolshevism and thus of Russia itself. Husson emphasizes the fact that Russia was the only country of the 1914 coalition that was actually *defeated* in 1918 by Germany and also that the Bolshevik regime itself signed a humiliating armistice with the Germans in March 1918 that ceded to the latter extensive lands in the East.[39] Under these circumstances, Hitler's monomaniacal "fear" of Russia and Bolshevism hardly seems plausible.

As for Nolte's "rational core" thesis, the criticism of other historians is equally sharp. Charles Maier dismisses the thesis on both counts cited by Nolte. Maier agrees with Nolte that there was a higher-than-proportional representation of Jews in Germany's and Central Europe's educated middle classes and that this made them "the natural targets of those who felt threatened" in their social situations. But while their persecution was "historically plausible," this did not make the burning of synagogues throughout Germany and the terrorizing of a group—most of whose members were "neither influential nor rich, and certainly not disloyal"—*rational*. And, Maier continues, as for the second count, is "the extermination of as many Jewish children as one could find" a *rational* response to the high correlation between Jews and the Bolshevik and Socialist leadership cadres?[40]

These (and other) criticisms of Nolte's work from a historical perspective are certainly telling. But for most historians and others who have taken Nolte on, what is most disturbing and in fact condemnable and unacceptable are the beliefs, attitudes, and prejudices that to all appearances underlie his historical interpretations as well as what might be described as the rhetorical practices and strategies he employs to make his points. Nolte was not trained as a historian, and although he was old enough to serve in Hilter's army, a minor medical condition prevented him from doing so. Thus, he did not experience the horrors of war directly. As he states in the foreword to the French edition of *The European Civil War*, in his view the combination of these factors reinforced his "desire for objectivity." But in other comments published recently, Nolte states lightheartedly that the first book he wrote as a child during the Weimar years was an attack on Bolshevism, which he recognized as the enemy of his and his family's staunch Catholicism. This "first encounter with Communism," as Nolte describes it, while merely anecdotal in nature, is hardly consonant with the later "desire for objectivity" that Nolte claims for himself.[41]

But Nolte's early animosity toward Communism is much less the issue than, obviously, his attitude toward Nazism, the Holocaust, and historical revisionism itself. As discussed earlier, a number of historians have underscored the fact that from its inception Nolte's historical project has served to de-Fascistize and de-Nazify German history by making Fascism a "European" phenomenon and Nazi crimes merely "imitations" of or "pale reactions" to the original crimes of others.[42] Moreover, the exchanges with François Furet suggest at best a thinly veiled sympathy, in the name of "truth," for a disturbing historical revisionism and even the arguments of Holocaust deniers.

In his "Open Letter to Ernst Nolte" published in *Le Débat*, Maier argues not only that Nolte's historical views are insidious—and politically motivated—but that his style of argumentation, his manner of posing "legitimate" historical questions and of making comparisons, is, in its deliberate ambiguity, designed to legitimize indefensible positions:

> The problem your work poses for me is [that] the thesis that you propose to defend is presented only in an indirect fashion and it remains intangible. This ambiguity is the result of several rhetorical strategies: first a strategy of misplaced interrogations; second, constant recourse to minimization; third, a fog of intermediate comparisons designed to displace the heart of the discussion of monstrous deaths onto other potential collective crimes. Some questions are not asked directly, but rather in the form of questions concerning the legitimacy of questions as, for example, in the following instance (permit me to paraphrase): "Far be it from me to deny the existence of the Holocaust, but is it truly false to observe that Zyklon B was used to exterminate vermin at Auschwitz or that the crematoriums could never have eliminated as many bodies as is claimed? Is it not legitimate to ask if . . . [?]" Because we believe in freedom of expression, we all feel ourselves constrained to recognize that we cannot censor questions. But all questions do not have the same status or equal legitimacy. The question that one asks as a specialist is, is it sincerely posed in order to forward research, or is it not simply a strategy of disculpation? . . . You ask all the questions that revisionists ask, without the shadow of a hesitation: your writing treats these pedantic obscenities as if they were slightly disagreeable speculations but imminently interesting nonetheless. . . . you deny anti-Semitism in the indicative all the while voicing it in the subjunctive, or on occasion, [you express], in the form of interrogatives, all sorts of anti-Semitic conjectures.[43]

Many of the strategies and tactics Maier describes here are also seen in, for example, Nolte's exchanges with Furet.

Ultimately, in stressing the originary nature of Bolshevik crimes and Nazism's "imitation" of them, as well as lending at least a veiled credence to the speculations of the Holocaust deniers, Nolte is, to all appearances, challenging the uniqueness of the Holocaust at the very least and at the outside insinuating that it may not have existed, certainly in the form and dimensions generally ascribed to it. For years both of these issues have been at the heart of historical debate and controversy, the broad parameters of which are beyond the scope of the present study. But what Enzo Traverso describes as Nolte's "wrong, ideologically insidious comparison"[44] of Bolshevik crimes and Nazi copies and the political implications of that linkage are very relevant to our purposes here. The comparison of Communist and Nazi crimes is at the very heart of the controversy surrounding Stéphane Courtois's introduction to the *Black Book*. Equally important, Courtois has endorsed many of Nolte's views and, in a number of ways, become a sponsor of sorts for his work in France. Courtois, in fact, wrote a laudatory preface to the French translation of *The European Civil*

War and, more recently, has published other texts by Nolte in the series he edits for the Monacan publisher the Éditions du Rocher.

In his preface to *The European Civil War,* Courtois begins with a favorable appreciation of Nolte's role in the Historians' Debate, arguing that the latter was "attempting to reinsert the history of Nazism in German and *European* history."[45] As the comments of Edouard Husson and Charles Maier cited earlier would suggest, many historians would question that this was indeed Nolte's role and aim.

But more importantly, Courtois also expresses his support for what he describes as Nolte's two key, controversial theses: first, the "causal link" among Soviet crimes, the Nazi Holocaust, and, more broadly, the attendant notion of the "European civil war," and second, the "rational core" of the Hitlerian anti-Semitism. On the first score, Courtois states simply that 1989, German reunification, and the collapse of the Berlin Wall all proved that Nolte was right. But he also offers what might be described as a "geographical reason" accounting for Nolte's perspicacity in the matter by stressing that Nolte, as a German, "had direct and often rough (*rugueux*) contact with the Slavic world." This allowed him (and Germans more generally) to understand "Bolshevik and Soviet reality." By contrast, the French, geographically removed from this reality, only had, and have, a "largely imaginary" vision of it. In collapsing Bolshevism and the Soviet regime into the "Slavic world" with its "rough contacts," Courtois also seems to be seconding Nolte's claim for Hitler's overriding—and justified—fear of a kind of Asiatic threat.[46]

On the second point, the "rational core" of Nazi anti-Semitism, Courtois states the following:

> Nolte advances the idea that, given the circumstances, Hitlerian anti-Semitism nourished itself on the powerful presence of militants of Jewish origin in both the German and the Russian Communist movements. In doing so, Nolte reminds us that the historian cannot content himself to evaluate men and facts solely in the light of his own values. If he truly wishes to explain a phenomenon and seek to render it intelligible, to uncover its "rational core," he must penetrate and understand the values and the logic of the actors themselves, no matter how far removed they are from those of the historian. Following this approach, moreover, in no way implies an allegiance to [the values or logic of the actors] nor a justification of the phenomenon itself.[47]

Whereas Maier (among many other historians) finds Nolte's "rational core thesis" preposterous and exposes its own irrationality, Courtois considers it the mark of the truly probing and objective historian.

In regard to Courtois's affirmation of the accuracy of Nolte's "causal nexus" and the overarching notion of the European civil war, Courtois's reasoning not only mirrors Nolte's own but runs counter to François Furet's views on Communism and Fascism in *The Passing of an Illusion*. Courtois recalls that for Furet, Communism and Fascism were both engendered by the terrible trauma of World War I; thus, the terrible confrontations and destruction of World War II originated in 1914. For Nolte, of course, they began in 1917 with the Bolshevik Revolution. Courtois argues, first, that Furet's thesis is inadequate because not all of the principal belligerents who shared the terrible experience of trench warfare subsequently embraced brutal and extremist ideologies. England and France, for example, "returned to normal," and there was therefore no "inevitable continuity of mass murder from the war to the postwar period." By contrast, Courtois continues, once Lenin declared a "global civil war," he inaugurated "an uncontrollable process."[48]

Where and how did this process end? Following Nolte again, Courtois argues that the conclusion of the "European civil war"—and the demise of Communism—got underway with the fall of the Soviet state's "partner adversaries," Fascist Italy in 1943 and especially Nazi Germany in 1945. Henceforth, the Soviets found themselves confronted with a democratic enemy that didn't desire or thrive on war but was not about to let itself be destroyed, either by "national civil wars" or by an international war. Deprived of partners that matched and opposed its own violent dynamic on equal terms, the Soviet state and the Communist system ended up imploding. Hence, the final proof of the validity of Nolte's "causal nexus" revealed itself in 1989.[49]

In seconding Nolte's principal theses in his preface to the French edition of *The European Civil War*, Stéphane Courtois embraces at the very least Nolte's myopic and schematic views of twentieth-century history as well as his deliberately and dangerously reductive approach to dealing with the origins and respective natures of Europe's totalitarian regimes. From the perspective of most historians of twentieth-century Europe, this makes Courtois guilty of poor historical judgment. But sharing someone's historical perspectives does not necessary imply sharing the political views or ideological positions underlying them. For example, there is no indication that Courtois can be accused of sharing what Maier, Husson, and others see as Nolte's not-so-secret intent to rid Germany of the historical responsibility of Nazism. If anything, given Courtois's focus on Communism's victims and the West's supposed amnesia where those crimes are concerned, his own overriding concern—his own "political motivation"—would be to emphasize the Soviets' overwhelming culpability rather than Germany's innocence. Of course, to a significant degree, this amounts to the same thing.

One could argue that in his preface to *The European Civil War* Courtois justifies and indeed endorses Nolte's "rational core" thesis, making him complicitous, at least from the perspective of what Nolte calls "Jewish thought," in justifying Nazi crimes by defending their "rationality." But as previous discussions should make clear, Courtois in effect neatly dodges this issue by arguing, in abstract terms, that the historian's search for such a "rational core" is his responsibility in the name of historical acuity and objectivity.

As these remarks suggest, Courtois's preface to *The European Civil War* does not necessarily implicate him in Nolte's ideologically loaded reading of history or his slippery, rhetorical lip service to revisionism and even negationism. But in other contexts as well as in the broader implications of the introduction of the *Black Book* itself, Courtois does ultimately reveal himself to be complicitous not only with a fundamentally anti-Semitic reading of history but, through some of the "evidence" provided in his introduction, with the French (and European) extreme Right today.

To begin with, Annette Wieviorka is accurate in her criticism that Courtois's statements concerning the constant promotion of the Holocaust by the "international Jewish community" is historically misleading and—although she does not state it explicitly—smacks of the Jewish conspiratorial stereotypes often invoked by anti-Semites to denounce supposed Jewish threats. She is also accurate in her claim that Courtois's use of the same terminology to describe Soviet and Nazi crimes is politically loaded and that Courtois can hardly be unaware of this. In fact, in his most recent book dealing with Communist crimes and the history and legacy of the *Black Book*, Courtois repeats the same technique, this time referring to the respective memories of these crimes—or, more accurately, their obfuscation. Courtois labels as "negationism" what he considers to be the denial of Communist crimes.[50]

But in a broader sense, Courtois is most substantially complicitous with Nolte's historical revisionism less because of the reasons for which Wieviorka condemns him than because of the ways in which the arguments and statistics he presents in his introduction to the *Black Book* coincide with, and even reinforce, Nolte's historical arguments. In effect, Courtois's arguments as well as much of the information provided in his introduction not only serve as *pièces à l'appui*—evidence in support of Nolte's reasoning—but provide, in a perverse fashion, the introduction and conclusion of Nolte's argument. Courtois's discussion of the sheer horror and number of Communism's crimes—and especially the crimes of Leninism and Stalinism—appears to lend credence to Nolte's assertion that Hitler and the Nazis had *every reason* to fear the Soviet menace. They had to come up with a radical and preemptive measure to stymie it, and hence their effort to "copy the Gulag."

At the other end of the process, Courtois's argument picks up the baton again. If the ferocity of Soviet oppression drove the Nazis to respond, and if the crimes of the two regimes were by and large on the same footing—as Courtois so tenaciously maintains—then the only logical and just thing to do is hold Nuremberg trials for the crimes of Communism.

In fairness to Courtois, it should be pointed out again that he does not follow Nolte in his pointed defense of the legitimacy and tactics of some Holocaust deniers. However, Courtois's insistence on and exaggeration of Communism's body count disturbingly echoes the tactics and approach of other negationists, especially those interested in grisly historical comparisons as a way of de-emphasizing the murderousness of the Holocaust to the point of insignificance.

As an example, in June 1996, a little more than a year before the *Livre noir* appeared, the French public was shocked when Father Abbé Pierre, the renowned advocate of the homeless, sprang to the defense of his old friend Roger Garaudy. A former Communist, then a Christian, and finally a devoted follower of Islam, Garaudy had recently published a book titled *Les mythes fondateurs de la politique israélienne* (The founding myths of Israeli politics). The book's main thesis is that Israel exploits the "myth" of the Holocaust in order to justify its own genocide of the Palestinians, which Garaudy labels "Zionist colonialism."[51]

But what is interesting about the book for our purposes is that one of Garaudy's strategies of downplaying and ultimately effacing the Nazi genocide of the Jews is to argue that it was nothing in comparison with the American genocide of black Africans. Following a perverse and convoluted logic that he nevertheless labels "scientific," Garaudy asserts that the number of victims of America's genocide of black Africans exceeded 100 million. He reasons that since America "deported" 10 million to 20 million Africans into slavery, and since it is safe to assume that ten Africans were killed trying to escape for each one captured, the real figure for the genocide is between 100 million and 200 million. The enormity of Garaudy's figure as well as the crudeness of his comparisons and calculations is reminiscent of Courtois's approach in the *Black Book.*

Finally, given the disturbing resonances of Courtois's introduction and the subject matter of the book itself, it is not surprising that *The Black Book of Communism* was welcomed by the extreme Right in France (and in the United States as well).[52] The New Right philosopher Alain de Benoist gleefully reiterated Courtois's figures for Communism's worldwide body count and even asserted that evidence suggests Courtois had been too conservative in his estimates. Without missing a beat, Benoist then took up the major theses of Nolte's approach and plugged in figures and arguments from the *Black Book* as needed.[53]

But as Anson Rabinbach points out, the uses to which the French far Right put the *Black Book* were not purely historical or academic. The National Front quickly included the book on its must-read list and advertised it with the slogan "We are awaiting an act of repentance from the French Communists." Aside from the propaganda possibilities for the likes of Le Pen, according to the Socialists at least, efforts by the traditional conservatives—the Union pour la Démocratie Française (UDF)—to exploit the *Black Book* to their advantage in denouncing their opponents in the national assembly would encourage, in the long run, an alliance between their own ranks and the far Right. While Le Pen's victory in the first round of the 2002 presidential elections certainly put a definitive end to any possibility of such an alliance, it is also true that renegade elements in the UDF did join forces with the National Front in regional elections in 1998 to ensure their own victory.

I am aware of no evidence that Stéphane Courtois—or any of his coauthors, for that matter—endorsed any of this, and writing historical studies denouncing the crimes of Communism in no way implies an engagement on behalf of France's extreme Right. However, it is hard to imagine that Courtois was ignorant of the propaganda potential of his inflammatory introduction to the *Black Book*. It is also hard to imagine that he was unaware that the publisher of Nolte's *European Civil War*, for which Courtois wrote the preface, also published "classic" Fascist texts by figures including the Belgian Rexist leader Léon Degrelle. In these contexts at least, it seems fair to say that Courtois was complicitous with political agendas and cultural and intellectual projects that hardly championed the values and principles of a liberal antiracist democracy.

But ultimately, it is perhaps accurate to say that Courtois's historical project as well as his commitment to the memory of Communism's victims is most *politically* tainted, and perhaps even compromised, by his allegiance to the intellectually insidious work of Ernst Nolte. And it is important to stress that Nolte's work is politically loaded in terms of both history and current political realities. Invoking in a recent interview his "rational core" thesis once again, Nolte chooses to apply it not to the historical context of Hitler's hatred and persecution of the Jews but to Jean-Marie Le Pen's first-round victory in the 2002 presidential elections. Nolte states that the 18 percent of the vote Le Pen received is not "a negligible quantity" and that "the citizens" who voted for Le Pen "were expressing something that must henceforth be seen as semi-legitimate, as possessing a sort of legitimacy." He concludes that because the Left is admitting "poor Third-Worlders," it is disenfranchising the nation's poor. For Nolte, this is the "rational core" of Le Pen's popularity, and his *legitimacy*.[54]

As is the case with the so-called rational core of Nazi anti-Semitism, Nolte's application of the notion here is schematic, selective, and profoundly misleading. It effectively brackets the racism and xenophobia of the National Front, and certainly many of its followers, while casting its very negative politics in an essentially *positive* light. This is hardly an example of the objectivity Nolte claims for himself, and one wonders if this dangerous application of his ideas to the circumstances of the present has given Courtois pause in regard to application of those ideas to the past.

Conclusion

The present study has dealt essentially with two topics: the complicity with reactionary, antidemocratic, and often racist politics of French writers and intellectuals from two different decades, and, especially with regard to the writers of the 1990s, what might best be described as the coercive power of memory. There are, of course, enormous differences between the two historical periods considered here, and it is only natural that the wages of political commitment and the reasons underlying complicitous involvements and attitudes should vary profoundly. The Nazi Occupation of the 1940s was worlds removed from the France of the 1990s, not only in terms of the dangers and hardships involved during the Dark Years but in the ways in which the individual *living under* Vichy and Nazism comprehended that experience, as opposed to someone fifty years later looking back on the period and its implications and lessons. The extraordinarily different and often fragmentary and misguided ways in which Henry de Montherlant, Alphonse de Châteaubriant, and Jean Giono understood the realities and aims of Hitler and Pétain, saw their interests and views coinciding with these aims, and "accommodated" themselves to them exemplify the divergence among those who experienced Vichy and the Nazi Occupation directly. By contrast, despite the range of their knowledge and understanding of Vichy and Nazism, and despite their very different choices as to how to *apply* that past to the present, Alain Finkielkraut, Régis Debray, and even Stéphane Courtois largely share a common view of the evil that past represents.

Although clear differences exist between the two periods and among the six writers, similarities are also evident. Despite Montherlant's taste for force, Châteaubriant's apocalyptic millenarianism, and Giono's pacifism, all three shared a similar vision of prewar French "decadence" that played a powerful role in their wartime allegiances. Like Debray, Finkielkraut, and Courtois fifty years later, all three sought to explain their political complicity with reference to their own visions of history—visions that, they believed, justified their choices in the present. Montherlant and Châteaubriant never renounced their visions and therefore never acknowledged the intellectual errors—and worse—of their political positions during the war. To a significant degree, the same is true of the choices of Finkielkraut, Debray, and Courtois in the 1990s.

The second major topic dealt with in this study concerns the power of memory, in this case the coercive influence of the memory of Vichy and Nazism as a hermeneutic device and moral compass in the intellectual discourse of 1990s France. In the chapters on Finkielkraut and Croatia, Debray and Kosovo, and Courtois and the *Black Book of Communism*, the power of that memory should be obvious. It was in fact a defining trait, if not *the* defining trait, of the decade, a continuation and intensification of what Henry Rousso labeled the "Obsession" phase of the Vichy syndrome that began in the 1970s.[1]

But now, in the early twenty-first century, the power of that memory is fading, if not already extinguished. Several important factors and events explain this development. The first was, undoubtedly, the Papon trial in 1997–1998. Maurice Papon was the last of the figures associated with Vichy to be charged with crimes against humanity for activities during the Occupation. After Papon was convicted and sentenced, there were no more well-known and widely discussed representatives—and living reminders—of France's criminal past, at least to serve as defendants in highly publicized and mediatized trials.

Aside from painful reminders of the Vichy past and the Nazi Final Solution, the trial itself created a general sense of malaise, frustration, and even failure that compromised its historical and moral efficacy and exemplariness. Rather than offering France a clear and uplifting opportunity to deal with the most terrible moment in its recent past, the Papon trial, which lasted a seemingly endless six months, presented instead the spectacle of needless histrionics by lawyers and inadequate and questionable memories from witnesses. More importantly, it failed to illuminate the Vichy past and make it comprehensible to the general public. And it failed as an exercise in justice as well. Papon's sentence was handed down by a jury too young to have firsthand experience of the historical circumstances surrounding the crimes of the accused. This struck many as ludicrous. And the sentence Papon received—ten years in prison—hardly seemed appropriate given the magnitude and horror of the crimes with which he was associated or the historical importance of the trial. Finally, the comic opera of Papon's flight to Switzerland under an assumed name a year later to avoid imprisonment lent, ex post facto, an air of ridiculousness to the entire proceedings. Added to this was outrage when Papon was the first prisoner in France to be freed in fall 2002 in the wake of a new statute that required the release of prisoners too frail to take the rigors of incarceration. Rather than provide an adequate and satisfying means for France to understand and come to terms with the historical and moral implications of its Vichy past, the Papon trial as well as the hopes invested in it ended, in the eyes of many, in futility.[2] Under these circumstances, why remember?

As the discussion of the *Black Book of Communism* also confirms, even at the moment that the Papon trial was getting underway, *other* memories and histories besides Vichy and Nazism were imposing themselves on the French national psyche and demanding their own role in how the present should be interpreted and judged. Stéphane Courtois's effort to "tear down the mental Berlin Wall" put the memory and history of Communism front and center and, in so doing, offered a rival place of memory to Vichy and Nazism that challenged their negative moral exemplariness.

Also during the Papon trial, the history and memory of the Algerian War of Independence (1954–1962) made its presence felt. Early in the proceedings in Bordeaux, Papon's role as prefect of the Paris police took center stage in regard to the deaths of arguably hundreds of Algerian protesters in Paris in October 1961. Vichy was supplanted briefly during the trial not only historically but legally and morally, since many argued (not unreasonably) that Papon should *also* be charged with crimes against humanity for his actions during the Algerian War.[3]

In the spring of 2001 the troubled memory of Algeria and its own ghosts received another jolt when General Paul Aussaresses published his memoirs, *Services Spéciaux: Algérie, 1955–1957*. An intelligence officer during the conflict, Aussaresses proudly discussed his activities in torturing and even executing Algerian rebels. He expressed no regrets, claiming that his actions were justified in the name of serving his country. To complicate matters, Aussaresses had also been in the Resistance during the Occupation. While the scandal provoked by Aussaresses did not last long, it did serve to put the so-called war without a name very much back in public view and suggested once again that the memory of Vichy and Nazism was not the *only* moral evil that could serve as a compass for interpreting the present.

But the impact of these events and the historical memories and traumas they brought to the surface were by no means the only incidents that, to a very significant extent, turned France away from the Vichy past and forced it to consider new moral and political dilemmas in the present. In a lecture delivered to a National Endowment for the Humanities summer 2003 seminar for schoolteachers held in Paris,

Henry Rousso argued that the "extreme violence" and global implications of the 11 September 2001 attacks in the United States had changed the stakes completely in France and the world at the start of the new century. After 9/11, Rousso argued, the issue could no longer be "assimilating the past"—it now had to be to "think the future" (*penser l'avenir*).

The necessity of thinking of the future in the wake of 9/11 had important implications in France. Tensions between the Muslim world and the West, cast dramatically into focus by the destruction of the World Trade Center and fueled by the interminable conflict between Israelis and Palestinians, certainly stimulated an increase in anti-Semitic violence and vandalism in France. But, as Alain Finkielkraut argued, this was a "new" anti-Semitism only tangentially linked to traditional, historical European forms of that prejudice and hatred.[4]

Tensions between Muslim and Western—and specifically French—outlooks and traditions also influenced the debate over the wearing of the *foulard* (scarf) by Muslim women in French public schools. The impact of the law forbidding the wearing of the traditional headdress in primary and secondary schools, enacted in fall 2004, is yet to be fully determined.

If 9/11 forced the French as well as the world to think of the future, or at least the present and not the past, so too, ultimately, did Jean-Marie Le Pen's stunning first-round victory in the presidential elections of spring 2002. Initially, of course, Le Pen's shocking success stirred memories of France's and Europe's dark past. This was natural enough, given the National Front's historical pedigree: a number of founding members were former collaborators and pro-Nazi zealots. Many of those who protested Le Pen's success made the linkage with Fascism's past explicit in the protest posters and banners they paraded in the streets of French cities. But in the final analysis, Le Pen's brief moment in the sun helped extinguish rather than revive historical ghosts. Galvanized by what it perceived as a *present* danger, the French electorate delivered a crushing blow to Le Pen and the extreme Right in the second round. The power of the memory of Vichy and Nazism had always benefitted from Le Pen's presence, but his defeat diminished that power.[5]

No event forced France and the world to look more at the present and toward the future than the Bush administration's decision to invade Iraq. French outrage in the face of the American action not only further riveted attention on the global dangers of the invasion but dredged up historical contexts to explain and judge the present in ways that cast America, not Vichy or Nazi Germany, in the role of evildoer in the world. Specifically, the same kind of visceral hatred of America that characterized most of the French intelligentsia during the cold war years returned in full force. And whereas in the 1990s innumerable books, television shows, and radio programs dealt with the history of Vichy, Nazism, and their multifaceted legacies, the tendency in the last few years has been to focus on American political, military, and cultural hegemony in order to denounce it.

Ultimately, what Tzvetan Todorov aptly describes as today's "New World Disorder," along with the many crises it engenders, is likely to continue to challenge the wisdom of constantly assimilating the past and relying too narrowly on its specific lessons.[6] To the degree that Finkielkraut, Debray, and Courtois did precisely that, their interpretations of events as well as the urgency of their involvements seem almost as removed from us today as do those of Montherlant, Châteaubriant, and Giono.

But if the historical crises of the recent and not-so-recent past seem to fade quickly from view in a new century dominated by a global and ill-defined "war on terror," the complicity of writers and intellectuals with antidemocratic politics seems more of a constant in terms of motives, expressions, and attendant blind spots. In all the cases studied here, political complicity derives from a combination of passions and ideals—whether positive or negative, whether emotional or intellectual (or sexual, in Montherlant's case)—as well as a desire to make the present conform to a particular and generally skewed vision of the past. In all cases, the full implications of these involvements or positions are neither fully grasped nor understood by their authors due to a lack of objectivity, rationality, or imagination or because of willful ignorance. The results are always unfortunate and often disastrous.

Nevertheless, each case of complicity offered here provides lessons for us today in a world in which we are all more cognizant of, and even implicated in, the political horrors and human disasters occurring around us. Together, these cases of complicity should serve to remind us that misguided political involvements are complicated and very dangerous things. Perhaps paradoxically, given the motivating historical circumstances, these cases of complicity should also remind us that political responsibility and action in the present are absolutely necessary.

Notes

INTRODUCTION

1. Burrin, *France under the Germans*, pp. 2–3.

2. As Mark Sanders demonstrates in his study of writers who resisted Apartheid in South Africa, complicity with political authority is often unavoidable even in the act of resistance to that authority. See *Complicities: The Intellectual and Apartheid*, especially the introduction.

3. Burrin, *France under the Germans*, p. viii.

4. Todorov, *L'Homme dépaysé*, p. 31.

5. Lefort, *La complication*, p. 11.

6. Todorov, *L'Homme dépaysé*, p. 36.

7. Baudrillard, *The Gulf War Did Not Take Place*, p. 23.

8. Kutz, *Complicity*, p. 1.

9. Ibid., pp. 1, 2.

10. Ibid., p. 271.

11. Mulisch, *The Assault*, p. 181.

12. Ibid., p. 184.

13. For an excellent discussion of these moments in Malle's films and their implication, see Higgins, *New Novel, New Wave, New Politics*, pp. 186–206.

14. Lilla, *The Reckless Mind*.

15. Witt, *The Search for Modern Tragedy*, p. 114.

16. Wolin, *Heidegger's Children*, pp. 191, 9.

17. For a discussion of Montherlant in the de Man affair, see my article "Find a Victim: Montherlant and the de Man Affair."

18. Burrin, *France under the Germans*, p. 2.

19. Wohl, *The Generation of 1914*, pp. 25–26.

20. Finkielkraut, *L'Imparfait du présent*, p. 3.

21. The original French title of Conan and Rousso's *Vichy: An Everpresent Past* is *Vichy: Un passé qui ne passe pas* (Vichy: A past that will not pass).

22. See Lecarme, *Drieu La Rochelle*.

23. Browning, *Ordinary Men*, p. xx.

24. Ibid.

25. Benhabib, "Taking Ideas Seriously."

26. Lilla, *The Reckless Mind*, pp. 193–216.

27. Stoekl, "Mark Lilla: *The Reckless Mind*," 89–93.

CHAPTER 1: HENRY DE MONTHERLANT

1. For a general discussion of Montherlant's theater as tragedy, see my *"Service inutile": A Study of the Tragic in the Theatre of Henry de Montherlant*. More recent discussions of Montherlant's plays along these lines and in the context of the Occupation will be discussed later in this chapter.

2. *Le songe* and *Les bestiaires* are contained in Montherlant, *Romans et oeuvres de fiction non théâtrales*.

3. Conversation with the author, December 6, 1980.

4. Beauvoir, "La pensée de droite, aujourd'hui."

5. See Wohl, *The Generation of 1914*, especially pp. 22–35.

6. Witt, *The Search for Modern Tragedy*, p. 17.

7. Guéhenno, *Journal des années noires*, p. 15.

8. Ibid., p. 58.

9. Ibid., p. 170.

10. Ibid., p. 75.

11. Ibid., p. 72.

12. Ibid., p. 208.

13. Ibid., p. 172.

14. Ibid., p. 147.

15. Ibid., p. 148.

16. Added, *Le théâtre dans les années Vichy*, pp. 321–322.

17. Montherlant, "Mémoire," p. 274.

18. Ibid., p. 277.

19. Sipriot, *Montherlant sans masque*, Vol. 1, *L'Enfant prodigue*, p. 99; Montherlant's emphasis.

20. Montherlant, "Jeunesse 1938."

21. Peyrefitte and Sipriot, *Henry de Montherlant-Roger Peyrefitte Correspondance*, p. 152.

22. Burrin, *France under the Germans*, p. 344.

23. The text in *Les Lettres Françaises* reads: "When Montherlant declines an invitation to Weimar after having solicited it, it is because of the announcement of the first Russian successes. Coward steeped in cowardice." All passages quoted from *Les Lettres Françaises* are quoted in Rosenberg, "Montherlant and the Critics of the French Resistance."

24. Guéhenno, *Journal des années noires*, p. 213.

25. The tribute is contained in Montherlant, *Essais*, pp. 1483–1489, although it is not identified as having originally appeared in the *Deutschland Frankreich*.

26. See Assouline, *L'Epuration des intellectuels*, p. 39.

27. Céline, *Lettres à son avocat*, p. 39.

28. Loiseaux, *La littérature de la défaite et de la collaboration*, p. 299.

29. Montherlant, "Mémoire," p. 300.

30. Montherlant, *Essais*, p. 929.

31. Ibid., pp. 932–933.

32. Montherlant, "Mémoire," p. 209.

33. Montherlant, *Essais*, p. 952.

34. Quoted in Verdès-Leroux, *Refus et violences*, p. 243.

35. Montherlant, *Essais*, p. 957.

36. Ibid., pp. 955–956.

37. Ibid., p. 960.

38. Belot, "Rebatet," p. 945.

39. Montherlant, "Mémoire," p. 301.

40. Ibid., p. 302.

41. Sipriot, *Montherlant sans masque*, Vol. 2, "*Écris avec ton sang*," pp. 175–176.

42. H.K.P.K., "Henry de Montherlant."

43. Montherlant, "Le goût d'attaquer."

44. Theweleit's massive two-volume study provides a great deal of evidence in support of the notion that hatred and fear of women are central to the Fascist mind set and are, in fact, the source of its violent impulses. For an excellent summary of Theweleit's project and the relation of his theory of Fascism to other such theories, see Benjamin and Rabinach, *Male Fantasies*, pp. ix–xxv.

45. Mort, "Montherlant devant lui-même."

46. Ibid.

47. This is the assessment of Richard Cobb, who lumps Montherlant together with the likes of Brasillach and Drieu La Rochelle. See Cobb, *French and Germans*, p. 161. As I shall argue here, Montherlant's case is more ambiguous than Cobb acknowledges.

48. Montherlant, *Romans et oeuvres de fiction non théâtrales*, p. 181.

49. Ibid., p. 139.

50. Simone de Beauvoir, *The Second Sex*, uses all of these descriptives to sum up Montherlant's attitude toward women. See the section titled "Montherlant on the Bread of Disgust," pp. 224–242.

51. Ibid., p. 226.

52. Ibid., p. 226.

53. Ibid., p. 225.

54. For Kaplan's discussion of the "fascist fantasy narrative" and Mafarka in particular, see her *Reproductions of Banality*, pp. 76–87.

55. Montherlant, *Essais*, p. 505.

56. Raimond, *Les romans de Montherlant*, p. 129.

57. Montherlant, *Essais*, p. 575.

58. Ibid., p. 578. It is important to note that *La rose de sable* and the essay "La sympathie" are not the only examples in Montherlant's prewar oeuvre where the spirit of charity leads to leftist sympathies. During the late 1920s, Montherlant wrote a novel titled *Moustique, ou l'hôpital*, which was sympathetic to the needs of the working class. The novel, however, was not published during the writer's lifetime.

59. Ibid., p. 586.

60. Perruchot, *Montherlant*, p. 153.

61. Montherlant, *Romans et oeuvres de fiction non théâtrales*, p. 1096.

62. Ibid., pp. 1090–1091.

63. *La reine morte* was inspired by Luis Vélez de Guevara's Spanish Golden Age play *Reinar después de morir*, which Montherlant read at the suggestion of Jean-Louis Vaudoyer, director of the Comédie Française.

64. Montherlant, *Théâtre*, p. 148.

65. Ibid., p. 151.

66. Ibid., p. 161.

67. Beauvoir, *The Second Sex*, pp. 240–241.

68. Frese Witt, *The Search for Modern Tragedy*, p. 204.

69. Krauss, *The Drama of Fallen France*, p. 159.

70. Jackson, *France*, p. 314.

71. Quoted in Verdès-Leroux, *Refus et violences*, p. 247.

72. Ibid., p. 392.

73. Ibid., p. 475.

74. Guerard, "Montherlant and the Collaborators," p. 98.

75. White, *Genet*, pp. 161–162.

76. Montherlant, *Essais*, p. 571.

77. The lead-off essay in *Service inutile* is titled "Chevalerie du néant" (The knighthood of nothingness). See Montherlant, *Essais*, pp. 595–599.

78. Ibid., p. 963.

79. Montherlant, "Mémoire," p. 311.

80. Ibid., p. 280.

81. Ibid., p. 283.

82. Quoted in Verdès-Leroux, *Refus et violences*, p. 392.

CHAPTER 2: ALPHONSE DE CHÂTEAUBRIANT

1. On the Hussards and their role in rehabilitating collaborationist writers, see Hewitt, *Literature and the Right in Postwar France*, pp. 5–35.

2. Paulhan, *De la paille et du grain*, p. 67.

3. Ibid., p. 107.

4. Ibid., p. 137.

5. Ibid., p. 136.

6. See, for example, Carroll, *French Literary Fascism*, and Kaplan, *Reproductions of Banality*.

7. The details of Châteaubriant's German trips are provided in Maugendre, *Alphonse de Châteaubriant*, chap. 3.

8. Châteaubriant quoted in ibid., p. 178.

9. Ibid., p. 190.

10. Châteaubriant, *La gerbe des forces*, p. 158.

11. Ibid., p. 140.

12. Châteaubriant, *Cahiers*, p. 205.

13. Châteaubriant, *La gerbe des forces*, p. 119.

14. Ibid., p. 24.

15. Editorial in *La Gerbe*, 10 December 1942.

16. Châteaubriant, *La gerbe des forces*, p. 136.

17. Ibid., p. 161.

18. Ibid., p. 160.

19. Ibid., p. 69.

20. Ibid., p. 136.

21. Châteaubriant, *Cahiers*, pp. 161–162. These passages are dated April 1936.

22. One favorable review of *La gerbe des forces* appeared in *l'Oeuvre*. The author of the review, a left-wing pacifist named M. G. Martin, praised the book for its pacifist message. See Serant, *Le romantisme fasciste*, p. 134.

23. Paulhan, *Choix de lettres II*, p. 196.

24. Quoted in Dioudonnat, *Je suis partout*, p. 159.

25. Lecarme, *Drieu La Rochelle ou le bal des maudits*, p. 374.

26. Quoted in Maugendre, *Alphonse de Châteaubriant*, p. 212.

27. Chadwick, *Alphonse de Châteaubriant*, pp. 1065–1066.

28. Quoted in Fouché, *L'Édition Française sous l'Occupation*, p. 396.

29. Gordon, *Collaborationism in France during World War II*, p. 230.

30. Ibid., p. 243.

31. Chadwick, *Alphonse de Châteaubriant*, p. 18.

32. For a discussion of Touvier's career as well as his 1994 trial for crimes against humanity, see my *Memory, the Holocaust, and French Justice*.

33. Ibid.

34. Paxton, *Vichy France*, p. 256.

35. Lucien Rebatet quoted in Sapiro, *La Guerre des écrivains*, p. 36.

36. Circulation figures are taken from Sapiro, *La guerre des écrivains*, p. 36.

37. For details of Brasillach's trajectory during the Occupation, see Kaplan, *The Collaborator*, especially chap. 2.

38. For a detailed discussion of literary collaboration at *La Gerbe*, see my "Ideology, Cultural Politics, and Literary Collaboration at *La Gerbe*."

39. Thiesse, *Écrire la France*, p. 207.

40. Combelle, *Péché d'orgueil*, p. 202.

41. Ibid., p. 213.

42. Ibid., p. 194.

43. Ory, *Les collaborateurs*, pp. 74–75.

44. Chadwick, *Alphonse de Châteaubriant*, pp. 289–291.

45. Châteaubriant, "Singapour."

46. Châteaubriant, "La Cante Rouge."

47. Châteaubriant, "Gerbe Française."

48. Châteaubriant, "L'Armee nouvelle allemande."

49. Châteaubriant, "Ordre de l'heure."

50. Châteaubriant, *Cahiers*, p. 184.

51. Ibid., p. 189.

52. Ibid., p. 186.

53. Quoted in Ory, *Les collaborateurs*, p. 146.

54. Ibid., p. 212.

55. Ibid., p. 209.

56. Quoted in Verdès-Lerroux, *Refus et violences*, p. 193.

57. Châteaubriant, *Cahiers*, p. 222.

58. Ibid., pp. 221–222.

59. The scene described here is in Céline, *Castle to Castle*, pp. 266–269.

60. Jackson, *France*, p. 553. This episode is discussed and the text of the petition provided in Rousso, *Pétain et la fin de la collaboration*, pp. 75–76.

61. Châteaubriant, "De Breughel à Beethoven," *La France*, 15 January 1945, in *Cahiers Romain Rolland*, pp. 432–433 (emphasis mine).

62. Chadwick, *Alphonse de Châteaubriant*, p. 13.

63. Quoted in ibid., p. 203.

64. See ibid., pp. 205–220.

65. Ibid., p. 205.

66. Châteaubriant, *Cahiers*, p. 322.

67. Quoted in Chadwick, *Alphonse de Châteaubriant*, p. 321.

68. Ibid., p. 207.

69. See ibid., pp. 243–280.

70. Maugendre, *Alphonse de Châteaubriant*, p. 191.

71. For this affirmation by Maugendre, see Chadwick, *Alphonse de Châteaubriant*, p. 246.

72. Ibid., p. 1078.

73. Verdès-Lerroux, *Refus et violences*, p. 192.

74. Ehrlich, *Cinema of Paradox*, p. 35.

75. Châteaubriant, *Monsieur des Lourdines*, p. 17.

76. Chadwick, *Alphonse de Châteaubriant*, p. 31.

77. Ibid.

78. Thiesse, *Écrire la France*, 154–155.

79. Jean de Pierrefeu, quoted in Chadwick, *Alphonse de Châteaubriant*, p. 162.

80. Ibid., p. 65.

81. This is the rather innocuous characterization of the novel offered in the introductory note to the 1985 *Cahier Rouge* edition published by Grasset.

82. Ory, *Les collaborateurs, 1940–1945*, p. 15.

83. See Kaplan, *The Collaborator*, pp. 17–20.

84. Steiner, "Cry Havoc," pp. 35–46.

85. De Man, "Chronique littéraire: Récits de guerre," p. 174.

86. Ibid., pp. 174–175.

87. Chadwick, *Alphonse de Châteaubriant*, p. 29.

88. Cohn, *The Pursuit of the Millennium*, p. 13.

89. Ibid., p. 14.

90. Ibid., p. 21.

CHAPTER 3: JEAN GIONO

1. Weber, *The Hollow Years*, p. 11.
2. Quoted in Green, *Fiction in the Historical Present*, p. 2.
3. Ibid., p. 4.
4. Ibid., p. 3.
5. Ibid., p. 5.
6. Citron, *Giono*, p. 74. Citron does suggest that this statement might be ironic on Giono's part, but this does not belie the fact that Giono appears to have been a patriotic soldier during the conflict.
7. Ibid., p. 64.
8. Peyre, *French Novelists of Today*, p. 131.
9. Giono, "Lettre aux paysans sur la pauvreté et la paix," p. 549.
10. Ibid., p. 553.
11. Ibid., p. 547.
12. Ibid., p. 551.
13. Ibid., p. 538.
14. Ibid., p. 539.
15. Ibid., p. 539.
16. Ibid., pp. 542–63.
17. Quoted in Citron, *Giono*, p. 291.
18. Pollès, *L'Opéra politique*, p. 207.
19. Quoted in Hebey, *La Nouvelle Revue Française des années noires*, p. 332.
20. Quoted in ibid., p. 333.
21. Weber, *The Hollow Years*, p. 24. The complete text of Giono's remarks was published in the *Cahiers du Contadour* in September 1937 and justifiably angered many. For a discussion of the episode, see the *Notice* for the *Lettre aux paysans sur la pauvreté et la paix* in Giono, *Récits et essais*, pp. 1159–1160.
22. Giono, "Lettre aux paysans sur la pauvreté la paix," p. 584.
23. Ibid., p. 585.
24. Giono, "Précisions," p. 611.
25. Ibid., p. 616.
26. See Citron's remark to this effect in the appendices to *Récits et essais*, p. 1208.
27. Quoted in Jackson, *France*, p. 87.
28. Giono, "Recherche de la pureté," p. 653.
29. Ibid., p. 654.
30. Quoted in Weber, *The Hollow Years*, p. 24.
31. See Golan, *Modernity and Nostalgia*.
32. Giono, *Regain*, p. 185.
33. Beauvoir, "La pensée de droite, aujourd'hui (fin)," p. 2253.
34. Quoted in Citron, *Giono*, p. 334.
35. Pierre Citron, "Jean Giono," p. 539.
36. For a discussion of *Le voyage en calèche* and the circumstances surrounding its censorship by the Germans, see Added, *Le Théâtre dans les années Vichy*, pp. 98–99.

37. Fabre-Luce, *Journal de la France août 1940–avril 1942*, p. 190.
38. Citron, *Giono*, p. 337.
39. Fabre-Luce, *Journal de la France août 1940–avril 1942*, p. 195.
40. Gordon, *Historical Dictionary of World War II France*, p. 61.
41. Fabre-Luce, *Journal de la France août 1940–avril 1942*, p. 195.
42. Ibid., p. 195.
43. Along these lines, see Hebey, *La nouvelle revue Français dea années noires*, pp. 345–349.
44. Citron, *Giono*, p. 349.
45. Assouline, *L'Épuration des intellectuels*, p. 24.
46. Denis de Rougemont quoted in Ory, *Les collaborateurs*, p. 30.
47. Hebey, *La nouvelle revue Français dea années noires*, p. 349.
48. Loiseaux, *La littérature de la défaite et de la collaboration*, 577.
49. Sipriot, *Montherlant san masque*, Vol. 2, "*Écris avec ton sang*," p. 194.
50. Loiseaux, *La littérature de la défaite et de la collaboration*, p. 588.
51. Fabre-Luce, *Journal de la France août 1940–avril 1942*, pp. 196–197.
52. Added, *Le Théâtre dans les années Vichy*, p. 277.
53. Fabre-Luce, *Journal de la France août 1940–avril 1942*, p. 196.
54. Giono's 1942 trip to Paris is described in detail in Citron, *Giono*, pp. 346–350.
55. Quoted in ibid., p. 556.
56. All references to *La Gerbe* are to microfilms of the periodical held at the Sterling C. Evans Library, Texas A&M University.
57. The title of Michelfelder's book was *Jean Giono et les religions de la terre*. Truc's laudatory essay "Jean Giono ou le salut par la terre" appeared in *La Gerbe* on 9 April 1942.
58. Paulhan, *Choix de lettres II*, pp. 267–272.
59. Quoted in Burrin, *La France à l'heure allemande*, p. 335.
60. Added, *Le théâtre dans les années Vichy*, p. 219.
61. Ibid., p. 301.
62. Gordon, *Collaborationism in France during World War II*, p. 256.
63. Citron, *Giono*, p. 338.
64. Ibid., pp. 346–353.
65. Ibid., p. 347.
66. Quoted in Burrin, *France under the Germans*, p. 350.
67. Richard, "Jean Giono."
68. Quoted in Burrin, *France under the Germans*, pp. 354–355.
69. Citron, *Giono*, p. 364.
70. Giono, "Journal de l'Occupation," p. 311.
71. Ibid., p. 312.
72. Ibid., p. 435.
73. Ibid., p. 312.
74. Ibid., p. 387.
75. Ibid., p. 395.
76. Ibid., p. 425.
77. Ibid., pp. 425–426.
78. Delperrié de Bayac, *Histoire de la Milice*, p. 266.

79. Ibid., p. 267.

80. See, for example, Giono, "Journal de l'Occupation," p. 382.

81. Ibid., p. 319–320.

82. Ibid., p. 354.

83. Ibid., p. 389.

84. Ibid., p. 476.

85. Ibid., p. 426.

86. Ibid., p. 319.

87. Giono, "Triomphe de la vie," p. 659.

88. Ibid., p. 680.

89. Ibid., p. 713.

90. Ibid., p. 670–671.

91. Ibid., p. 680.

92. Richard, "Jean Giono."

93. A recent challenge to this view of Giono and his work can be found in Godard, *D'Un Giono l'autre.*

CHAPTER 4: ALAIN FINKIELKRAUT

1. Khilnani, *Arguing Revolution*, p. 176.

2. For a discussion of Le Pen's first-round victory in the presidential elections of spring 2002 as well as its political and cultural implications, see my "The Le Pen Moment."

3. Lévy, *La pureté dangereuse*, pp. 26–27.

4. Ibid., p. 31.

5. Ibid., p. 32.

6. Tanner, *Croatia*, p. 239.

7. Ibid., pp. 239–240.

8. Ibid., p. 267.

9. Martel, "Pour servir à l'histoire de notre défaite: 'L'Élite intellectuelle et morale' et la guerre en ex-Yougoslavie," p. 151.

10. The text of the petition is published in Lévy's diary of the conflict, *Le Lys et la cendre*, pp. 68–69.

11. Martel, "Pour servir à l'histoire de notre défaite," pp. 131–132.

12. Quoted in Finkielkraut, *Dispatches from the Balkan War and Other Writings*, pp. 24–25. This text includes Finkielkraut's major writings on the breakup of the former Yugoslavia including *Comment peut-on être Croate?* and *Le crime d'être né.* All subsequent references to these text will be to this translation.

13. Morin's writings on the conflict have been published in book form under the title *Le Fratricides.*

14. For Lévy's account of Izetbegovic's visit, see *Le Lys et la cendre*, pp. 133–137.

15. Ibid., p. 515.

16. Finkielkraut, *L'Ingratitude*, p. 44.

17. Finkielkraut, *Dispatches from the Balkan War*, p. 60.

18. Finkielkraut, *L'Ingratitude*, pp. 41–42.

19. Finkielkraut, *Dispatches from the Balkan War*, p. 203.

20. Finkielkraut, *The Defeat of the Mind*, p. 111.

21. Ibid., p. 135.

22. Finkielkraut, *Remembering in Vain*, pp. 66–67.

23. Ibid., p. 70.

24. Finkielkraut, *Dispatches from the Balkan War*, p. 18.

25. Ibid., p. 1.

26. Ibid., p. 148.

27. Ibid., p. 155.

28. Ibid., p. 32.

29. Ibid., p. 86.

30. Quoted in Tanner, *Croatia*, p. 136.

31. Ibid., p. 144.

32. Ibid., p. 152.

33. Ibid., p. 149.

34. Ibid., p. 148.

35. Ibid., p. 223.

36. See excerpts from Tudjman's autobiography "Wastelands: Historical Truth," at http://www.srpska-mreza.com/library/facts/Tudjman.html.

37. Ibid.

38. Ibid., p. 228.

39. Glenny, *The Balkans*, p. 631.

40. Tanner, *Croatia*, p. 222.

41. Ibid., p. 230.

42. Ibid., p. 231.

43. Glenny, *The Balkans*, p. 645.

44. Finkielkraut, *Dispatches from the Balkan War*, p. 31 (emphasis in original).

45. For Girard's theories on violence and scapegoating, see especially his *Violence and the Sacred*.

46. Ibid., p. 29.

47. Ibid., p. 31.

48. Finkielkraut, *L'Imparfait du présent*, p. 181.

49. Ibid., p. 23.

CHAPTER 5: RÉGIS DEBRAY

1. For a discussion of these engagements, see chapter 4 as well as my "From Sarajevo to Vichy: French Intellectuals and the Wages of Commitment in the Balkans."

2. The petition was published in *Le Monde* on 3 April 1999.

3. Lévy, "Faire la guerre à la guerre."

4. Julliard, "Priorité absolue," p. 63.

5. Finkielkraut, "Inévitable."

6. Faubert, "Rendez-nous de Gaulle," p. 16.

7. Sagot-Duvauroux, "L'Empire et la barbarie."

8. Dutourd, "Nos amis, nos frères d'armes."

9. Bourdieu, "Arrêt de bombardements, autodétermination."

10. Besson, "Il n'y a pas que les Serbes qui assassinent."

11. Salvaing, "Comme dans un fauteuil."

12. Debray would reveal later in an article titled "Une Machine de guerre," published in *Le Monde diplomatique* in June 1999, that the original title of his letter had been "Lettre d'un voyageur au Président sur une guerre insensée" but that this title had been altered by *Le Monde*.

13. Debray, "Lettre d'un voyageur au président de la République."

14. Ibid.

15. Ibid.

16. Ibid.

17. Debray, "Ce que j'ai vraiment dit."

18. Debray, "Lettre d'un voyageur au président de la République."

19. Ibid.

20. Ibid.

21. Ibid.

22. Ibid.

23. Daeninckx, Fajandic, and Staraselski, "Debray, ou le révisionnisme au présent."

24. Debray, "Lettre d'un voyageur au président de la République."

25. Ibid.

26. The essay was originally published in German in 1999, the same year as Peter Handke's *Eine Winterliche Reise zu den Flüssen, Save, Morawa, und Driner Oder Gerechtigkeit für Serbien.*

27. Kahn, "L'affaire Debray: Les dessous d'un lynchage raté," pp. 14–20.

28. Rayski, "L'affaire Debray: La trahison des intellectuels," pp. 57–63.

29. See Couturier, "Régis Debray: Le retour du proscrit," pp. 16–19.

30. Péan and Cohen, *La face cachée du monde,* p. 528–531.

31. Amalric, "Pourquoi répondre."

32. Debray, "Une machine de guerre."

33. Lévy, "Adieu, Régis Debray."

34. Interview with Max Gallo in *Le Figaro,* 17 May 1999.

35. Rayski, "L'affaire Debray: La trahison des intellectuels," p. 57.

36. Tordjman, "Le Régis Debray sans peine," p. 63.

37. Glucksmann, "Vous n'avez pas vu ce que vous avez vu," p. 63.

38. Brauman, "Debray voit ce qu'il croit."

39. Finkielkraut, *Une voix vient de l'autre rive,* pp. 45–46.

40. Ibid., p. 47.

41. Debray, *Les masques,* p. 174.

42. See the discussion of Drieu's trajectory during the Occupation in Lecarme, *Drieu la Rochelle, ou le bal des maudits,* pp. 403–425.

43. Péan and Cohen, *La face cachée du monde,* p. 534.

44. Finkielkraut, *Une voix vient de l'autre rive,* pp. 40–41.

45. Debray, *Charles de Gaulle,* p. ix.

46. Reader, *Régis Debray*, p. ix.
47. Reid, "Régis Debray: Republican in a Democratic Age," p. 134.
48. Debray, *Charles de Gaulle*, pp. 4–5.
49. Debray, *Que vive la République!*, pp. 13–14.
50. Debray, *La République expliquée à ma fille*, p. 55.
51. Debray, *Le Code et la glaive*, pp. 73–94.
52. Ibid., pp. 90–91 (emphasis in original).
53. Ibid., p. 111.
54. Glucksmann, "Europe, an 1."
55. Julliard, "Adieu!", p. 59.

CHAPTER 6: STÉPHANE COURTOIS

1. Julliard, *L'année des fantômes*.
2. All references are to the American edition: Courtois, Werth, Panné, Paczkowski, Bartošek, and Margolin, *The Black Book of Communism*.
3. My thanks to Nicholas Werth for background information concerning the publication of the *Black Book*, which he provided during a conversation at his home in Paris on 26 May 2004.
4. "M. Jospin se déclare 'fier' que le PCF soit représenté au sein de son gouvernement," *Le Monde*, 14 November 1997.
5. Revel, "Jospin a commis deux erreurs historiques."
6. Hue, "Aux morts du communsme, Robert Hue répentant."
7. Courtois et al., *The Black Book of Communism*, p. 4.
8. Werth, "Le Communisme: L'heure du bilan?", p. 8.
9. Courtois et al., *The Black Book of Communism*, p. 8.
10. Ibid., p. 9. It seems clear from this and the previous quote from Courtois's introduction that despite his assertions as to the equivalency of class and race genocide, he is not entirely comfortable with that equation. Otherwise, why would he use quotation marks around the expression "is equal to" and the terms "class" and "race"?
11. Ibid., p. 5.
12. Margolin and Werth, "Communisme: Retour à l'histoire."
13. Rabinbach, "Communist Crimes and French Intellectuals," p. 61.
14. Courtois, "Comprendre la tragédie communiste."
15. Julliard, "Ne dites plus jamais 'jamais'!", p. 49.
16. Rousso, "The Legitimacy of an Empirical Comparison," p. 4.
17. Ibid.
18. Ibid., p. 5.
19. In France, Margarete Buber-Neumann's *Déportée en Sibérie* (Deported to Siberia) appeared as early as 1948. Solzhenitsyn's *L'Archipel du Goulag* appeared in French translation in June 1974. The publication of the latter work created a huge controversy in France. Many former supporters of the USSR abandoned their support following the book's publication.
20. Rabinbach, "Communist Crimes and French Intellectuals," p. 63.
21. Wieviorka, "Stéphane Courtois, en un combat douteux."

22. Courtois, "Comprendre la tragédie communiste."

23. I would like to thank Henry Rousso for providing me with a copy of the manuscript of Kershaw's lecture.

24. The original French version, *Fascisme et communisme*, was published by Plon in 1998.

25. Furet and Nolte, *Fascism and Communism*, p. 53.

26. For the term "eliminationist anti-Semitism" and its application to the Nazi genocide of the Jews, see Goldhagen, *Hitler's Willing Execusioners*, pp. 80–128.

27. Furet and Nolte, *Fascism and Communism*, pp. 54–55.

28. Ibid., p. 52.

29. Ibid., pp. 90–96.

30. Ibid., p. 47.

31. Trierweiller, "Un spectre hante Ernst Nolte," p. 166.

32. Husson, "Le 'noyau rationel' de l'oeuvre de Nolte," p. 142.

33. Nolte, "Fascisme, communisme, histoire et controverses."

34. Nolte, "Avant-propos d'Ernst Nolte à l'Édition Française," p. 20.

35. Nolte, "Fascisme, communisme, histoire et controverses."

36. Ibid.

37. Maier, "Lettre ouverte à Ernst Nolte," p. 161.

38. Husson, "Le 'noyau rationel' de l'oeuvre de Nolte," p. 149.

39. Ibid., p. 151.

40. Maier, "Lettre ouverte à Ernst Nolte," p. 158.

41. Nolte, "Fascisme, communisme, histoire et controverses."

42. Maier, "Lettre ouverte à Ernst Nolte," p. 161.

43. Ibid., pp. 156–157.

44. Traverso, *Understanding the Nazi Genocide*, p. 77.

45. Courtois, *La Guerre civile européenne*, p. 7.

46. Ibid., p. 10.

47. Courtois, *La Guerre civile européenne*, pp. 11–12.

48. Ibid., p. 11.

49. Ibid., p. 13.

50. Courtois, *Du passé faisons table rase*, p. 55.

51. Garaudy's book and the Abbé Pierre-Garaudy affair are discussed in detail in my *Vichy's Afterlife*, chap. 7.

52. Along these lines, see Thiessen, "Why We Fought." Thiessen's praise of the *Livre noir* is cast in such a way as to justify Pinochet's actions in Chile.

53. Benoist, "Nazisme et communisme: vrais ou faux jumeaux?", pp. 14–36.

54. Nolte, "Fascisme, communisme, histoire et controverses."

CONCLUSION

1. Rousso discusses the intensification of the Vichy syndrome in 1990s France in *Vichy: An Everpresent Past* and in the introduction to *Vichy: L'Evénement, la mémoire, l'histoire*, pp. 43–51.

2. These issues are discussed in a number of the essays and interviews in my *The Papon Affair*.

3. For a discussion of Papon's actions as prefect of the Paris police in 1961 and the impact of these actions on the proceedings in Bordeaux, see my *Vichy's Afterlife*, pp. 156–180.

4. See the discussion of Finkielkraut's *Au nom de l'autre* in chapter 4.

5. For a discussion of Le Pen' first-round victory in the presidential election of 2002, see my "The Le Pen Moment."

6. See Todorov, *Le nouveau désordre mondial.*

Bibliography

Added, Serge. *Le théâtre des années Vichy, 1940–1944.* Paris: Ramsay, 1992.

Allen, Beverly. *Rape Warfare: The Hidden Genocide in Bosnia-Herzegovina and Croatia.* Minneapolis: University of Minneapolis Press, 1996.

Amalric, Jacques. "Pourquoi répondre." *Libération,* 14 May 1999.

Anguelov, Zlatko. *Communism and the Remorse of an Innocent Victimizer.* College Station: Texas A&M University Press, 2002.

Argelès, Jean-Marie, et al. *Communisme.* Paris: L'Age d'Homme, 1999.

Aron, Raymond. *Démocratie et totalitarisme.* Paris: Gallimard, 1965.

Ash, Timothy G. *In Europe's Name: Germany and the Divided Continent.* New York: Vintage Books, 1993.

———. *History of the Present: Essays, Sketches and Despatches from Europe in the 1990s.* New York: Penguin, 1999.

Assouline, Pierre. *L'Epuration des intellectuels.* Brussells: Editions Complexe, 1985.

Aussaresses, General Paul. *Services Spéciaux: Algérie, 1995–57.* Paris: Perrin, 2001.

Balibar, Etienne. *Droit de cité: Culture et politique en démocratie.* Saint-Etienne: L'Aube, 1998.

Banac, Ivo, ed. *Eastern Europe in Revolution.* Ithaca: Cornell University Press, 1992.

Barrett, William. *Irrational Man: A Study in Existential Philosophy.* New York: Doubleday Anchor, 1962.

Baudrillard, Jean. *Fragments: Cool Memories III, 1990–1995.* Trans. Emily Agar. London: Verso, 1997.

———. *The Gulf War Did Not Take Place.* Trans. and introduced by Paul Patton. Bloomington: Indiana University Press, 1995.

———. *Paroxysm: Interviews with Philippe Petit.* Trans. Chris Turner. London: Verso, 1998.

Beauvoir, Simone de. "La pensée de droite, aujourd'hui." *Les Temps modernes* 112–113 (1954): 1539–1575, and 114–115 (1955): 2219–2261.

———. *The Second Sex.* Trans. H. M. Parshley. New York: Vintage, 1974.

Belot, Robert. *Lucien Rebatet: Un itinéraire fasciste.* Paris: Seuil, 1994.

———. "Rebatet." In *Dictionnaire des intellectuels Français,* ed. Jacques Julliard and Michel Winock. Paris: Seuil 1996.

Benhabib, Seyla. "Taking Ideas Seriously: Can We Distinguish Political Choices from Philosophical Truths?" *Boston Review,* 15 January 2003, http://bostonreview.net/BR27.6/benhabib.html.

Benjamin, Jessica, and Anson Rabinach. "Foreword." *Male Fantasies*, Vol. 2, *Male Bodies: Psychoanalyzing the White Terror.* Minneapolis: University of Minnesota Press, 1989.

Benoist, Alain de. "Nazisme et communisme: Vrais ou faux jumeaux?" *Eléments* 92 (July 1998): 14–36.

Besançon, Alain. *Le malheur de siècle: Sur le communisme le Nazisme et l'unicité de la Shoah.* Fayard, 1998.

Besson, Partrick. "Il n'y a pas que les Serbes qui assassinent." *Le Figaro*, 29 March 1999.

Betz, Albrecht, and Stefan Martens, eds. *Les intellectuels et l'Occupation: Collaborer, partir, résister.* Paris: Autrement, 2004.

Bonnafous, Simone, Pierre Fiala, and Alice Krieg, eds. *Mots: Les langages du politique.* Paris: Presses des Sciences Po, June 1996.

Bourdieu, Pierre. "Arrêt de bombardements, autodétermination." *Le Monde*, 31 March 1999.

Brauman, Rony. "Debray voit ce qu'il croit." *Libération*, 15–16 May 1999.

Bronner, Stephan Eric. *Camus: Portrait of a Moralist.* Minneapolis: University of Minnesota Press, 1999.

Browning, Christopher R. *Nazi Policy, Jewish Workers, German Killers.* Cambridge: Cambridge University Press, 2000.

———. *Ordinary Men: Reserve Police Battalion 101 and the Final Solution in Poland.* New York: Harper Perennial, 1993.

Bruckner, Pascal. *La mélancolie démocratique: Comment vivre sans ennemis?* Paris: Seuil, 1990.

———. *La tentation de l'innocence.* Paris: Grasset, 1995.

———. *Misère de la prospérité: La religion marchande et ses ennemis.* Paris: Grasset, 2002.

Burrin, Philippe. *France under the Germans.* Trans. Janet Lloyd. New York: New Press, 1996.

———. *La France à l'heure allemande.* Paris: Seuil, 1995.

Camus, Albert. *Between Hell and Reason: Essays from the Resistance Newspaper* Combat, *1944–1947.* Trans. Alexandre de Gramont. Hanover: University Press of New England, 1991.

———. *Lyrical and Critical Essays.* Trans. Ellen Conroy Kennedy. New York: Knopf, 1968.

———. *Notebooks: 1935–1942.* Trans. Philip Thody. New York: Modern Library, 1965.

———. *Notebooks: 1942–1951.* Trans. Justin O'Brian. New York: Modern Library, 1965.

Carroll, David. *French Literary Fascism: Nationalism, Anti-Semitism, and the Ideology of Culture.* Princeton: Princeton University Press, 1995.

Céline, Louis-Ferdinand. *Castle to Castle.* Trans. Ralph Mannheim. New York: Dell, 1968.

———. *Lettres à son avocat.* Paris: La Flute de Pan, 1984.

Chadwick, Kay. *Alphonse de Châteaubriant: Catholic Collaborator.* Oxford: Peter Lang, 2002.

Châteaubriant, Alphonse de. *Cahiers, 1906–1951.* Paris: Grasset, 1955.

———. "Gerbe Française." *La Gerbe*, 22 March 1944.

———. *La brière.* Paris: Grasset, 1923.

———. "La Carte Rouge." *La Gerbe*, 9 October 1941.

———. *La gerbe des forces.* Paris: Grasset, 1937.

———. "L'Armée nouvelle allemande." *La Gerbe*, 22 June 1944.

———. "Ordre de l'heure." *La Gerbe*, 3 December 1942.

———. "Singapour." *La Gerbe*, 14 February 1942.

Cigar, Norman. *Genocide in Bosnia: The Policy of Ethnic Cleansing.* College Station: Texas A&M University Press, 1995.

Citron, Pierre. *Giono, 1895–1970.* Paris: Seuil, 1990.

———. "Jean Giono." In *Dictionnaire des intellectuels Français,* ed. Jacques Julliard and Michel Winock. Paris: Seuil, 1996.

Citron, Pierre, Henri Godard, Violaine de Montmollin, and Mireille Sacotte, eds. *Jean Giono: Journal, poèmes, essais.* Paris: Gallimard, 1995.

———, eds. *Jean Giono: Récits et essais.* Paris: Gallimard, 1989.

Cobb, Richard. *French and Germans, Germans and French: A Personal Interpretation of France under Two Occupations.* Hanover: University Press of New England, 1983.

Cohen, Philip. *Serbia's Secret War: Propaganda and the Deceit of History.* College Station: Texas A&M University Press, 1996.

Cohn, Norman. *The Pursuit of the Millennium.* London: Paladin Press, 1970.

Combelle, Lucien. *Péché d'orgueil.* Paris: Orban, 1978.

Conan, Eric, and Henry Rousso. *Vichy: An Everpresent Past.* Trans. Nathan Bracher. Hanover, NH: University Press of New England, 1998.

Conquest, Robert. *Reflections on a Ravaged Century.* New York: Norton, 2000.

Courtois, Stéphane. "Comprendre la tragédie communiste." *Le Monde,* 20 December 1997.

———, ed. *Du passé faisons table rase: Histoire et mémoire du communisme en Europe.* Paris: Laffont, 2002.

———. "*Le livre noir* et le travail historien sur le communisme." *Communisme* 59/60 (1999): 93–126.

Courtois, Stéphane, Nicolas Werth, Jean-Louis Panné, Andrzej Paczkowski, Karel Bartošek, and Jean-Louis Margolin. *The Black Book of Communism: Crimes, Terror, Repression.* Trans. Jonathan Murphy and Mark Kramer. Cambridge: Harvard University Press, 1999.

Couturier, Brice. "Régis Debray: Le retour du proscrit." *L'Evénement du Jeudi,* 13–19 April 2000.

Cushman, Thomas, and Stjepan Meštrovic, eds. *This Time We Knew: Western Responses to Genocide in Bosnia.* New York: New York University Press, 1996.

Daeninckx, Didier, Frédéric Fajandic, and Valère Staraselski. "Debray, ou le révisionnisme au présent." *Libération,* 18 May 1999.

Debray, Régis. "Ce que j'ai vraiment dit." *Le Nouvel Observateur,* 20–26 May 1999, p. 8.

———. *Charles de Gaulle: Futurist of the Nation.* Trans. John Howe. London: Verso, 1994.

———. *Dieu, un itinéraire.* Paris: Editions Odile Jacob, 2001.

———. *I.F. suite et fin.* Paris: Gallimard, 2000.

———. *La république expliquée à ma fille.* Paris: Seuil, 1998.

———. *Le code et le glaive: Après l'Europe, la nation?* Paris: Albin Michel, 1999.

———. *L'Emprise.* Paris: Gallimard, 2000.

———. *Les masques.* Paris: Gallimard, 1987.

———. "Lettre d'un voyageur au président de la République." *Le Monde,* 13 May 1999.

———. *Loués soient nos seigneurs: Une education politique.* Paris: Gallimard, 1996.

———. *Que vive la République!* Paris: Odile Jacob, 1989.

———. "Une machine de guerre." *Le Monde diplomatique.* June 1999.

Del Castillo, Michel. *L'Adieu au siècle.* Paris: Seuil, 2000.

Delperrié de Bayac, Jacques. *Histoire de la Milice, 1918–1945*. Paris: Fayard, 1969.

Denitch, Bogdan. *Ethnic Nationalism: The Tragic Death of Yugoslavia*. Minneapolis: University of Minnesota Press, 1994.

Dioudonnat, Pierre-Marie. *Je suis partout, 1930–1944: Les maurassiens devant la tantation fasciste*. Paris: La Table Ronde, 1973.

Djilas, Aleksa. *The Contested Country: Yugoslav Unity and Communist Revolution, 1919–1953*. Cambridge: Harvard University Press, 1991.

Donia, Robert J., and John V. A. Fine. *Bosnia and Hercegovina: A Tradition Betrayed*. New York: Columbia University Press, 1994.

Dorman, Joseph. *Arguing the World: The New York Intellectuals in Their Own Words*. Chicago: University of Chicago Press, 2000.

Dreyfus, Michel, et al. *Le siècle des communismes*. Paris: L'Atelier, 2000.

Dutourd, Jean. "Nos amis, nos frères d'armes." *Le Figaro*, 29 March 1999.

Ehrlich, Evelyn. *Cinema of Paradox: French Filmmaking under the German Occupation*. New York: Columbian University Press, 1985.

Fabre-Luce, Alfred. *Journal de la France août 1940–avril 1942*. Paris: JEP, 1942.

Faubert, Serge. "Rendez-vous de Gaulle." *L'Evénement du Jeudi*. 1–6 April 1999.

Ferro, Marc, ed. *Nazisme et communisme*. Paris: Hachette, 1999.

Ferry, Luc, and Alain Renaut. *French Philosophy of the Sixties: An Essay on Antihumanism*. Amherst: University of Massachusetts Press, 1985.

Finkielkraut, Alain. *Au nom de l'autre: Réflexions sur l'antisémitisme qui vient*. Paris: Gallimard, 2003.

———. *Comment peut-on être Croate?* Paris: Gallimard, 1992.

———. *The Defeat of the Mind*. Trans. Judith Friedlander. New York: Columbia University Press, 1995.

———. *Dispatches from the Balkan War and Other Writings*. Trans. Peter S. Rogers and Richard Golsan. London: University of Nebraska Press, 1999.

———. "Inévitable." *Libération*, 26 March 1999.

———. *La réprobation d'Israël*. Paris: Denoël/Gonthier, 1983.

———. *L'Avenir d'une négation: Réflexion sur la question du génocide*. Paris: Seuil, 1982.

———. *Le crime d'etre né: L'Europe, les nations, la guerre*. Paris: Arléa, 1994.

———. *Le Juif imaginaire*. Paris: Seuil, 1980.

———. *L'Humanité perdue: Essai sur le XXe siècle*. Paris: Seuil, 1996.

———. *L'Imparfait du présent*. Paris: Gallimard, 2002.

———. *L'Ingratitude: Conversation sur notre temps*. Paris: Gallimard, 1999.

———. *Remembering in Vain: The Klaus Barbie Trial and Crimes against Humanity*. Trans. Roxanne Lapidus and Sima Godfrey. New York: Columbia University Press, 1992.

———. *Une voix vient de l'autre rive*. Paris: Gallimard, 2000.

Finkielkraut, Alain, and Peter Sloterdijk. *Les battements du monde: Dialogue*. Paris: Pauvert, 2003.

Fisher, David. *Romain Rolland and the Politics of Intellectual Engagement*. Berkeley: University of California Press, 1988.

Flood, Christopher, and Laurence Bell. *Political Ideologies in Contemporary France*. London: Pinter, 1997.

Fouché, Pascal. *L'Edition Française sous l'Occupation*. Vol 1. Paris: Bibliothèque de la littérature contemporaine de l'Université de Paris VII, 1987.

Frese Witt, Mary Ann. *The Search for Modern Tragedy: Aesthetic Fascism in Italy and France*. Ithaca: Cornell University Press, 2001.

Friedlander, Judith. *Vilna on the Seine: Jewish Intellectuals in France since 1968*. New Haven: Yale University Press, 1990.

Furet, François. *La révolution en débat*. Paris: Gallimard, 1999.

——. *Le passé d'Une illusion: Essai sur l'idée communiste au XXe siècle*. Paris: Laffont, 1995.

——. *Un itinéraire intellectuel: L'Historien journaliste, de* France-Observateur *au* Nouvel Observateur *(1958–1997)*. Paris: Calmann-Lévy, 1999.

Furet, François, and Ernst Nolte. *Fascism & Communism*. Trans. Katherine Golsan. Lincoln: University of Nebraska Press, 2001.

Furet, François, Jacques Julliard, and Pierre Rosanvallon. *La république de centre: La fin de l'exception Française*. Paris: Calmann-Lévy, 1988.

Garapon, Antoine, and Olivier Mongin, eds. *Kosovo: Un drame annoncé*. Paris: Michalon, 1999.

Garaudy, Roger. *Les mythes fondateurs de la politique Israélienne*. Paris: Samizdat Garaudy, 1998.

Garde, Paul. *Vie et mort de la Yougoslavie*. Paris: Fayard, 1992.

Gentile, Emilio. *Le religioni della politica: Fra democrazie e totalitarismi*. Rome: Gius. Laterza & Figli Spa, 2001.

Geyer, Michael, ed. *The Power of Intellectuals in Contemporary Germany*. Chicago: University of Chicago Press, 2001.

Gilman, Richard. *Decadence: The Strange Life of an Epithet*. New York: Farrar, Staus and Giroux, 1975.

Ginsborg, Paul. *A History of Comtemporary Italy: Society and Politics, 1943–1988*. New York: Penguin, 1990.

Giono, Jean. "Journal de l'Occupation." In *Journal, poèmes, essais*. Paris: Gallimard, Éditions de la Pléiade, 1995.

——. "Lettre aux paysans sur la pauvreté et la paix." In *Récits et essais*. Paris: Gallimard, Éditions de la Pléiade, 1989.

——. "Précisions." In *Récits et essais*. Paris: Gallimard, Éditions de la Pléiade, 1989.

——. "Recherche de la pureté." In *Récits et essais*. Paris: Gallimard, Éditions de la Pléiade, 1989.

——. *Regain*. Paris: Grasset, 1930.

——. "Triomphe de la vie." In *Récits et essais*. Paris: Gallimard, Éditions de la Pléiade, 1989.

Girard, René. *Violence and the Sacred*. Baltimore: Johns Hopkins University Press, 1977.

Glenny, Misha. *The Balkans: Nationalism, War and the Great Powers, 1804–1999*. New York: Viking, 1999.

——. *The Fall of Yugoslavia: The Third Balkan War*. New York: Penguin, 1992.

Glucksmann, André. *De Gaulle, où es-tu?* Paris: Jean-Claude Lattès, 1995.

——. *Dostoïevski à Manhattan*. Paris: Laffont, 2002.

——. "Europe, an 1." *L'Express*, 4 April 1999.

———. *La bêtise.* Paris: Grasset, 1985.

———. *La fêlure du monde: Ethique et sida.* Paris: Flammarion, 1994.

———. *La force du Vertige.* Paris: Grasset, 1983.

———. *Ouest contre Ouest.* Paris: Plon, 2003.

———. "Vous n'avez pas vu ce que vous avez vu." *L'Express.* 20 May 1999.

Godard, Henri. *D'un Giono l'autre.* Paris: Gallimard, 1995.

Golan, Romy. *Modernity and Nostalgia: Art and Politics in France between the Wars.* New Haven: Yale University Press, 1995.

Goldhagen, Daniel Jonah. *Hitler's Willing Executioners: Ordinary Germans and the Holocaust.* New York: Knopf, 1996.

Golsan, Richard J. *Fascism, Aesthetics, and Culture.* Hanover: University Press of New England, 1992.

———. "Find a Victim: Montherlant and the de Man Affair." *French Review* 66(3) (1993): 393–400.

———, ed. "The French Intellectual: New Engagements." *L'Esprit Créateur* 37(2) (Summer 1997). Special issue. Lexington: L'Esprit Créateur.

———. "From Sarajevo to Vichy: French Intellectuals and the Wages of Commitment in the Balkans." *L'Esprit Créateur* 37(2) (Summer 1997): 79–89.

———. "Ideology, Cultural Politics, and Literary Collaboration at *La Gerbe.*" *Journal of European Studies* 23(1–2) (1993): 27–47.

———. "The Le Pen Moment." *Substance* 32(1) (2003): 128–143.

———. *The Papon Affair: Memory and Justice on Trial.* New York: Routledge, 2000.

———. *"Service inutile": A Study of the Tragic in the Theatre of Henry de Montherlant.* Mississippi: Romance Monographs, 1986.

———. *Vichy's Afterlife: History and Counterhistory in Postwar France.* Lincoln: University of Nebraska Press, 2000.

Gordon, Bertram. *Collaborationism in France during World War II.* Ithaca: Cornell University Press, 1980.

———, ed. *Historical Dictionary of World War II France: The Occupation, Vichy, the Resistance, 1938–1946.* Westport: Greenwood, 1998.

Goux, Jean-Joseph, and Philip Wood, eds. *Terror and Consensus: Vicissitudes of French Thought.* Stanford: Stanford University Press, 1998.

Goytisolo, Juan. *Cahier de Sarajevo.* Translated from Spanish by François Maspero. Bar le Duc: La Nuée Bleue, 1993.

Green, Mary Jean. *Fiction in the Historical Present: French Writers and the Thirties.* Hanover: University Press of New England, 1986.

Grossman, Vassili, and Ilya Ehrenbourg. *Le Livre Noir: Sur l'extermination des Juifs en URSS et en Pologne (1941–1945).* 2 vols. Paris: Solin/Actes Sud, 1995.

Guéhenno, Jean. *Journal des années noires.* Paris: Gallimard, 1947; Folio edition, 1973.

Guerard, Albert J. "Montherlant and the Collaborators." *Yale Review* 35(1) (1945): 93–98.

Handke, Peter. *Un voyage hivernal vers le Danube, la Save, la Morava, et la Drina.* Paris: Gallimard, 1996.

Hebey, Pierre. *La nouvelle revue Française des années noires, 1940–1941.* Paris: Gallimard, 1992.

Hewitt, Nicolas. *Literature and the Right in Postwar France*. Oxford: Berg, 1996.

Higgins, Lynn A. *New Novel, New Wave, New Politics: Fiction and the Representation of History in Postwar France*. Lincoln: University of Nebraska Press, 1996.

Hilberg, Raul. *Perpetrators, Victims, Bystanders: The Jewish Catastrophe, 1933–1945*. New York: HarperCollins, 1992.

H.K.P.K. "Henry de Montherlant," *La Gerbe*, 23 April 1942.

Hue, Robert. "Aux morts du communisme, Robert Hue répentant." *Libération*, 9 November 1997.

Husson, Edouard. "Le 'noyau rationel' de l'oeuvre de Nolte." *Le Débat* 122 (November–December 2002): 141–153.

Ignatieff, Michael. *Virtual War: Kosovo and Beyond*. New York: Metropolotan, 2000.

Jackson, Julian. *France: The Dark Years, 1940–1944*. Oxford: Oxford University Press, 2001.

Joffrin, Laurent. *Mai 68: Histoire des evénements*. Paris: Seuil, 1988.

Jouary, Jean-Paul, and Arnaud Spire, eds. *Grammaire du pluralisme*. Paris: Editions Sociales, 1993.

Judah, Tim. *The Serbs: History, Myth, & the Destruction of Yugoslavia*. New Haven: Yale University Press, 1997.

Judt, Tony. *The Burden of Responsibility: Blum, Camus, Aron, and the French Twentieth Century*. Chicago: University of Chicago Press, 1998.

Julliard, Jacques. "Adieu!" *Le Nouvel Observateur*, 15–20 April 1999.

——. *Ce fascisme qui vient . . .* Paris: Seuil, 1994.

——. *L'Année des dupes*. Paris: Seuil, 1996.

——. *L'Année des fantômes: Journal 1997*. Paris: Grasset, 1998.

——. "Ne dites plus jamais 'jamais'!" *Le Nouvel Observateur*, 20–26 November 1997.

——. *Pour la Bosnie*. Paris: Seuil, 1996.

——. "Priorité absolue." *Le Nouvel Observateur*, 8–14 April 1999.

Kahn, Jean-François. "L'affaire Debray: Les dessous d'un lynchage raté." *Marianne*, 24–30 May 1999.

Kaplan, Alice. *The Collaborator: The Trial and Execution of Robert Brasillach*. Chicago: University of Chicago Press, 2000.

——. *Reproductions of Banality: Fascism, Literature and French Intellectual Life*. Minneapolis: University of Minnesota Press, 1986.

Kaplan, Steven. *Farewell, Revolution: The Historians' Feud, France, 1789/1989*. Ithaca: Cornell University Press, 1995.

Keane, Fergal. *Season of Blood: A Rwandan Journey*. New York: Penguin, 1995.

Kershaw, Ian, and Moshe Lewin. *Stalinism and Nazism: Dictatorships in Comparison*. Cambridge: Cambridge University Press, 1977.

Khilnani, Sunil. *Arguing Revolution: The Intellectual Left in Postwar France*. New Haven: Yale University Press, 1993.

Kiernan, Ben. *The Pol Pot Regime: Race, Power, and Genocide in Cambodia under the Khmer Rouge, 1975–79*. New Haven: Yale University Press, 1996.

Krauss, Kenneth. *The Drama of Fallen France: Reading la Comédie sans Tickets*. Albany: State University of New York Press, 2004.

Kristeva, Julia. *Contre la dépression nationale*. Paris: Textuel, 1998.

Kutz, Christopher. *Complicity: Ethics and Law for a Collective Age*. Cambridge: Cambridge University Press, 2000.

Lecarme, Jacques. *Drieu La Rochelle, ou le bal des maudits*. Paris: Presses Universitaires de France, 2001.

Lefort, Claude. *La complication: Retour sur le communisme*. Paris: Fayard, 1999.

———. *La découverte du politique*. Paris: Michalon, 1997.

Lehman, David. *Signs of the Times: Deconstruction and the Fall of Paul de Man*. New York: Poseidon, 1991.

Lévy, Bernard-Henri. "Adieu, Régis Debray." *Le Monde*, 14 May 1999.

———. "Faire la guerre à la guerre." *Libération*, 26 March 1999.

———. *La pureté dangereuse*. Paris: Grasset, 1994.

———. *Le lys et la cendre*. Paris: Grasset, 1996.

———. *Le siècle de Sartre*. Paris: Grasset, 2000.

———. *Les aventures de La liberté: Une histoire subjective des intellectuels*. Paris: Grasset, 1991.

———. *L'Idéologie Française*. Paris: Grasset & Fasquelle, 1981.

———. *Mémoire vive: Questions de principe sept*. Paris: Le Livre de Poche, 2001.

Lilla, Mark. *The Reckless Mind: Intellectuals in Politics*. New York: New York Review of Books, 2001.

Lindenberg, Daniel. *Le rappel a l'ordre: Enquête sur les nouveaux réactionnaires*. Paris: Seuil, 2002.

Loiseaux, Gérard. *La littérature de la défaite et de la collaboration*. Paris: Fayard, 1995.

Maier, Charles S. "Lettre ouverte à Ernst Nolte." *Le Débat* 122 (November–December 2002): 154–164.

Malia, Martin. *The Soviet Tragedy: A History of Socialism in Russia, 1917–1991*. New York: Free Press, 1994.

Man, Paul de. "Chronique littéature: Récits de guerre." *Le Soir*, 23 December 1941.

Margolin, Jean-Louis, and Nicholas Werth. "Communisme: Retour à l'histoire." *Le Monde*, 18 November 1997.

Martel, Frédéric. "Pour servir à l'histoire de notre défaite: 'L'Elite intellectuelle et morale' et la guerre en ex-Yougoslavie." *Le Messager Européen* 8 (1994): 127–154.

Mathy, Jean-Philippe. *French Resistance: The French-American Culture Wars*. Minneapolis: University of Minnesota Press, 2000.

Maugendre, L.-A. *Alphonse de Châteaubriant, 1877–1951*. Paris: André Bonne, 1977.

McCarthy, Patrick. *The Crisis of the Italian State: From the Origins of the Cold War to the Fall of Berlusconi*. New York: St. Martin's, 1995.

Michelfelder, Christian. *Jean Giono et les religions de la terre*. Paris: Gallimard, 1938.

Mills, Nicolaus, and Kira Brunner, eds. *The New Killing Fields: Massacre and the Politics of Intervention*. New York: Basic Books, 2002.

Minc, Alain. *Le nouveau moyen age*. Paris: Gallimard, 1993.

Montherlant, Henry de. *Essais*. Paris: Gallimard, Éditions de la Pléiade, 1963.

———. *Henry de Montherlant-Roger Peyrefitte Correspondance* Paris: Laffont, 1983.

———. "Jeunesse 1938." *Je suis partout*, 18 March 1938.

———. "Le goût d'attaquer." *La Gerbe*, 28 August 1941.

———. "L'Équinoxe de Septembre" suivi de "Le Solstice de Juin." Paris: Gallimard, 1976.

———. "Mémoire." In "L'Équinoxe de Septembre" suivi de "le solstice de Juin." Paris: Gallimard, 1976.

———. Romans et oeuvres de fiction non théâtrales. Paris: Gallimard, Éditions de la Pléiade, 1959.

———. Théâtre. Paris: Gallimard, Éditions de la Pléiade, 1972.

Morin, Edgar. Le fratricides: Yugoslavie-Bosnie, 1991–1995. Paris: Arléa, 1995.

Mort, Noël de la. "Montherlant devant lui-même." La Gerbe, 8 January 1942.

Mousavizadeh, Nader. The Black Book of Bosnia: The Consequences of Appeasement. New York: New Republic, 1996.

Mulisch, Harry. The Assault. Trans. Claire Nicolas White. New York: Pantheon, 1985.

Muray, Philippe. Chers djihadistes . . . Paris: Mille et Une Nuits, 2001.

Nietzsche, Friedrich. Beyond Good and Evil. Trans. Walter Kaufmann. New York: Vintage, 1966.

———. The Birth of Tragedy and the Case of Wagner. Trans. Walter Kaufmann. New York: Vintage, 1967.

Nolte, Ernst. "Fascisme, communisme, histoire et controverses . . . Un entretien avec Ernst Nolte." Parutions, 22 October 2002, http://www.parutions.com/pages/1-6-82-3331.html.

———. La guerre civile européenne, 1917–1945: National-socialisme et Bolchevisme. Trans. Jean-Marie Argelès. Paris: Editions des Syrtes, 1997.

Nora, Pierre, ed. Le débat. Paris: Gallimard, No. 107, November/December 1999.

Ory, Pascal. Les collaborateurs, 1940–1944. Paris: Seuil, 1976.

Osiel, Mark J. Mass Atrocity, Ordinary Evil, and Hannah Arendt: Criminal Consciousness in Argentina's Dirty War. New Haven: Yale University Press, 2001.

Paris, Erna. Unhealed Wounds: France and the Klaus Barbie Affair. New York: Grove, 1985.

Paulhan, Jean. Choix de lettres II, 1937–1945. Paris: Gallimard, 1992.

———. De la paille et du grain. Paris: Gallimard, 1948.

Paxton, Robert. Vichy France: Old Guard and New Order. New York: Columbia University Press, 1972.

Péan, Pierre, and Philippe Cohen. La face cachée "du monde": Du contre-pouvoir aux abus du pouvoir. Paris: Mille et une nuits/Fayard, 2003.

Perruchot, Henri. Montherlant. Paris: Gallimard, 1963.

Peyre, Henri. French Novelists of Today. New York: Oxford University Press, 1967.

Peyrefitte, Roger, and Pierre Sipriot, eds. Henry de Montherlant-Roger Peyrefitte Correspondance. Paris: Laffont, 1983.

Plenel, Edwy. L'Epreuve. Paris: Stock, 1999.

———. Secrets de jeunesse. Paris: Stock, 2001.

Pollès, Henri. L'Opéra politique. Paris: Gallimard, 1937.

Rabinbach, Anson. "Communist Crimes and French Intellectuals." Dissent (Fall 1998): 61–66.

Raimond, Michel. Les romans de Montherlant. Paris: CEDES, 1982.

Ramet, Sabrina. Balkan Babel: The Distinction of Yugoslavia from the Death of Tito to Ethnic War. Boulder: Westview Press, 1996.

Ramonet, Ignacio. Guerres du XXIe siècle. Paris: Galilée, 2002.

Rayski, Benoît. "L'affaire Debray: La trahison des intellectuels." *L'Evénement du Jeudi*, 20–26 May 1999.

Reader, Keith. *Régis Debray: A Critical Introduction*. London: Pluto, 1995.

Reid, Donald. "Régis Debray: Republican in a Democratic age." In *Intellectuals and Public Life: Between Radicalism and Reform*, ed. Leon Fink, Stephen T. Leonard, and Donald M. Reid, 121–141. Ithaca: Cornell University Press, 1996..

Revel, Jean-François. "Jospin a commis deux erreurs historiques." *Le Figaro*, 15 November 1997.

Richard, Marius. "Jean Giono." *La Gerbe*, 19 March 1942.

Rieff, David. *Slaughterhouse: Bosnia and the Failure of the West*. New York: Simon & Schuster, 1995.

Rigoulot, Pierre, and Ilios Yannakakis. *Un pavé dans l'histoire: Le débat français sur Le Livre Noir du Communisme*. Paris: Laffont, 1998.

Rioux, Jean-Pierre, ed. *Vingtième siècle: Revue d'histoire*. Paris: Presses des Sciences Po, No. 69, January/March 2001.

Rohde, David. *End Game: The Betrayal and Fall of Srebrenica: Europe's Worst Massacre since World War II*. New York: Farrar, Straus, and Giroux, 1997.

Rolland, Romain. *Cahiers Romain Rolland*, No. 30. Paris: Albin Michel, 1996.

Rosenberg, Merrill, A. "Montherlant and the Critics of the French Resistance." *French Review* 44 (1971): 839–851.

Ross, Kristin. *May '68 and Its Afterlives*. Chicago: University of Chicago Press, 2002.

Rousso, Henry. *The Haunting Past*. Trans. Ralph Schoolcraft. Philadelphia: University of Pennsylvania Press, 2002.

——. *Pétain et la fin de la collaboration: Sigmaringen, 1944–1945*. Brussels: Editions Complexes, 1984.

——. *Stalinism and Nazism: History and Memory Compared*. Trans. Thomas Hilde, Lucy Golsan, Richard J. Golsan, and Peter Rogers. Ed. Richard J. Golsan. Lincoln: University of Nebraska Press, 2004.

——. *Vichy: L'événement, la mémoire, l'histoire*. Paris: Gallimard, 2001.

——. *The Vichy Syndrome: History and Memory in France since 1944*. Trans. Arthur Goldhammer. Cambridge: Harvard University Press, 1991.

Roy, Claude. *Défense de la littérature*. Paris: Gallimard, 1968.

Sagot-Duvauroux, Jean-Louis. "L'Empire et la barbarie." *L'Humanité*, 19 April 1999.

Said, Edward W. *Representations of the Intellectual*. New York: Vintage, 1994.

Salvaing, François. "Comme dans un fauteuil." *L'Humanité*, 19 May 1999.

Sanders, Mark. *Complicities: The Intellectual and Apartheid*. Durham: Duke University Press, 2002.

Sapiro, Gisèle. *La guerre des écrivains, 1940–1953*. Paris: Fayard, 1999.

Sartre, Jean-Paul. *"What Is Literature?" and Other Essays*. Cambridge: Harvard University Press, 1988.

Savage Brosman, Catherine. *Art as Testimony: The Work of Jules Roy*. Gainesville: University of Florida Press, 1989.

Schalk, David L. *War and the Ivory Tower: Algeria and Vietnam.* New York: Oxford University Press, 1991.

Schlink, Bernhard. *The Reader.* New York: Vintage, 1998.

Serant, Paul. *Le romantisme fasciste: Etude sur l'oeuvre politique de quelques écrivains français.* Paris: Fasquelle, 1959.

Silber, Laura, and Allan Little. *The Death of Yugoslavia.* London: Penguin, 1995.

Singleton, Fred. *A Short History of the Yugoslav Peoples.* Cambridge: Cambridge University Press, 1985.

Sipriot, Pierre. *Montherlant sans masque,* Vol. 1, *L'Enfant prodigue, 1895–1932.* Paris: Laffont, 1982.

———. *Montherlant sans masque,* Vol. 2, *Ecris avec ton sang, 1932–1972.* Paris: Laffont, 1990.

Steiner, George. "Cry Havoc." In *Extraterritorial: Papers on Literature and the Language Revolution.* New York: Atheneum, 1971.

Stoekl, Allan. "Mark Lilla: The Reckless Mind." *South Central Review* 20(2) (Summer 2004): 89–93.

Stora, Benjamin. *Histoire de la guerre d'Algérie (1954–1962).* Paris: La Découverte, 1993.

Tanner, Marcus. *Croatia: A Nation Forged in War.* New Haven: Yale University Press, 1997.

Thiesse, Anne-Marie. *Ecrire la France: Le mouvement littéraire régionaliste de langue Française entre la belle epoque et la Libération.* Paris: Presses Universitaires de France, 1991.

Thiessen, Marc A. "Why We Fought." *National Review,* 24 January 2000.

Tillion, Germaine. *A la recherche du vrai et du juste.* Paris: Seuil, 2001.

Todorov, Tzvetan. *Le Nouveau désordre mondial: Réflexions d'un Européen.* Paris: Laffont, 2003.

———. *Benjamin Constant: La passion démocratique.* Paris: Hachette, 1997.

———. *Devoirs et délices: Une vie de passeur.* Paris: Seuil, 2002.

———. *La fragilité du bien: Le sauvetage des juifs bulgares.* Paris: Albin Michel, 1999.

———. *Le jardin imparfait: La pensée humaniste en France.* Paris: Grasset, 1998.

———. "Le totalitarisme encore une fois." *Communisme* 59/60 (1999): 29–44.

———. *L'Homme dépaysé.* Paris: Seuil, 1996.

———. *Life in Common: An Essay in General Anthropology.* Trans. Katherine Golsan and Lucy Golsan. Lincoln: University of Nebraska Press, 2001.

———. *Mémoire du mal, tentation du bien: Enquête sur le siècle.* Paris: Seuil, 2000.

———. *The Morals of History.* Trans. Alyson Waters. Minneapolis: University of Minnesota Press, 1995.

———. *On Human Diversity: Nationalism, Racism, and Exoticism in French Thought.* Trans. Catherine Porter. Cambridge: Harvard University Press, 1993.

Tordjman, Gilles. "Le Régis Debray sans peine." *L'Evénement du Jeudi,* 20–26 May 1999.

Traverso, Enzo. *Understanding the Nazi Genocide: Marxism after Auschwitz.* London: Pluto, 1999.

———, ed. *Le totalitarisme: Le XXe siècle en débat.* Paris: Seuil, 2001.

Trierweiller, Denis. "Un spectre hante Ernst Nolte." *Le Débat* 122 (November–December 2002): 165–174.

Ugrešic, Dubravka. *The Culture of Lies*. University Park: Pennsylvania State University Press, 1998.

Van Kley, Dale, ed. *The French Idea of Freedom: The Old Regime and the Declaration of Rights of 1789*. Stanford: Stanford University Press, 1994.

Verdès-Leroux, Jeannine. *Refus et violences: Politique et littérature à l'extrème droite des années trente aux retombées de la Libération*. Paris: Gallimard, 1996.

Weber, Eugene. *The Hollow Years: France in the 1930s*. New York: Norton, 1994.

Werth, Nicholas. "Le communisme: L'heure du bilan?" *L'Histoire* 217 (January 1998): 6–8.

White, Edmund. *Genet: Autobiography*. New York: Knopf, 1993.

Wieviorka, Annette. "Stéphane Courtois, en un combat douteux." *Le Monde*, 27 November 1997.

Winock, Michel. *Le siècle des intellectuels*. Paris: Seuil, 1997.

Wittmann, Rebecca. *Beyond Justice: The Auschwitz Trial*. Boston: Harvard University Press, 2005.

Wohl, Robert. *The Generation of 1914*. Cambridge: Harvard University Press, 1979.

Wolin, Richard. *Heidegger's Children: Hannah Arendt, Karl Löwith, Hans Jonas, Herbert Marcuse*. Princeton: Princeton University Press, 2001

———. *The Seduction of Unreason: The Intellectual Romance with Fascism from Nietzsche to Postmodernism*. Princeton: Princeton University Press, 2004.

Wolton, Thierry. *Rouge-Brun: Le mal du siècle*. Paris: J-C Lattès, 1999.

Woodward, Susan L. *Balkan Tragedy: Chaos and Dissolution after the Cold War*. Washington: Brookings Institution, 1995.

Yaeger-Kaplan, Alice. *Reproductions of Banality: Fascism, Literature, and French Intellectual Life*, Vol. 36, *Theory and History of Literature*. Minneapolis: University of Minnesota Press, 1986.

Yakovlev, Alexander N. *A Century of Violence in Soviet Russia*. New Haven: Yale University Press, 2000.

Index